SAS

A STORY OF LOVE AND SURVIVAL

SASCHA

A STORY OF LOVE AND SURVIVAL

INGEBORG HESSE

BANTAM BOOKS
SYDNEY • AUCKLAND • TORONTO • NEW YORK • LONDON

To Sascha

SASCHA
A BANTAM BOOK

First published in Australia and New Zealand in 1991 by Bantam

National Library of Australia
Cataloguing-in-Publication Entry
Hesse, Ingeborg.
Sascha
ISBN 0 947189 93 9.
1. Hesse, Ingeborg. 2. Roschmann, Eduard. 3. War criminals
— Germany — Biography. 4. World War, 1939–1945 — Latvia
— Riga — Atrocities. 4. Holocaust, Jewish (1939–1945)
Latvia — Riga — Personal narratives. I. Title.
940.5405092

Bantam Books are published by

Transworld Publishers (Aust.) Pty Limited
15–25 Helles Avenue, Moorebank, NSW 2170
Transworld Publishers (NZ) Limited
Crn Moselle and Waipareira Avenues, Henderson, Auckland
Transworld Publishers (UK) Limited
61–63 Uxbridge Road, Ealing London W5 5SA
Bantam Doubleday Dell Publishing Group Inc.
666 Fifth Avenue, New York New York 10103
Cover design by Peter Bollinger

Text design by Trevor Hood

Typeset by Midland Typesetters, Maryborough, Victoria.

Printed in Singapore by Fong & Sons Printers Pte Ltd

Acknowledgements

THERE ARE MANY I want to thank for their encouragement, moral support, and belief in my writing ability, not to mention their pride in my accomplishment.

My son Alex was the first to convince me that my life story would make an interesting book, and that I was capable of putting it into words.

My author friend John Bierman, after reading my synopsis, saw a book in it and gave me valuable advice.

My friend Wendy was unshakable in her encouragement throughout and was the first at my door with flowers and congratulations at the news that my book would be published.

My dear late friend Nina helped me many times to persevere when I was ready to give up due to the pain typing caused in my hands and wrists, which are crippled by rheumatoid arthritis.

My daughter Sylvia, my grandchildren Michelle and Tony and my friends Merilyn, Joy, Hertha, Gertrude, Wilga and Tammy to name a few, all have my thanks for their expression of confidence in my ability to write this book without anybody's help. I seemed to be the only one in doubt.

I also want to thank Angelo from Transworld Publishers who, after reading my manuscript, rang me to assure me that it was a good book, and that they would like to publish it. It was a happy moment in my life.

Last, but not least I thank Jacqueline my editor, who showed a remarkable understanding of the drama and depth of feeling I express in this book.

BALTIC
SEA

ESTONIA

RUSSIA

Kirbishof (Kirbeli)

Rujen (Ruijena)

Wolmar (Valmiera)

Saulkrasti
Meluzi

● Riga

LATVIA

Leipāja

LITHUANIA

Prologue

IN AUGUST 1977, I read this news item in the *Australian* newspaper. It was headed 'Nazi mass killer dies a pauper' and datelined New York:

NAZI MASS KILLER DIES A PAUPER

NEW YORK, Sat.—A man believed to be the infamous Nazi war criminal, Eduard Roschmann—known as The Butcher of Riga—has died in a hospital for down-and-outs in Paraguay.

An SS captain in the Jewish ghetto of Riga, Latvia, during World War II, Roschmann is said to have ordered the slaughter of 40,000 Jews.

The Butcher fled Europe in 1948 and lived in Argentina until recently, using the alias Federico Bernardo Wegener.

The war crimes tribunal in Hamburg last year asked Argentina to extradite Wegener and they agreed to the request last month. But by then the alleged murderer had disappeared.

A month ago he turned up in Ascunsion the Paraguayan capital, and rented a small shabby room.

MISSING LINK

Two weeks ago he fell ill and he checked into a paupers' hospital complaining of lung trouble.

Paraguayan, Argentine and German authorities are convinced Wegener was Roschmann.

The dead man had three toes missing from his left foot and two from his right—as did Roschmann.

The original story about Roschmann's death, published in the Australian *in August 1977.*

Reading those words brought back a flood of painful memories. My resentment, hatred and bitterness towards Roschmann had lain buried for more than thirty years. But I had not forgiven or forgotten the twelve months in 1943–44 when my baby daughter and I were at the complete mercy of the Butcher of Riga. Learning that he had enjoyed years of freedom, gone unpunished for his crimes and died of natural causes made me feel again the enormous injustice of many things.

I began to consider letting people know about the Nazi years in Latvia and their tragic impact on our lives. But many emotional and other barriers had yet to be overcome.

At the request of my son, I told the story on tape. After listening to it, he and my daughter persuaded me to write it down in the form of a book. I researched the historical facts about the period I was going to write about and spent a couple of years typing and editing. Throughout, I found my memory was very clear about most of the past. I also read countless books about the Nazi era.

Even after all those years, dwelling on the past and writing about it were painful. I was reliving again the happiness as well as the sorrow, tragedy and loss.

I was not able to bury Sascha physically. I have not been able to put flowers on his grave, or to mourn his death openly and normally. Neither could I bury him emotionally for over half a century. By writing this book, I feel I have built a memorial of faithful memories and true love that express more grief over the loss of his precious life than any granite or marble slab over his unknown grave ever could.

Most of all I want to show how love and loyalty can prevail over nationality, religion, and even death itself.

Speaking of the Nazi persecution of the Jews, Leon Uris wrote: 'The world is guilty by the conspiracy of silence'. I am speaking out on behalf of one who has been silenced forever.

Ingeborg Hesse

1

Innocent Years

My FIRST CLEAR memories are of Kirbishof (Kirbeli in the Latvian language) a small village about 30 kilometres from the town of Rujen (Rujiena) in northwest Latvia.

My father came from a line of Germans who had settled in Latvia at the beginning of the nineteenth century. He was born in the town of Wolmar (Valmiera).

As a young man, he went to Tsarist Russia, where the opportunities for foreigners were limitless, especially for Germans willing to work. He became the manager of huge properties owned by wealthy Russian noblemen who, disdaining any kind of work, spent their time mostly in St Petersburg (now Leningrad) pursuing every kind of pleasure. It was father's responsibility to see that the peasants worked the land, looked after horses, cattle and so on. He handled the purchase and sale of livestock and crops, sending the profits to the landowners. He was capable, honest and very much respected by the peasants. He could go where he pleased, and his income was enormous.

In 1909, he found himself managing just such a property near the Ukrainian city of Minsk. On a visit to St Petersburg, he was introduced to a beautiful girl of twenty-three. After a whirlwind courtship they married and father whisked her off to the country property.

My mother came from a wealthy German family, originally from Koenigsburg, established in St Petersburg as second-generation bankers. She had grown up pampered and spoiled by her parents and two elder brothers, waited on by nannies and governesses. Her young life consisted of riding in a carriage along the Nevsky Prospekt, discussing clothes with her dressmaker, reading French novels and playing the piano. As the etiquette of her time demanded, she was not allowed much freedom, being always escorted by her parents or by one of her brothers when attending the theatre, ballet and balls.

Young ladies of her era were expected only to look pretty, dress well, have good manners and marry and have children at the right time. My mother was no exception. However, she learned from her many nannies somehow that sex, the intimacy of marriage, was an ordeal, only wanted and enjoyed by men. According to these 'experts', women had to endure it.

My mother had had many eligible suitors, but had refused the young men, trying to postpone this ordeal of sex. When my father came along, he impressed her with his romantic, persistent and extravagant courtship (on her twenty-third birthday he sent her twenty-three white baskets full of roses). But more important, he was fifteen years her senior. She reasoned that, at the age of nearly forty, he would not be particularly interested in the physical side of marriage.

How wrong she was! My father was a very passionate and sensual man. I learned from him later that he suffered greatly because he could not break down my mother's resistance to sexual relations.

My sister Liz and I were born in Russia before the Revolution. However, during 1918, the government decreed that foreign nationals should go back to their place of birth. We were in great danger because my father occupied a position of privilege, and the Bolsheviks considered anyone with wealth and position to be an enemy. Thousands of people were slaughtered because they were rich, and for people like my parents to get out, despite the government decree, was little short of miraculous. My parents' decency towards the peasants and servants on the estate saved our lives.

I was four when we were allowed to leave Russia for Latvia, my father's place of birth. We joined thousands of other refugees fleeing westward. We used whatever transport was available; sometimes we spent days waiting for trains.

We had to leave all our worldly possessions behind. However, my father hid some of my mother's jewellery, mostly rings and earrings, in her hair, concealed under the upswept bun she always wore. She also sewed gold coins into the rims of the bonnets my sister and I wore. Guards searched us several times but they didn't find anything.

Once we arrived in Latvia, we had to endure extreme hardship. Sometimes we almost starved. My father bartered jewellery for food; farmers always do best in famine because they control the food supply. Father would exchange a diamond ring for potato peelings, our staple food. Eventually he bartered all mother's beautiful jewellery, and had nothing left.

My father managed to find temporary jobs, and sometimes his relatives helped us. I remember that one of our aunts gave a rabbit to Liz and me as a pet. But times were hard, and one day we found the rabbit's paws and head in the garden. The rest of him was destined for the dinner table! We cried and cried—how could anybody do such a thing? It was horrible! We buried what was left of the rabbit with a cross marking the grave—and of course we refused to have rabbit for dinner. We hated the aunt after that.

I was eight when we came to Kirbishof. My father had been appointed forester for the area. Having spent all his adult life in Russia, he had forgotten most of the Latvian language. Now, having to work in Latvia, it was imperative for him to learn to speak it again fluently. He did accomplish it, even though he retained a slight foreign accent. He was a government employee, in charge of a large area of forest, and he wore a grey uniform with green lapels and cuffs. It was his responsibility to know about and keep a record of every tree in his area; the peasants of the district would come to see him to ask about buying firewood and building materials. It was his job to tell them what trees they could have, and set a price according to the age and condition of the tree. Four or five people worked under him; they would go around the forest and report on the state of the trees.

My brightest and happiest memories of childhood and adolescence are interwoven with Kirbishof. Our house was old, its rooms very large, its windowsills wide, its ceilings high. We only lived in five of the many rooms. Another large room was converted into my father's office and the big ballroom, which had a beautiful parquet floor, was used to store apples on long shelves during the winter. The aroma of apples, freshly baked bread, pickled cucumbers, steaming buckwheat—all these things, mixed with the smell of an open wood fire—I can still bring forth from some chamber of my memory.

The front verandah was surrounded by a graceful wrought-iron balustrade. Wide steps led down to a semicircle of stone paving bordered by flower beds. All summer long carnations, stocks and pansies flourished in these beds, tended by a farmer's daughter and myself. Behind these flowerbeds, as far as the eye could see, every kind of fruit tree covered an enormous area. There were cherries, plums, pears and above all apples. I counted the apple trees; there were ninety.

In the spaces between the trees were berry bushes, currants, gooseberries and raspberries. Where the fruit trees ended, various other trees covered more land in a kind of well-kept forest which we called 'our park'. Enclosing the lot was a high paling fence, preserving our absolute privacy. Along all of this fence grew white and purple lilacs. In May, when the lilac was in bloom, the sight and aroma were truly overwhelming.

Between two birch trees my father had built a swing for me. A hammock was strung between two others. There were many old and magnificent trees with trunks that needed four men to span. Under one such old majestic oak my father had built a wooden table and seats where we often gathered on summer evenings. High up in the branches of this oak father had placed an old cartwheel so storks could build their nests. A pair of storks did just that, returning each spring.

Standing on the verandah and looking at this garden never failed to enchant me during all the years we lived there. I always found it breathtaking, no matter what the season. In spring the hundreds of fruit trees in even rows were covered in white and pink rich bloom, adding to the display of colour and perfume of the lilacs. In summer everything was so green, the bees were humming, the birds chirping, and fragile butterflies flittered from flower to flower, adding beauty during their short lives. In autumn the scene changed to deeper colours. The trees bent under the weight of the fruit, the bushes were covered in their multicoloured berries. To this was added the spectacle of leaves—bright yellow, orange and red, slowly fluttering to the ground. In winter all this colour and life enjoyed a rest under the soft blanket of snow. There was a different beauty. Every branch was encrusted as if dipped into sugar. A peaceful silence reigned. Only the sparrows chirped away busily, their cousins gone to warmer lands.

More than half a century has passed since I could feast my eyes on this beautiful garden, but in my mind I see it more clearly than places I have seen only recently. Everybody must surely have their idea of the Garden of Eden—this is mine! All through my life it was tucked away in a corner of my mind, and countless times, while distressed and despairing, I mentally fled back to it to find comfort. It still lives in all its beauty with me, a paradise of my own.

Before we settled down in Kirbishof, we had moved from place to place, and so I did not go to school until I was eight. My father had taught me to read and write in German, Russian and Latvian, as well as teaching me mathematics. Now father felt he had a secure job, it was time to think about my education. Kirbishof was a village without a school, so I was enrolled in a German private school in Rujen. It was half an hour's train ride from Kirbishof, and it was another twenty minutes from Kirbishof station to our place by horse and buggy. My parents therefore decided to board me with a German family in Rujen during the week. The school week lasted five and a half days and I went home on Saturday afternoon, returning on Sunday evening. At the beginning I suffered from homesickness and shed many tears lying in a strange bed, in a strange house among strangers.

But gradually I adjusted to the new life. The foundation for my entire education was laid in that school, and the teaching was very thorough. The school gave Russian lessons, but I was exempt from them because my knowledge of the language was way ahead of the others'. I had already read the Russian classics.

My mother, who never learned to speak Latvian, spoke German, Russian and French. My sister and I mixed with Latvian children and picked up their language easily. We preferred the Russian language, but were *not* allowed to use it in the presence of our parents. We still correspond and talk in Russian.

I did well at school and made friends. I boarded with three other girls, two German and one Norwegian, Borgi. She was frail and thin, with big blue eyes and a soft voice. We liked each other very much and developed a close friendship, which lasted well beyond our schooldays. Unfortunately, we were unable to spend the school holidays together because Borgi's parents lived far from Kirbishof. School holidays were three months in summer, two weeks at Christmas and a week in October.

Borgi and I formed a particularly close bond because we were the only two girls in that school of about sixty pupils whose parents could not afford to pay the fees. Father's job as a forester brought in very little money. After being approached by our parents, the school committee had granted both Borgi and me the 'privilege' of attending the school free of charge. We were made aware of this 'privilege' more than once, and it hurt.

Before I went to this school, I had accepted that we were poor without much thought, as a child will. But some remarks made by other children, and various incidents, often made me ashamed of it. Borgi and I never had any pocket money, our clothes were plain and our books acquired secondhand. During gymnastics, as we all bent and jumped, I was acutely aware of my mended panties, and my cheeks burned with shame.

Another painful experience was my brief encounter with piano music. I was very keen to learn to play the piano and in my first year at school my father paid for lessons. I was overjoyed, and made good progress. But to my great disappointment my father decided after a year he could no longer afford my lessons, so I stopped. On that occasion, being poor hurt me very deeply. Pride prevented me from showing the hurt as I grew older, and I said that the piano did not interest me. From that time, I practised disguising my real feelings in front of my well-to-do schoolmates.

From the age of six, Liz had a governess in Russia who started her education. It was interrupted for a year when we arrived in Latvia, where everything was uncertain and the main preoccupation was to find shelter and food. Mother's parents had settled in Riga, where grandfather secured a good job in a bank. They offered to take in Liz, to ease the burden on my parents. So from the age of nine Liz lived with our grandparents, who completely supported her. She was educated in an exclusive Russian gymnasium and grandfather paid for her education, clothing and even for her train fare when she visited us occasionally.

When I was an adult my father told me that he resented not been able to support both his children. He was ashamed and humiliated, but allowed Liz to stay on with the grandparents for her sake. My mother visited her parents sometimes, but I was not permitted to go with her, and father never did see them over the years Liz lived with them.

It was to be only a temporary arrangement, until father got a permanent job. But even when we settled down in Kirbishof, Liz remained with the grandparents in Riga, visiting only occasionally. As a result I knew my only sister very little, although we corresponded during the years we lived apart.

So when I was home, I was left very much to myself, seeing my parents at mealtimes and in the evenings.

My mother had greyish hair from a young age, but she was beautiful, with classic chiselled features. She looked years younger than she was, even when she was quite old. But my relationship with her was difficult for me to understand, and hard to explain. She was good-hearted and affectionate, but she never fulfilled the role of a mother towards me. Possibly because of her upbringing, she remained a spoiled child all her life, unable to make decisions and absolutely lacking any authority. I was a headstrong, rebellious child, and whenever I disobeyed her, she would call out to my father: "Atcy, Atcy, Inge won't do as I tell her!" So my father had to do all the disciplining.

I loved my mother, and got a lot of cuddles and kisses from her, but she never attempted to talk to me about matters I was interested in, referring me to father. As I was growing up

myself I sensed her immaturity, and knew there was no point
in turning to her with any questions I might have had.

I will never forget one incident which, more than anything
else, influenced my attitude towards my mother. I was twelve
years old and spending my summer vacation in Kirbishof, as
usual, crouching by the vegetable garden picking some fresh
cucumbers. When I straightened up, I noticed a red rivulet
travelling down my naked leg. Puzzled, I investigated the cause
and discovered to my horror that my panties were soaked in
blood. I had no idea about menstruation: school, girlfriends,
and my mother and sister had failed to enlighten me. Fearing
that some terrible disease had befallen me, I was at a loss what
to do. By some unfathomed instinctive feeling I knew this had
something to do with the many sexual taboos, and I was terrified.

I sneaked into the bathroom, washed myself and the bloodied
panties and changed into a clean pair. My mother was taking
her afternoon nap, and I left again unnoticed. I walked deep
into the garden, hoping it would all go away somehow. But
the bleeding did not stop and I developed a headache, and some
strange pains in my stomach. I felt guilty of something and
very lonely, and began to cry bitterly.

It turned dusk, and my mother called me from the verandah,
forcing me to return to the house. I walked slowly up the steps,
approached my mother, and hanging my head in shame
whispered: "Mutti, I do not feel well, I have some blood here."
I lifted my skirt, and pleaded for help with my eyes, red from
crying.

My mother's reaction forever precluded the possibility of my
respecting her. She stared at me aghast, then without a word,
turned and ran inside, calling in panic to my father: "Atcy,
Atcy! Imagine how terrible, Inge already has her periods!"

I stood transfixed. Periods? What kind of horrible illness was
it? Why did she say 'already'? Was I to get the illness later?
What had I done wrong?

I could hear a discussion going on inside, and eventually my
mother reappeared and took me into my bedroom. She was
obviously ill at ease and upset. In a few unconvincing words
she told me that I would bleed like this once a month. She

gave me some linen pads and said this was not an illness, but something all women had to endure. She pointed out, however, that she and most girls did not start until they were at least fourteen years old. With the relief of not having some horrid disease was mingled the feeling of guilt, that I had 'it' while only twelve, which was wrong, and caused my mother's disapproval.

Lacking any intelligent explanations, it was left to me as a child and teenager to find answers to many questions by observing, overhearing and imagining. Thus I created my own distorted picture of my parents' love life.

My parents had separate bedrooms. Mother's was next to mine, with a connecting door, which always stood open. My father's bedroom was across the hall.

Many times I was awakened by strange noises coming from father's bedroom at night, or sometimes in the morning. There were obvious arguments, with father apparently entreating, mother lamenting. Then I heard my father's heavy breathing and often some muttered words. Most distressing to me was that after a seemingly endless time, my mother started to weep. After my mother returned to her room, there were usually a few sniffles, and then all was quiet.

Listening to all this I cried, convinced father was doing something terrible to mother. I could not imagine what it was, but with the unerring instinct of a child I sensed that I was not supposed to know.

I lay sleepless and disturbed, pitying my mother, and feeling resentment towards father, whom I loved and respected.

I puzzled me no end that after these mysterious night episodes my parents seemed quite normal the next day, both behaving as though nothing at all unusual had happened the previous night. I could find no trace of suffering in mother.

It was normal that in arguments father humoured mother in almost everything. If I did not show enough respect towards her, he reprimanded me severely.

My father smoked a pipe and his hair was always very short, an inch-long crew cut. He was broad and stocky in build, though not tall. Ever since I can remember he wore a short white beard.

He was a real gentleman of the old style. He kissed mother's hand after meals, although she was anything but a good cook and we were restricted to the simplest dishes. He made a big fuss over her birthdays, and never refused if she asked for his help. This even meant that he would give her a manicure or a pedicure whenever she wanted one.

I had long since accepted the fact that when we went shopping in Rujen, father would always find the money to buy mother new clothes, although he repeatedly claimed he could not afford to spend money on me.

Putting all my thoughts together, I had finally formed the opinion that because my mother submitted to father, who obviously inflicted pain on her during her visits to his bedroom, he was bound to make it up to her by spoiling her.

It was many years before I learned the facts of life. Not having a brother, not ever having seen a naked boy, let alone a man, I was at a loss to comprehend how men and women were different, apart from the clothes they wore. I must have been about thirteen when I came across a book by accident. Father had always encouraged me to read, but he chose my books, which were mostly Russian classics and historical books about the Roman Empire and the early Christian era. I was also allowed to read 'clean' German novels.

The book I was flipping through now contained pictures of sculptures, and suddenly I came across a print of the statue of Michelangelo's David. Blood rushed to my face and I stood transfixed, staring at the phenomenon between David's legs. When my heart stopped thundering I put the book back, and spent days and nights pondering over this mystery. After this episode I managed to have many more staring sessions with David, my imagination running wild.

Absolutely everything remotely connected with sex was 'taboo' in my young life. When I saw a rooster jumping on a hen, I was told they were fighting. The same explanation was applied if I witnessed a close encounter between birds or butterflies. Pregnant women in advanced stages avoided being seen in public and for many years the birth of a child involved storks, kisses between husband and wife and a mysterious happening in the hospital. Any direct question was met with: "When you grow up, you will know."

One day while dusting the top of mother's wardrobe I managed to find a book that looked exciting. I went into 'our park', and sitting on an old wooden bench half hidden between bushes, I felt wicked as I pressed the precious book to my budding breasts. My heart beat in anticipation and I opened the book with reverence. It turned out to be a very sentimental love story: a young man and a girl became engaged and behaved beyond reproach, as they did in the other novels I read, mostly looking into each other's eyes and touching hands.

Disappointed, I was ready to put the book away when my desire for excitement was fulfilled. 'They are alone in the moonlit garden, he puts his strong arms around her, whispering words of love into her tiny ear. She trembles. His lips touch hers, passionately, tenderly . . . His hand cups her breast . . . Slowly they sink on to the soft grass . . . "You are mine . . . At last . . . " She closes her eyes . . . A cloud glides over the moon.' End of story.

My cheeks burning, I read the exciting words over and over. What mystery there must be in love! When will a man touch my lips passionately with his? I wondered. Will I tremble? The book dropped to the ground, my hands cupped my young breasts . . . Unknown emotions stirred in my body. There was so much I wanted to know, feel, experience . . .

In spite of all the unanswered questions and unsolved mysteries, I was a happy child. In my beloved garden I dreamed all my dreams, brought my childish sorrows and joys, and tried to fathom the meaning of life.

Unforgettable are the long, lazy, carefree days of all the summers in my enchanted garden. I lay for hours on the soft grass, on the swing, swinging higher and higher, experiencing the excitement of daring. I lay in my hammock reading, or just looking at the deep blue sky, watching little fleecy clouds chasing each other like playful children.

Sometimes the pair of storks were slowly circling above. I listened to the eternal conversation of the whispering leaves of the trees. The trees and the grass and the birds were my friends. I was content to retreat into my fertile imagination, full of vivid images.

My father made me aware of the beauty of nature at a very early stage in my life. He encouraged my love for animals, and taught me never to hurt even an ant. I loved all creatures, and it sometimes proved quite a problem. Over the years I cried many tears over injured birds who did not respond to our treatment, not to mention the several dogs we lost for various reasons.

One of the most intelligent of our dogs was a dachshund, Picko, who, while I was in Kirbishof, did not leave my side. In summer he ran with me through the garden, sat with me on the swing, slept with me in the hammock, and barked, when I said, "Speak."

In winter I taught Picko to sit on the back of my skis, while I would ski on the gentle slopes around the property. We had endless fun together, and fortunately Picko lived to a ripe age.

A year after we arrived in Kirbishof my father's sister, Aunty Ally, joined us and stayed on for the next eight years. She was a childless widow and in contrast to my mother, very practical. She helped father in the office, did all the sewing and knitting, baked bread and cakes and took over cooking our meals, to the immense relief of my mother and to my delight.

I came to love Aunty Ally very much. She was not in the least good-looking, rather mousy and plain, but her figure was truly magnificent. I also remember her beautiful hands, soft, like a kitten, with long fingers and beautifully formed nails. Her voice was deep and melodious.

On summer evenings we often had our dinner outside on the table under the oak tree. Afterwards father would bring out his guitar, and he, Aunty Ally and I would sing, mostly Russian love songs, into the quiet summer night. My father was extremely gifted musically. He played the piano, the violin and the flute, besides having a magnificent baritone voice.

Sadly, neither my sister nor I inherited his gift for singing. He spent a lot of time teaching me many Russian and German ballads, but my voice never developed into anything, although I loved to sing with him.

The winter evenings were even more enjoyable for me, when we would all gather in the large living room. There was a huge brick oven, nearly a metre and a half wide, two-thirds of a metre deep and reaching to the ceiling. These ovens were situated between two rooms, warming both. The fire was lit with large logs of wood, the door left open till the wood turned into gleaming coal. Then the door was shut and the hot bricks of the oven threw out warmth for many hours.

All four of us would sit around the large dining table, covered with a lacy tablecloth, a kerosene lamp in the middle, burning bright. More often than not, father would do some woodcarving and under his deft fingers the most delicately carved flowers appeared on the handle of a paperknife. Aunty Ally would sew or knit, and I usually embroidered some endless tablecloth. Mother sat with her hands folded in her lap, as she did not like doing handicrafts.

On these evenings I learned a lot about my parents' past. Mother liked to reminisce about the good old times when they had been rich and lived in luxury. She talked about the dozens of servants at her disposal, her fabulous dresses, her grand piano, her silver and crystal, and her jewellery. Her eyes would shine when she talked about the gala performances she loved to attend in St Petersburg, and her rides in a 'troika' along the Nevsky Prospekt. She never tired of dwelling on that part of her life, sighing sadly that life now was so hard to bear.

I learned about my nanny, Dasha, a Russian peasant woman, who nursed first my sister and then me, and whom my mother claimed she loved like a sister. Mother told us that she would call into the dining room some of her servants to eat in front of her, hoping they would stimulate her own appetite. My father would let her talk, and smiled indulgently. If she grew too morbid, he would interrupt, reminding her of when he serenaded her on his knees as he courted her. Once he became impatient with her and said angrily that we should thank God that we all got out of Russia alive, as thousands of bourgeois who were rich like us had been slaughtered during the Revolution. Thus I learned that when a group of Bolshevik sailors stormed our house in 1918 with the obvious intention of killing us, our

servants and peasants stood up for our parents, claiming they
were 'good *burzui*' and had treated them well. Father was
philosophical about our fate, but mother never stopped
complaining that the 'horrible Bolsheviks' had ruined our lives.

After mother had her turn, father also recounted episodes
from his life in Russia. I remember one tale that fascinated
me. He had been riding home one night through a dark forest,
alone on his favourite horse. Suddenly the horse started
trembling, slowed down and stopped. Looking around father
saw countless little gleaming specks of green light surrounding
him from all sides. He realised it was a pack of wolves, intending
to attack him and his horse. He knew his shotgun was useless
for so many wolves, as he had only two cartridges and would
not have time to reload. He sat very quietly, slowly taking out
a box of matches from his pocket. Striking one, he flicked it
into the pack, immediately following it up with another and
another of the little flames. As wolves are afraid of fire, they
gradually retreated and father was saved by his presence of mind
and ingenuity.

Then there was the story of the orphaned bear cub he found
and took home for a pet. The cuddly little brown ball of fur
grew into a formidable animal and father had to give him to
a zoo.

Once he was lost in a snowstorm and had passed out in the
sleigh, convinced he would soon freeze to death. But his faithful
horse had struggled through the storm and snow, heading for
home by instinct. Father was still unconscious and half frozen
when the horse pulled up by the front entrance of his house.
Whinnying loudly, it attracted the attention of sleeping servants,
and saved father's life.

Father told many such fascinating stories of their lives in
Russia. I liked his adventures more than mother's tales of the
splendour of their life in St Petersburg. Aunty Ally usually joined
in with memories of her and father's childhood in Wolmar.
She made me wince when she described how their father used
a heavy stick on them for the slightest misbehaviour. I was
soaking all this knowledge up like a sponge, my imagination
filling in the gaps.

About ten o'clock my mother would retire to bed, insisting that I do the same, though knowing from long experience that I would not, as father did not support her in this demand.

As soon as mother had left the room, Aunty Ally would put away her knitting and take a book from the shelf.

My father is carving an intricate rose and my head is bent over my embroidery. Aunty clears her throat and begins to read aloud. During these sessions, which usually last till two in the morning, mother wakes up several times, each time calling out in vain that I should be in bed.

The book Aunty is reading is one of the volumes by Karl Mai, my father's favourite author, whose works I have heard over the years several times. This one is about the American Indians and their fight for survival when the mostly bad whites take over their country. The author is sympathetic to the oppressed, and his strong religious beliefs are evident in all his works. These books do not fail to exert a lasting influence on me, and to develop in me a strong sense of justice due to every human being.

The hours tick away. Picko's head rests on my feet. I feel warm and secure and cosy. Christmas is approaching. Father and I will walk through the forest soon, picking a huge Christmas tree. I will decorate it with candles and gaily wrapped candy. There will be little presents under the tree for everybody. Life is really so good! . . .

My hands are busy with the needle, Aunty's pleasant voice rises slightly. She is coming to the part now where the Red Indian, Winitoo, the hero of the book, is mortally wounded by a white scoundrel. He lies dying in the arms of his white true friend, Shatterhand. Aunty's voice falters, her lip quivers, and she reads on with difficulty: "My friend . . . Winitoo . . . dies . . . a Christian . . . " Shatterhand cradles his friend, weeping.

Aunty Ally stops reading and reaches for a glass of water. Father takes out his handkerchief and blows his nose loudly. My head is bowed low over my work, and my tears are dripping on to the cloth unchecked, like spring rain. Sweet tears of innocent compassion . . .

After I finished at the German primary school, I went to a Latvian public high school. There was no German high school in Rujen and most of my classmates went to Riga to continue their education. Borgi transferred with me and we both found it difficult that all lessons from then on were given in the Latvian language, although we spoke it well. Borgi and I stayed on with the same German family, who were nice people and did not charge too much for board.

My parents had made some friends in Rujen among the German community: the Lutheran minister, the chemist, the doctor, the miller, several teachers and their families. All these people were well off financially, and my mother was embarrassed by our modest circumstances. In the beginning she resisted any involvement with these families, rejecting their invitations. As they continued to invite us, mother gave in, and we became a part of Rujen's German society. Over the years my parents and I attended many festive gatherings in the homes of these people. But it was one-sided, as my mother refused to invite anybody to Kirbishof, ashamed of our less-than-elegant home.

I believe the main reason that these German families continuously invited us into their homes was because my father had become the life of each function. He willingly entertained with songs, played the piano and was a brilliant conversationalist. As I grew older I started to resent the somewhat condescending attitude these German people had towards us, and felt my father humbled himself before them unnecessarily by providing all the entertainment for them as a matter of course.

I often found excuses not to take part in these visits, and when I had to, I was aloof and even arrogant in my behaviour.

As most German young people were in Riga pursuing their careers or education, Borgi was the only person of my age I was close to. Somehow we did not fit into the predominantly Latvian pupils of the high school, mostly keeping to ourselves. Several boys showed interest in me, during the four years I attended the high school, but I remained completely indifferent towards them, feeling much more mature than they and superior to boys my age.

On my thirteenth birthday I was given two valuable gifts; a pair of skates from Aunty Ally and an old men's bike father had acquired for me. I quickly learnt to skate, and Borgi and I spent our free hours from school on the iced-over river in Rujen. In summer we both rode our bikes.

There were few diversions in the life of a small country town like Rujen. Every Saturday a film was shown in the hall, or a dance was organised. But the German community disdained such amusements, and so did my father.

Once a year there was a *Jahrmarkt*, a travelling fair that went from town to town, lasting for several days. There were stalls with various goods and foods, a circus in a tent and in general it was an opportunity for people of the area to gather and enjoy themselves.

I was fifteen when at such a *Jahrmarkt* a gipsy read my palm. Among many good things she predicted for me was that I would marry someone of a different race and religion. Immediately I conjured up an Arab sheik asking for my hand in marriage, followed by a life of eastern splendour.

Many years later I remembered the gipsy's words.

2

First Love

By the time I reached sixteen, I had grown into a shapely girl, with a pretty face, dominated by a pair of sparkling dark eyes. I wore my thick curly black hair in two plaits to my waist.

That winter, a new and exciting person arrived in Rujen. He was Valodja, a twenty-two year-old Russian, who had lived and studied in Riga and now returned to work with his father who was a dentist. Valodja drew everybody's immediate attention by roaring through the streets on a shiny big motorbike. Even when he was not riding this most impressive machine, he was hard to overlook. He always appeared in riding breeches, knee-high highly polished boots and a trendy polo neck sweater, with dark goggles dangling around his neck. He soon became the talk of the town, especially among the local girls.

I was no exception, but well aware that he was a grown man, while I was still a schoolgirl with pigtails hanging down my back, I was content to admire him from a distance.

As fate wanted it, we were thrown together. Borgi and I were skating on the river one day, and Valodja appeared. I had not seen him on the ice before, and when I stumbled and fell, doing a figure, Valodja picked me up, brushed the snow off me, and after looking me over from head to toe, skated alongside me for a considerable distance. He introduced himself and I pretended I had not seen him before. I told him my name, and we made small talk for a while. I noticed Borgi ahead, and skating up to her, introduced them. After a few more minutes, Valodja excused himself and left.

After that, he often came to the ice rink, always greeting me and spending some time talking to me and Borgi, and then skating away to talk to other people, including girls. I blushed painfully each time we met, hoping he would skate with me again.

He was blond, with blue eyes and a disproportionately large mouth. He joked a lot, skated well and seemed to know many of the young skaters. Sometimes he would help me take off my skates, but he did not offer to accompany me and Borgi, even if we left the rink at the same time. Gradually I learned to relax in Valodja's presence and my awe turned into a new feeling I could not define.

I started to record our meetings in my diary; everything he said to me, every move he made. I counted the hours before I could go to the rink and was bitterly disappointed if he did not show up, as often happened. Sometimes he would take my hand or my arm and skate with me a few rounds, or he would skate backwards in front of me, daring me to catch him. These occasions were mentioned in my diary, at length.

By the time spring came—I was in love!

The ice started melting, I started panicking. The rink was roped off, and I did not see Valodja for weeks. Borgi was my confidante, and loyally accompanied me on extensive bike rides in the hope of encountering my heartthrob. We saw him several times on his motorbike, but he did not stop, either ignoring us or not noticing us.

Time passed, it was May, and spring had arrived. One day after school, Borgi and I were riding our bikes in the park when we heard the now familiar roar of the motorbike and saw Valodja stop and alight from it in the street alongside the park. He appeared in front of us, and spreading out his arms shouted: "Stop, stop, you are in a forbidden area!" We jumped off our bikes and exchanged greetings. After a few minutes, Valodja took my arm and led me away from Borgi: "Meet me tonight at the cafe," (there was only one cafe in Rujen) "come alone, please!" His lips were curved in a teasing smile, his hand pressed my arm. My heart jumped and stopped, then hammered so loud I could not hear myself talking.

I stammered, "I am not allowed to go out at night alone."

He laughed: "I understand. You name the time and place, and I will be there."

The only place I could think of away from prying eyes was the old cemetery on the outskirts of town. Timidly I said I could be there the next day at dusk. Valodja threw back his head and laughed loudly. I was very embarrassed and turned to go, convinced that he thought me a little fool.

Valodja stopped laughing at once, and taking my hand brushed my fingers with his lips: "Forgive me, the place struck me as funny. Don't be angry. I will be there for sure." I tried to smile, and then he was gone.

My emotions were in turmoil. I desperately wanted to be alone with Valodja, but I knew it was not the 'right' thing to do. Borgi, whom I trusted implicitly, sat with me that night for hours discussing the situation and working out a plan.

Next day after school we told the woman we boarded with that we had to spend some hours at the library and would be a little later than usual. Together we rode our pushbikes to a clump of trees within sight of the iron gates of the cemetery. We had decided that Borgi would wait here for my return. We hugged each other in silence, then I rode on, my heart singing . . .

Entering the cemetery I wheeled the bike inside and looked around. White fences, surrounding family plots, headstones, crosses and various statues of angels created an eerie scene. Stories I had read about ghosts haunting people who disturbed the peace of the departed made my skin crawl with goosebumps. But before panic could take hold of me, the sound of an approaching motor engine blew away all my anxiety. A few minutes later Valodja stepped through the gates.

I don't know what I expected or whether I knew what to do, but when Valodja opened his arms, I flew into them. He held me tightly and his arms felt strong and reassuring. As he was very tall, my head reached only his chin. "My little kitten, my little black kitten!" I felt his lips brushing my temple, while his hand stroked my hair, my arms, my neck.

I trembled, every nerve vibrating in my young body. Listening to Valodja's murmuring endearments and feeling his caressing hands, I lost all sense of time. I did not notice when he manoeuvred me towards a large marble headstone, leaning my back against it.

I felt very hot. Valodja's hand travelled down my back, and touched my bare thigh. My flesh was tingling; I could feel my skin coming alive to his touch. He tilted my head back, gazing at me with strangely dark eyes.

He started to plant quick, light kisses on my face, eyes, hair and neck. It was sheer magic, filling me with a new feeling of melting submission. In a strange state of trance, I watched as Valodja's mouth paused a hairbreadth away from my tremulous lips. *His lips touched hers, passionately, tenderly . . .* flashed through my mind, and I closed my eyes.

Then—his mouth came down hard on mine, covering it, squashing it, his lips burrowing into mine, his tongue trying to part them, forcing its way in, and touching my tongue.

I felt nauseated, suffocating. Trying to free myself, I found I had the cold marble headstone at my back and Valodja's hot body in front, and was unable to move. His mouth still kept devouring mine relentlessly, his teeth biting into my lips, wetness running down my chin. There was a ringing in my ears and I felt myself going limp.

Suddenly my mouth was free, and I gulped air in, frantically, opening my eyes. Valodja was holding me now by the shoulders, staring at me with astonishment, disbelief and amusement in his face. He asked softly, "Have you never been kissed before?"

I wanted to scream at him, "No, no, no, and I *hate* it!" But I only shook my head feebly.

I felt disappointed, ashamed, disgusted, but at the same time strangely excited. Averting my face I whispered, "I have to go," and was relieved when Valodja picked up my bike and, taking my hand, led me to the gates.

Stopping, he took my chin and lifted my face, forcing me to look at him. "Tomorrow, same time, here again? Please, kitten?" His voice was low and tender, his eyes unreadable in the near darkness. I managed only, "I don't know," swung onto the bike and pedalled away.

My first kiss! Tears filled my eyes and rolled down my hot

cheeks. My first, longed-for kiss! For months I had been dreaming
about Valodja kissing me. But not like this! I could not shake
off the feeling of disgust. I had a bitter taste in my mouth,
my tongue felt furry and foreign, my lips were bruised and sore.
His lips touched hers tenderly . . . What a lie!

I reached Borgi but did not stop and she followed me. Dear,
faithful Borgi! She had no romance of her own yet, and I let
her share in mine. But later, not then . . .

My tears kept coming all the way home. We sneaked up the
stairs, and I made for the bathroom. I went to work vigorously,
brushing my teeth, rinsing my mouth again and again. I rubbed
my tongue and lips, submerged my face in cool water. At last
I stopped and looked into the mirror. Staring back at me was
a face that did not look in the least extraordinary—the usual
appearance after a brisk bike ride. The red cheeks, the puffed
eyelids, could easily be attributed to the wind. There was nothing
new, mysterious or different in my face. After my first kiss,
why did I not look at all special? How was it possible that tonight's
experience did not show? There *ought* to have been *some*
difference.

That night I only partly confided to Borgi what had happened
in the cemetery. But I poured out to my diary all the tumultuous,
bitter-sweet emotions, which I could not even fully put into
words.

At last I stretched out between the cool sheets, reliving once
again the shattering experience of my first kiss. I had hated
it, but I knew that tomorrow I would go back for more . . .

And I did. I learned to kiss. I learned to like it, to enjoy
it, and developed the desire for more.

During May, with Borgi's help, Valodja and I met several
more times in the silent, shady cemetery. We kissed and cuddled,
but never went further. The place of our meetings, and the
fact that we had kept them necessarily brief, precluded a more
intimate relationship. Besides, Valodja no doubt realised how
young I was, and kissing had become so exciting for me that
I did not think further.

But as school summer holidays began, our love affair had
to come to an end, at least for three months, while I returned

to Kirbishof. There was no way I could have come to Rujen alone, and I did not dare to meet Valodja in Kirbishof as he suggested. I had never given my father any reason to suspect me of wrongdoing, but as I matured, he restricted me more and more. I had no doubt what ever that he would be furious if he as much as suspected what was going on between me and Valodja.

But before I left to go to Kirbishof for three months, Valodja and I made tentative arrangements to meet. On the fifteenth of every month my father was extremely busy in his office, as the peasants from the area came to buy timber, and father, with the help of Aunty Ally, worked hard till late. So on 15 June, July and August, Valodja was to come on his motorbike to a small brook near the ruins of a church about five kilometres from Kirbishof. With a bit of luck I could get away with my old pushbike and meet him at that place in the early afternoon.

At our last meeting in the cemetery I cried, miserable at the prospect of not seeing my love for so long. But Valodja comforted me, promising not to look at another girl, and to wait for his 'little black kitten' for ever.

Unfortunately for me, on 15 June father was in bed with a cold. There was no way I could have left unnoticed, as he liked me to read to him when he was ill.

A month passed. I still loved my garden, spending my days there, as I had in previous years. But this summer there was a new dimension to my childish dreams. There was the reality of Valodja, the memories of his kisses, the new feelings awakened by him in me, filling me with an aching longing.

At last 15 July arrived, and I was in luck. Father was in his office, which was crowded with people, and would be there all day. I told my mother casually that I was going for a ride on my bike, just down the road. She shrugged her shoulders, saying that she would never understand how I could enjoy "that old thing".

That old thing developed wings when I peddled down the rough narrow road leading to the brook. And Valodja was there! His motorbike was leaning against a tree, a rug was spread on the grassy bank of the brook, and he opened his arms to me, wide. For the first time we stretched out on the rug, our bodies close. We kissed and kissed, saying how much we had missed each other. Valodja's hands were busy all over my body, suddenly he turned me onto my back, and was on top of me. I distinctly felt a part of his body hard against me, and remembering the picture of Michelangelo's David, I knew what it was. A yearning surged through me, but Valodja sat up abruptly and lit a cigarette.

After some more cuddling and kissing, we parted, as I did not dare to be away from home for too long. We arranged to meet again in August, if I could manage it. It was very hot, and pushing the old bike to its limits, I arrived home with perspiration running down my face and back. My dress was soaked, and taking it off I dropped onto my bed, my heart still pounding from the excitement and exertion. I drifted off to sleep. When I opened my eyes, I was staring right into my father's face, bending over me. "Mother told me you were asleep. That is unusual for you. What is the matter?" I had only my slip on, and father's eyes travelled over me. I was speechless with fear, and prayed silently that Valodja's love-bite (the first one ever) on my neck was hidden by my dishevelled hair. I blushed deeply, and stammered that I had been out on my bike, it was so hot, I got tired . . .

But I knew father's suspicion was aroused, and my worries proved right. My father asked me to help him in the office, claiming Aunty Ally needed a break. Next he declared that the old bike was not safe any more, and gave it to the farmer for "repairs". It was never repaired, and my meeting in August with Valodja did not take place. Somehow I lived through the next six weeks, with my books, my soaring dreams, my beloved garden and my memories of Valodja.

September arrived, and it was back to Rujen and my last year at school. Never before had I welcomed that day so eagerly.

Valodja had not forgotten me, and we resumed our clandestine meetings again. As I did not have my own bike any more, we had to improvise. Borgi doubled me to the usual place, she stayed behind, and I rode on to the cemetery alone.

When winter came Valodja and I met on the ice rink again. I was happy and content in my first love.

I had learned a bit more about what happened between man and woman, in a vague way. I knew a child was a result of some act between them, after which the child grew in the body of the woman. Obviously prompted by father, my mother had told me in a shy and embarrassed manner that a girl had to be a virgin till she married. That meant never to be touched by a man "there". If she let it happen, she would be despised, a "fallen woman", and no man would ever marry such a girl. It was not clear to me what part of me constituted the virgin, and what a man was going to do "there".

Valodja never touched me "there", obviously not intending to make me a "fallen woman", and apart from bruised lips and an occasional love-bite I remained unharmed.

Christmas came and went. I turned seventeen and was confirmed in the Lutheran church with several other young girls, one of them the daughter of the miller. This was another occasion on which I was ashamed of our poverty. I needed a new dress; all the other girls had beautiful white dresses. Mine was the cheapest father could get, see-through and made of a very thin material like georgette. Other girls had beautiful petticoats; I wore a singlet with a cut-down nightgown underneath it, so nobody could see my legs.

The miller gave a large party for his daughter and my parents and I were invited. The miller's son, Herbert, had come from Riga for the occasion. I remembered him as a freckled awkward boy, with red hair. His hair was still the colour of carrots, the freckles were there too, but he had grown into a tall, well-mannered and self-assured young man. During the party Herbert did not leave my side, and he paid me a lot of compliments. He told me he was studying in Riga to become a lawyer, was interested in poetry and music, and would like very much to correspond with me, if my father and I would permit it. I thought him very unattractive and boring and told him I had little time to write letters, as it was my last year and I had to study hard for the final exams. But Herbert did not leave it at that, and actually asked my father's permission to write to me, insisting he had the most honourable intentions. Father was delighted, and lost no time in telling me that it was my duty to reply to the letters of a "nice German boy" who came from a good family. He added with a stern face that unless I had "someone else" in mind, he saw no reason for my refusal. I agreed meekly, hoping to keep father happy and my secret safe. Herbert's letters were as dull as he was, and I hated having to make up some suitable reply. In his letter before Easter he promised to come to Rujen again.

But as things turned out, I never was to set eyes on Herbert again. The miller, aware of his son's interest in me, decided to make some enquiries about his possible future daughter-in-law. Rujen was a very small town, and no matter how very discreet Valodja and I were, somehow some gossip must have reached the miller's ears. The result was predictable for a narrow-minded provincial German. He wrote a letter to my father, informing him "with regret", that he saw it as his duty to alert him to the dangers his daughter was exposed to by associating with a Russian. Under the circumstances he had naturally advised Herbert to discontinue correspondence with me.

For poor me, all hell broke loose. I was summoned home from school in the middle of the week and father gave me a dressing-down I never forgot. He was furious, particularly as Valodja was "just a Russian", and I had spoiled my chances with a "decent German boy". He made me swear on the Bible that I was still "untouched", whatever that meant. He threatened to take me out of the school, and keep me in Kirbishof behind locked doors. If "that Russian" came near me again, he said he would beat the daylights out of him.

In his blind rage, father had slapped my face, for the first time in my life, and I was devastated. My cheek burning, weeping, I admitted only that I knew Valodja from the skating rink and we had done nothing wrong.

After I had promised never to see Valodja again, I could return to Rujen for the last two months of school. Father had a discussion with my landlady, no doubt instructing her to watch over me more strictly in future. Then father took me to our minister for a 'chat', and he gave me a sermon on obedience to parents, God's love of pure woman and the importance of high morals.

At last, left alone, I sat on my bed with Borgi and told her about the whole sorry mess.

I did not have the slightest intention of not seeing Valodja. The only question was how? I was filled with rebellious thoughts and feelings. No doubt my father's intentions were meant for my own good, but he awoke in me only the desire for freedom. The submissive, obedient child had become a rebellious woman, aching to throw off the shackles holding her back. For the first time in my young life I felt strong resentment towards my father.

The last months at school were very difficult for me. Most of the time was taken up by studying for the final exams. After the scene with father, I managed to see Valodja only a few times. Our meetings were brief and hurried, as I felt everybody was watching us, ready to betray us. Valodja assured me things would be different once I finished school. He would talk to my father, ask for my hand in marriage. I was in love with Valodja, convinced he was the only man for me and longed to be with him—but I was not quite sure I wanted to get married.

I passed the exams, and my parents attended my graduation. Then it was back to Kirbishof. It was to be my last summer in my beloved garden. Father was friendly towards me, but watched me constantly. If I went to the local shop or post office, or to a farmer in the neighbourhood, he often met me at the front door with his watch in hand, pointing out I had been gone too long, and wanting to know why. The restrictions on my freedom made me very unhappy, and I was determined to do something about them.

Father suggested I help him in the office, which I did. My future was not discussed. When I raised the question of my going to Riga, where Liz was living and working, father said it was out of the question. I was only seventeen, and in his opinion my place was with my parents.

Liz was my only hope of ever getting away. She had lived with our grandparents since our arrival in Latvia. After graduating from school, she had taken a position in the government medical insurance office, did well and was promoted. Our grandfather died suddenly, which changed Liz's life. Grandmother went to live in a private home for the elderly.

Liz stayed for a while with some cousins of father's, but then decided to rent her own apartment, and now lived by herself.

Liz's visits to us had always been brief, but once she started working we hardly saw her. She and I exchanged letters for years. Her letters told me very little about her personal life, but I was open and frank, letting her into all my secrets, including Valodja. Knowing that our father usually asked me to let him read her letters to me, Liz was cautious in her replies. I looked up to her and respected her as being much older and wiser than I. Besides, she was living in the capital, while I was growing up a real country girl who had seen nothing.

During that last summer in Kirbishof I wrote sad letters to Liz, telling her of my wish to leave home and come to Riga. I kept asking her to help me. She did advise me to be patient, did not promise anything, and usually closed the letter by saying that she wished she could spend some time at home as the big city had its drawbacks. I was disappointed at her lack of response to my pleas, and was sure our father had written to her that he was against my going to Riga.

Towards the end of summer something unexpected happened that changed our lives, particularly mine. Father was suddenly pensioned off. He had hoped to stay on longer. We had to vacate our house for his successor. During the nine years father had been employed in Kirbishof, we had had plenty of good food, but his actual salary had been small. Now his pension was to be even smaller.

Everything happened very quickly. Aunty Ally packed and went back to Riga to live on her own pension. Father rented a small cottage in Rujen and with my help packed our belongings. Mother walked around wringing her hands and complaining about her lot.

I stood on the verandah looking at the leaves silently floating to the ground, yellow, orange, red. Autumn had arrived. I walked among the so-familiar trees, caressing their bark. I stretched out on the now cool ground, pressing my face into the high grass. I sat on the old swing; the wooden benches, touched the table father had made under the old oak tree. I found the young birch, deep in the park, where I had carved a heart and the letters "V" and "I". It was painful to say goodbye. In leaving that house and garden, I was saying farewell forever to a dear friend.

A difficult time followed for all three of us. Father felt very confined in the small cottage and miniature garden we found in Rujen. Mother never stopped lamenting, nagging him to find another job. I tried and failed to obtain a position, although I was given some promises for the future. Rujen was a very small town. Most of the young people went to Riga to find work or to go to university. The jobs available in Rujen were held by the same people for years.

The German families still invited us to their homes, even the miller. My parents were grateful for the company and diversion, but I hated these occasions. Borgi had gone to Riga to study to become a nurse. In a roundabout way I learned that Valodja had been gone for months, replacing an ill dentist in Walka, another country town, several hours' train ride from Rujen.

I became moody, irritable and more rebellious than ever. We had a miserable Christmas. I went skating, hoping to meet Valodja when he returned from Walka. But father started to turn up casually to watch me skate, and I abandoned that.

In January I turned eighteen and was offered by the German chemist the job of hand painting some porcelain jars containing medicines. This involved writing Latin names in intricate letters with black and red Indian ink. He offered to pay me a reasonable price. I performed the work at home, and its monotony drove me to despair.

At last I reached the limit of my patience, and confronted my father in earnest, begging him to let me go to Riga to find a decent job. He still refused to discuss it. I wrote to Liz, pleading with her to persuade him. Father became upset when he received her letter. Getting bolder, I argued with him, pointing out that he could not keep me on his pension, that I was an adult now. I even threatened to go to Riga against his will. Gradually his resistance weakened. Liz wrote that she could easily get me a job, and I could live with her. In the end father consented, an old beaten man.

I was delirious with excitement, packing my few belongings. I made my courtesy rounds to all the German families, saying goodbye. As if to mock me, the day before my planned departure, I was on my way home when I ran headlong into Valodja. Throwing all caution to the wind, we walked openly together. We had not seen each other for ten months, there was so much to say and ask. Our feeling for each other was still there, though slightly weakened by long separation. It was ironical Valodja was coming back to stay in Rujen with his father's practice again while I was going away. But I would not cancel my plans to go to Riga, not even for Valodja. He understood, knowing my reasons, and we could both see a future for us now. I promised to write as soon as I was settled, and he promised to come to me in Riga.

After a very emotional goodbye to my parents I set out on the first long journey by train alone. Including a change of trains in Walka, the trip lasted about twelve hours. Liz met me at the Riga station, a very well dressed, cool and composed young lady. I, on the contrary, was ecstatic. At last I had thrown off my chains, and was free! I knew Liz would try to supervise me, but that could never be like living with father. Liz's apartment was small, though luxurious in comparison to my parents' cottage.

Liz was kind to me, indulging my endless questions and my childish wonder and admiration for the big city. I had seen Riga only as a small child, and the impact now was colossal. The city was beautiful and exciting and I could hardly believe my eyes. So many people, so many shops, cinemas, theatres and restaurants! The big parks, monuments, multi-storeyed buildings, streetcars and horse-drawn carriages—endless wonders. It was weeks before I could settle down and stop marvelling at everything.

3

Freedom

I WAS OVERWHELMED by everything I saw and experienced in Riga after my arrival. Liz, having grown up in this city, took it for granted, and was amused by my delight and sheer awe. She assumed the role of my fairy godmother, literally transforming me from an awkward, plainly dressed girl into a young lady.

A month went by in a dream. Liz and her friends introduced me to all the endless wonders of a large city; the opera, the ballet, the many theatres, the circus, countless restaurants and cafes. I was enchanted also by the beauty of the wide boulevards, especially Freedom Boulevard with its monument, with many figures on the bottom and on its top a woman with raised arms, holding up three golden stars.

The old city with its extremely narrow streets, its rough cobblestones and dark uneven buildings, held a fascination of its own for me. Wandering among the old storehouses with closed shutters, unusually designed entrances, narrow windows with iron bars and strangely protruding attic balconies, I could feel the breath of the Middle Ages around me.

Kaltu (Chalk) Street lay like a jewel among the rest of the streets of the old city. It boasted the most exclusive fashion shops in Riga for women and men. Their sparkling plate glass windows displayed the latest Paris and London fashions. This street was the Fifth Avenue of Riga, where you could find the latest, the most elegant, and the most expensive of clothing, shoes, hats and jewellery.

Some of the most popular restaurants could be found in the

old city. There was the famous Rome Keller, luxurious, discreet, each table with its individual waiter in tails, for exclusive service. The food was reputed to be the best in town. Unobtrusive outside but exquisite inside was the Kloster Keller (Monastery Cellar) presenting floor shows with exotic overseas dancers. The new part of the city had all the cultural delights; theatres, art galleries, cinemas and clubs. There were also restaurants and night clubs for every taste and pocket. All night clubs, humble or elegant, were open as long as there were customers who wished to stay on for another drink or cup of coffee. In the small hours of the morning, at dawn or after sunrise, whenever required by tired, tipsy people, a droshky waited to take them home. There was the choice of a carriage in summer and sleigh in winter, with one, two or three horses.

Riga was alive day and night: trams clanged, *izvoschiki* (carriage drivers) shouted, crowds filled the streets. Hundreds of shops were open from morning till seven at night, their window displays brightly lit until morning. In the evenings well-dressed crowds went for leisurely walks along the wide boulevards, paved with narrow black bricks, making the surface as smooth as a floor.

The popular City Canal was well lit all night, its banks a beautiful garden on both sides. There was the huge Werman Park in the centre of the new part of the city, with trees, shrubs and lovingly tended flowerbeds. Nearby were two restaurants, one catering exclusively for vegetarians. There were numerous smaller parks with many seats and sandpits, inviting mothers with children, old couples and young lovers to find joy, sunshine or seclusion.

I loved this beautiful vibrant city, loved being one of the thousands of people who gave it life, part of the crowd hastening to work, the crowds bound for home, crowds spilling out in the evenings, bound again for other pleasures to finish the night. In time I got to know all this splendour well, and became a happy part of it. But on arrival, and during the first months of my initiation into city life, I was bewildered and incredulous, as only the child I still was at heart could be.

The quiet garden in Kirbishof was a dream of the past. The modest boarding house run by the middle-class German couple, the puritan German society of Rujen with its boring functions, and the whole sleepy, petty, backward speck of a country town—these things were also thankfully in the past. Life had just opened its doors to me and I was walking, running through them. Nothing and nobody could have held me back, least of all Liz. I was starved for excitement, eager to find answers to all my secret questions about the mysteries of life. I had inherited my father's passionate, stubborn and strong nature. I was also impetuous, curious and lacking a sense of fear of the unknown.

Siblings are often different, but Liz and I were the limit. I had black thick curly hair; hers was very long, straight and ash blond. She wore it in a thick plait around her head like a crown. My eyes were the darkest brown, large and sparkling, hers were soft pools of grey-green. My complexion was dark, in summer deeply tanned, Liz's skin was a delicate white, and she avoided the sun constantly. I was well shaped with a tiny waist, Liz was already showing a tendency towards plumpness.

As well as having all these outward difference, we were also entirely different by nature and in our likes and dislikes. Where I loved animals passionately, Liz was indifferent to them. I liked bright colours, she preferred paler shades. I was very impulsive, she was cautious. I was impatient, she had the patience of an angel. Liz had a level head, a cool temperament and a lot of commonsense—I was an undefused timebomb.

Our grandmother was a very intelligent woman, and had made sure Liz had no stupid fantasies like mine. Though she had not told her own daughter—our mother—the facts of life, she had told Liz, who in general had been given the freedom to decide for herself what she wanted to do, or be. As a result Liz managed to obtain a good job, respect from her bosses and colleagues, and had several promotions. She had many friends, and as she was very attractive did not lack attention from men. But she had her own plans for her future, and I have seen her put a forward man in his place by just one cold look, without words.

On my arrival Liz told me she would look after me, get me a job, and I could live with her. But she also stipulated that I respect her authority and listen to her advice. I was grateful to her for getting me out of Rujen and was prepared to promise anything.

First of all Liz spent some of her money buying me "decent" clothes. Then she made me take a crash course in typing. In three weeks' time I became a good touch typist. She introduced me to her boss, and I got the job of a junior office girl, with reasonable wages.

I learned that Liz liked social life, enjoyed going to theatres and concerts, had nice friends, liked reading, cooking and was a perfectionist in anything she did. Like me she also loved skating.

In summer she rented a cottage by the sea.

My father had forbidden me to cut my waist-long hair into a *bubikopf* (a short pageboy bob) as was then fashionable. My first act of defiance against my father, a week after I arrived in Riga, was to cut my hair. Liz advised me against it, but she did not forbid it. That became the pattern of our lives together; Liz advised me to do the right thing and I always got my way by pleading, pointing out to her how much I had suffered from our father's strictness. I loved Liz, it was easy to love her, as she had a generous and soft heart and a forgiving nature. She made it easy for me to get around her with affection, but it was a genuine affection.

I had arrived in Riga in May. By July I was established in my office job, and had got over my first excitement. Liz and I lived in a small cottage in Meluzi, one of the seaside resorts. In Riga during the summer, the whole population effectively moved to the seaside, commuting from there to their jobs in the city, twenty minutes away by train. Like other people, we stayed in our Riga apartment only on rainy days.

Liz bought a swimsuit for me, the first in my life. (During outings to the river with my parents, I swam in my underwear.) I frolicked for hours on the beach. The Baltic Sea has no surf, its waves rolling quietly onto the shore. There are several sandbanks, starting a few feet from the shore and determining the depth; knee-deep between the first and second sandbank, waist-deep between the second and third, and so on. Needless to say, the endless sea was another of life's wonders for me. I could wade into the clear waters, walk along the beach, feeling the warm sand under my bare feet, picking up lovely shells and little pieces of amber. Colourfully dressed people were everywhere, swimming, walking, playing ball or lazing in the numerous deckchairs all along the beach, enjoying the sun.

There were about ten developed beach resorts, stretching over miles along the sea and running into each other, like neighbouring villages. Each had its different name and a railway station. The different resorts resembled each other in layout; from the seashore stretched a wide band of fine, nearly white, sand, which rose up gradually into dunes, covered with coarse grass and tall pine trees. Behind the dunes were rows of hundreds of small cottages, separated in the middle by a wide road used for pedestrians and transport. Between the cottages were shops of every kind of merchandise, cafes and restaurants, many open twenty-four hours a day. Everywhere were teeming crowds, escaping from city life to relax and rest for the three to four months of summer. Come autumn the area was wrapped in silence. The shops and restaurants closed, the deckchairs were stored away, the cottages locked up.

So my protective cocoon had burst into a thousand pieces. Rujen's caterpillar had turned into a butterfly, swaying intoxicated through the bright lights of Riga and Meluzi.

During all this excitement, I had not forgotten Valodja. Liz knew from my letters about my romance with him, and the difficulties we had encountered. She pointed out that father had allowed me to leave only on condition that she looked after me. She intended to keep her promise and see to it that I did not rush into anything just because I no longer had father breathing down my neck. Without saying it in so many words, Liz made it clear that I would not be able to stay on with her unless I showed some sense and restraint concerning Valodja. After calm reasoning from her and tears from me, she extracted a promise that I would wait for three months before seeing Valodja again. I could write to him but he was not to come to Riga. I had no choice, and gave in to her demands.

As the first months proved so full of activity and excitement anyway, I did not really miss Valodja too much. I met many young men, and very soon found that they were attracted to me. My obvious innocence, my youth and my good looks, unspoiled by artificial means (Liz strictly forbade any makeup), were attractions in themselves. So were my eagerness for everything new, my zest for life and my thinly disguised passionate nature, all combined created a combination hard to resist by men. Flattered by the attention I tried my hand at flirting, but at that stage I thought of Valodja as my true and only love.

Towards the end of summer Liz, true to her word, agreed to have Valodja come to Riga to see me again, and meet her. After I wrote to him about the change of events, Valodja arrived without delay, booked into a hotel, and came to our apartment. He brought flowers for Liz, chocolates for me, was well behaved, full of respect towards Liz and affectionate towards me. I was happy to see him again and the fact that I could do so openly gave it a special meaning. No more looking over my shoulder, no more damp headstones in the cemetery, but most of all no more feelings of guilt. Valodja spoke of his desire to marry me and his plans to open a dental practice in Riga; in general he painted a rosy future for us. Liz was friendly but reserved, as was her way. After Valodja had left, she said she liked him, but as I was so very young, she thought we should have a long engagement. She also suggested I should tell our parents the truth, to which I objected immediately, remembering father's reaction the previous year.

For the first time since my arrival in Riga, Liz and I had a really serious, intimate conversation, and suddenly I was able to pour out my heart to her. I told her all that had been on my mind so long, unanswered questions, my thoughts, feelings and dreams about love, and life in general. It was wonderful to be able to open up, to speak freely, to question. Everything I had kept inside for many years came tumbling out, even what I had overheard in father's bedroom.

Liz answered all my questions, dispelled many doubts, and set me right about many things. For the first time I was told about sex, the risks of pregnancy, and about the biological difference of the sexes. She, made me realise that father was not cruel but normal, and mother had not suffered, but was just cold. Liz called our society hypocritical because it tried to pretend sex did not exist among 'decent' people. She told me matter-of-factly that some of her girlfriends had affairs and that in her opinion it was every woman's right to decide about her own body. She for her part had decided not to play around, as she wanted to wait for the man she would really love. So far she had not met that man, although she had been infatuated a few times, though she recognised it for what it was.

How long ago it was, and how clearly I remember that talk with my wise sister! She took both my hands into hers, and her eyes were shimmering green in the subdued lamplight; "My little Froggy" (her nickname for me since early childhood) "don't lose your head. You are only eighteen. Be very sure that what you feel for Valodja is love."

After that intimate talk with Liz, I felt grown up and mature. Valodja came every evening to visit us, and Liz left us mostly alone, going out or staying in the other room. Valodja and I went back to cuddling and kissing, and desire was roused in me once more. He took an apartment and made enquiries about working in Riga with a dentist; he also gave me a ring with a pearl to show we were engaged. I persuaded Liz not to say anything in her letters to our parents yet. It was a 'secret engagement', I said, till my nineteenth birthday, next January.

As time passed Valodja's embraces grew more and more passionate, and so did my response. He would open my blouse, cup my breasts, and caress and kiss them. That sent the blood rushing through me, and filled me with an unbearable longing to feel him with all of my body. The day came, as it had to, when I no longer wanted to wait, did not want to be sensible or cautious. I wanted to know—I *had* to know what sex was all about, what I would feel, giving my body to a man. I reasoned that the virginity father had guarded with an iron hand was mine, to keep or give away as I chose. The feeling of freedom was still new and intoxicating to me, and I was set to use and misuse it.

One evening Valodja took me to dinner and to a club afterwards. We danced, his arm tight around me, we had wine, we spoke of our future, our love . . . I am not sure whose suggestion it was, his or mine, but before the night was over we were in Valodja's apartment. His strong arms held me and he kissed me long and passionately. Slowly he undressed me, his breath hot, his hands trembling. Lifting me in his arms he placed me gently on the big bed. I did not protest; my heart was thundering and I was numb with desire and expectation. He tore at his own clothes, and suddenly he stood in front of me, naked. He had an athletic figure, broad shoulders, narrow hips, the muscles rippling in his arms and thighs. I lay there looking in fascination at him. David!

Everything happened as in a dream. "I love you, Inochka, God, how I love you, I waited for so long. Now you are mine at last, mine for ever . . . " "I love you too . . ." I felt a slight pain, something hard penetrating me, Valodja convulsed in a few moments, then it was over. Suddenly I was very clearheaded. The ecstasy that I had felt a moment before was gone! I felt nothing! A strange complete emptiness engulfed me, a deep disappointment and anger towards Valodja.

I sat up and noticed some bloody marks on the green bedcover. Valodja lay on his back, his chest heaving, his face flushed. He grabbed me and burying his head in my lap, started mumbling: "Darling, forgive me, I could not help myself. It is all my fault, forgive me. I love you. Let's get married at once." I felt no regret, no feeling of guilt—just an emptiness I had never felt before.

While Valodja kept apologising and kissing me, my mind reasoned coldly. Was this all? Was this *all* there was to sex? Was this supposed to be the culmination of love? The mysterious virginity was supposed to be the greatest gift a woman could give a man; I had just given it to Valodja. But what did he give me? Was this supposed to give me unknown pleasure? *What* pleasure?

A few minutes later Valodja was ready again, and once more he completely failed to do anything for me. Through the night he took me several times, lasting each time only a few minutes. His kisses and fondling excited and aroused me, but when we united, it was each time a dreadful letdown for me.

Towards morning Valodja fell asleep while I lay wide awake trying to work out what had happened. Valodja seemed so happy and content; why wasn't I? What was wrong? Was it me? Instinctively I knew that there must be a pleasure in the sex act. I had felt the desire—there *must* be fulfilment! I looked at Valodja and suddenly I knew it very clearly; he was not the man who would give me the fulfilment I was looking for. I did not know why, I just knew it was not he and I also knew that I had to find this fulfilment, experience it . . .

In the morning Valodja again assured me of his undying love and asked me whether I was happy to be his. I said 'yes' not meaning it, and 'yes' to his suggestion to get married soon, meaning it even less.

When Valodja took me back to our apartment, Liz was not there. I was unable to go to work, but spent some hours in a restless sleep. It was the first time I had stayed away all night, and I knew I would have to face Liz with the truth. When she came home from work and entered my room with a stern expression on her face, I just told her what had happened.

She sank next to me onto my bed, and there were tears in her eyes. But her voice was cold when she told me I was not worthy of her trust, and that she was bitterly disappointed in me and Valodja. She started lecturing me on the stupidity of our actions, but when I broke down and wept she became all compassion. Taking me into her arms, she stroked my hair and tried to comfort me. Liz did not know, and I did not tell her, that I was not crying over my lost virginity, but because of the realisation that Valodja was not the man for me. All of a sudden I did not even love him, but felt hostility towards him for disappointing me so deeply. Remembering how I had also been disappointed in my first kiss, I let myself hope that things might improve.

I slept with Valodja every night for the next week or so but all he achieved was to arouse me to the point where I wanted him, but he was unable to help me reach a climax. After a while I positively disliked the sex act, and as a consequence my dislike was transferred to Valodja, as the cause of my dissatisfaction.

Much later I realised Valodja was not to blame. At twenty-four, he was very inexperienced in lovemaking. Before me, he had had only one brief affair and he obviously knew nothing of the needs of a woman. He was a sportsman, working out regularly in a gym. His body and muscles were well developed, but his manhood was far from that.

When Valodja raised the question of our marriage once more, I told him unflinchingly that I had realised I did not love him any more. He was thunderstruck and argued that I did not know what I was saying. Now, after I had become his he wanted to marry me, more than ever.

A difficult time followed for both of us. I denied myself to him, assured him that I blamed him for nothing and asked him to accept the fact that I was not in love with him any longer, and really did not want to marry him. He looked to Liz for help, pleaded with me, blamed himself mercilessly, but I would not, could not relent. I felt nothing for him, nothing at all. Liz tried to reason with me, like Valodja harping on the fact that I had made 'that irreversible step', and should be married. In the end they both gave in; Liz with a heavy heart, saying she had failed me, Valodja bewildered and unhappy, not knowing where he had gone wrong. When he eventually accepted my decision to part, he went back to Rujen.

I was not quite nineteen yet, bewildered and unhappy myself. Like a gold digger who has found only fools' gold and who keeps digging and hoping for real gold, I put Valodja out of my mind and faced life determined to find what I was seeking.

After Valodja and I parted, Liz gave up any pretence of controlling my life. I was no longer her baby sister looking to her for advice and guidance, but my own person, not prepared to tolerate any interference in my life. Over the next years I changed jobs several times, getting bored or improving myself. I continued to live with Liz, finding her tolerant and understanding, although we lived two completely different lifestyles.

I am not proud of the period of my life after the breakup of my romance with Valodja. This affair, and subsequent disappointment had left a deep wound in my character. Something warm and vulnerable had died and a cold ring of indifference encircled my young heart. I was not bitter, just

My sister Liz in 1935.

cynical about love in general. Immersed in pursuit of pleasure I lost my sense of honesty and sincerity, as well as consideration for the feelings of the men I grew to know. I had several affairs, some more satisfactory than others; I picked men I was interested in or infatuated with, calling it 'being in love'. I experienced enjoyable sex, found physical satisfaction, but that is all it was, purely physical.

Regrettably I found it too easy to make the men I wanted fall in love with me. I had the advantage over them each time, as my sex drive alone was involved, not my emotions. To my amusement I found that the more indifference I displayed, the more the men desired me; a strange and unexplained phenomenon of human nature. I had no lasting relationships and would walk away from a man without any hesitation or compassion. Easy conquests gradually made me very spoiled, heartless and frivolous.

And all the time I knew I had not reached the peak. I knew somewhere there was real love, and sex was part of it. I was sure this 'whole love' was still waiting for me, if I could only find it.

Liz was concerned about me and my lack of feeling for the 'loves' I regularly introduced to her. Often she felt sorry for the men I discarded and hurt. She tried to arouse my conscience, and occasionally we quarrelled. Often when an unhappy lover came to the door asking for me, Liz would tell a lie to spare his feelings for a while longer.

By the time I was twenty-one, I was an experienced, sophisticated and cynical young woman of the world. There was no trace in me of the naive innocent country girl, dreaming her silly dreams in an enchanted garden. I had become a real city dweller, intimately acquainted with all the good as well as bad aspects of city life. Taking my victories over men for granted, I took from life and people much more than I gave in return. I avoided looking into myself, preferring to accept the arrogant belief that life owed me something.

At this time I was introduced to Vitja. His father was Latvian, his mother Russian. He was a construction engineer, thirty-two years of age, single and very attractive. It was not long till I let him 'seduce' me. He was a good lover, had an easygoing nature, was considerate, and genuinely fell in love with me.

As time went by, I felt comfortable with him, liked him very much, and deciding that my crazy fantasies were unobtainable, stayed with Vitja for the next two years. I still flirted a lot and took pleasure in playing around. But being eleven years my senior, Vitja showed a fatherly indulgence towards my ways and my youthful friends. He was not a jealous man, and he trusted me. I was faithful to him and we had an understanding that we would marry, but he knew he could not rush me.

By the time the summer of 1937 neared its end, I thought of Vitja as the man I would settle down with.

Fate decided differently.

4

Sascha

IT WAS A lovely sunny Sunday morning in August 1937 and I was having my weekly riding lesson. Vachramejev, the teacher, rode next to me, his excellent horsemanship evident in his posture. A Russian emigrant, he had the reputation of being a ladies' man, though I could not see why. He was elderly, skinny and blind in one eye, which he covered with a ridiculous monocle. But his riding lessons were good and cheap. I loved horses and riding, and felt relaxed and happy moving through the tall pine trees whose shadows made intricate patterns on the horse and myself.

Vachramejev told me to fall into a trot, and I gave the message to my horse with a light pressure of my knees. It was a small obedient pony, and responded readily. Suddenly a shrill train whistle cut the still air and my pony took off without warning, galloping blindly through the pines. We were riding parallel to the train track that ran from the seashore to Riga and my horse obviously hated locomotive whistles. I was not prepared for the sudden gallop, and could not avoid a brush against a tree that gave me a nasty gash to my left knee. After bringing my horse under control, I rode back to the stables, shaken up and angry, followed by an amused Vachramejev.

Liz attended to my knee, scolding me for being reckless again. Later we went down to the beach and rested on deckchairs. Not being a lover of the sun, as I was, Liz soon left, instructing me to take it easy. With my cut and bandaged knee I was unable to swim and growing bored, I let my eyes wander over the

About to begin my riding lesson with Vachramejev at the seaside resort of Meluzi on the day I met Sascha in August 1937.

colourful crowd. There were many pretty girls, some in sedate swimsuits, others in more daring costumes, as well as fat old women and men stretched out on towels, or chairs. Children were building sandcastles on the edge of the water, and hundreds of swimmers broke the blue, glittering surface of the calm sea.

My eyes began to close, but snapped open in hearing a jumble of laughter and deep male voices. A group of young men were kicking, throwing and catching a beach ball a few feet from me. Watching them, I immediately singled out one of the players and followed his movements with interest. I became quite fascinated. His body was beautifully proportioned—broad shoulders, slim waist, narrow hips and strong legs. What kind of face crowned this fantastic body? With all the furious activity it was difficult to get a good look. When I finally succeeded, I was not disappointed; dark hair fell onto the forehead, white teeth flashed in a broad smile, the face as bronze-tanned as the body . . .

It was a pity that none of the ball players were familiar to me. I wanted to meet that man, but I needed to be formally introduced by a mutual acquaintance, according to etiquette.

My gaze wandered—there were always plenty of young people I mixed with at the beach. I spotted a group I knew, and lifting myself up, I hobbled towards them. But after a few steps I froze, finding myself face to face with the handsome stranger who had been on my mind. He stood in front of me, the ball in his hands, looking straight into my eyes. Perspiration was glistening on his brow, his eyes were squinting against the sun, just dark blue slits between long golden lashes. I felt hot and cold at the same time. A strange exaltation gripped my body— a crazy desire to touch him. But he turned away and broke the spell.

I walked over to the group of my casual friends. After some small talk and jokes about my injury, I asked whether any of them knew the athletic man in the blue swimming trunks playing ball. Nobody did. The girls were interested, the boys teased me. After a while they all went swimming and I returned to my deckchair.

By then the ball players had moved along the beach, and I could hardly make out the one I liked so much. Disappointed, I stared out to sea, trying to think about Vitja, who was coming from Riga that evening.

A familiar voice interrupted my thoughts. "Inge, what are you doing here alone? What happened to your knee? I want you to meet Sascha, a friend of mine." It was Michael, a former colleague. The fascinating stranger stood by his side.

"Nice to meet you, Sascha." I stretched out my hand, smiling politely. "Didn't I see you playing ball just now?" I hoped I sounded casual. He was still holding my hand.

"Yes, I was. But I felt sorry, seeing you sitting alone with that injured knee. I could not concentrate on the game, wandering what had happened to you."

"Ha, ha, he could not take his eyes off you, my girl! When he found out I knew you, there was no holding him back!" Michael winked at me mischievously. "Another broken heart for your collection!"

After a few more minutes of frivolous talk, jokes and laughter, Michael left, claiming he was dying for a swim.

Sascha crouched down next to me, putting his hand lightly over mine on the chair arm: "I had to meet you. Are you free for dinner tonight?" My heart missed a beat, then leaped to my throat. My thoughts raced; he must not leave; must not lose interest! "I am sorry. I am expecting a friend and I promised to have dinner with him." His beautifully shaped, sensual lips parted in a slow smile.

"How about meeting me later to go dancing at the Mushroom?" The words sounded casual, but I could sense an urgency behind them. I shrugged my shoulders and, holding his eyes with mine, said I could not give a definite time when I would be free to meet him.

"I will wait for you till ten in my flat. Come if you can. Please!" Again the slow tantalising smile, and the dark blue insisting eyes. He gave me his address and his fingers squeezed mine briefly. "I will only wait till ten!"

My gaze followed his tall slowly receding figure. My head was spinning, my heart singing . . .

Later I stormed into our cottage where Liz sat reading, and threw myself into a chair.

"I have just fallen in love with the most beautiful man I have ever met!" I declared.

Liz did not bother to look up from her book. "Again? Congratulations." The sarcasm was undisguised.

I fell silent. I understood Liz's reaction only too well. But somehow I knew, this time it was different. Sascha's image would not leave me—every detail of his face was firmly imprinted on my mind. I yearned to see that face again.

I went through the motions of showering and dressing, and went to the railway station to meet Vitja at the arranged time. We had dinner at an intimate seaside restaurant, and Vitja told me about his last job. As a construction engineer he sometimes had to travel to different places along the coast to assess and supervise the work of strengthening the shore where necessary. Occasionally I went with him on such trips, and I was usually interested in his work. But tonight I could not force myself to concentrate, was irritable and absentminded. When Vitja noticed it, I told him I had a headache as a result of my accident that morning with the horse.

I kept watching the time. We went for a stroll along the beach, Vitja's arm through mine. Another hour over coffee in a little cafe. Would he leave before ten o'clock?

Vitja expressed concern over my strange mood, arranging to meet me tomorrow in Riga after work. My heart fluttered and ached, watching the clock on the wall showing ten-fifteen. With his usual show of affection and concern for me, Vitja offered to take me home, catch a later train, stay the night . . .

Close to tears, I insisted that I see him off at the station. Giving in to me, as usual, Vitja was going to take the train due to leave at 10.45. He kissed me goodbye tenderly. I waved.

At last! I ran from the station, grabbing the first horse-carriage I saw and, giving the driver Sascha's address, exclaimed urgently, "*Please* hurry. I will pay double fare!"

The long promenade connecting all the seaside resorts is crowded as usual with people and carriages. It is about one kilometre to Sascha's place, where he has said he has a flat upstairs.

He will be gone! He said he would only wait till ten, but it is now eleven! I did not catch his surname. Every fibre of my being wants him still to be there. I shiver, feel feverish, but my hands are ice-cold.

"Please hurry!"

"Relax miss, we are nearly there," the coachman growls. It is a big house, several lights are on upstairs. Which is his flat?

A couple sitting in the front garden are laughing and cuddling.

"Could you tell me which flat is Sascha's?" I hope they are familiar with his first name. The man stares at me, but the girl seems friendly.

"Upstairs, second to the right. But I don't think he is in." Too late, too late . . . My feet fill with lead as I climb the stairs. Second to the right—there is a light under the door.

Blood throbbing in my temples, I knock softly. Nothing! I knock again, louder. The door opens, and he stands there outlined by the light behind him. He is wearing a white open-necked shirt,

the sleeves pushed up, and a pair of light grey slacks. His suntanned
face looks mildly surprised:
"Oh, hello! What is the time? I was so engrossed in reading
. . . Please come in . . . Would you care for a drink before we
go?" I step into a large room. A settee with scattered cushions,
a coat over a chair. On the table a reading lamp, an open book,
an ashtray with many cigarette butts. Another door leading to
a room that is in darkness.

Sascha takes off the white coat I am wearing over the sleeveless
summer dress. The touch of his hands on my bare arms is like
an electric current.

"I was detained and did not think you would be still here. But
on my way home I decided to see where you live." My words sound
phoney, the explanation ridiculous—and I know it.

"I am glad I forgot about the time. I will just put on a tie
and jacket, and we can go. The night is still young!"

A forced laugh . . . We are both hiding behind a pretence of
indifference. The casual talk, our efforts to sound nonchalant, the
covering up of our real feelings—the demands of silly conventions,
observed by habit.

Suddenly we face each other—our eyes meet and lock. We are
touched by the force of life itself, all barriers invented by society
are swept away.

Surrendering to this force, we both step forward. Without a word
we cling to each other in our first embrace—two human beings,
stripped of all falsehood . . .

We made love, forgetting time and place and the world outside.
Our bodies united, throbbing with passion, parted, and clung
to each other with renewed desire to be united once more.
I felt a delicious sensation of melting into Sascha. He was a
magnificent lover, and took me with finesse, tender and wild,
to the magic peaks of ecstasy and fulfilment I had sought in
vain for so long. It was a completely new experience for me
and in return I gave all I had to give, all that till this moment
I had not realised I had in me to give. It was a mutual and
complete surrender of body and soul—a true act of love.

The rosy glow of dawn shimmered behind the window, the

golden rays of the sun entered the room—we still floated on the wave that had swept us so powerfully into each other's arms. It was late afternoon when we came down to earth, feeling thirst and hunger, and realising we had missed going to work.

Apart from our names, we knew nothing of each other. During all the hours of our lovemaking, only words of endearment and passion were uttered. But while we dressed, went out to dinner, and returned to Sascha's flat, I did not feel the slightest embarrassment. On the contrary. I felt I had known Sascha since my life's beginning. Everything about him was familiar, dear and wonderful, and being with him seemed the most natural thing to do.

Somehow I remembered to ring Liz, asking her not to worry.

Another blissful night of love followed, our passion undiminished. At dawn Sascha took me to Liz's and my cottage. On parting he took my face in his hands and kissed me long and deeply. We did not exchange any platitudes, any promises, or make any plans. We just knew we would be together again.

In the days and weeks that followed those first incredible hours of our togetherness, Sascha and I both realised that it was more than an infatuation. We had spontaneously yielded to a very strong mutual physical attraction, not questioning why. But this attraction so quickly developed into a deep feeling that we both recognised as much more than only sexual that it took us by surprise. In the beginning we made some effort to treat our relationship more lightly than we knew it was.

I had never really loved a man. All my previous relationships had been lighthearted, even with Vitja. I was always motivated by rebellion, physical attraction or curiosity, and the ever-present search for fulfilment. To this was added the excitement of new conquests that had become necessary to my ego. My new feeling of abandonment to Sascha frightened me by its intensity, taking complete possession of me.

I came alive only when I was with Sascha. Nothing and nobody else mattered. I had a constant need to be with him, look at him, listen to his deep voice, touch him. Parting, I lived for our next meeting; meeting him, I forgot the rest of the world existed.

So many have described love, in so many glowing words, I can't do it any better or different. I can only say that what I felt for Sascha was all that has ever been said by writers and poets—and more!

When I told Vitja it was finished between us, and why, he did not take me seriously. Having weathered a few of my 'loves', he, like Liz, refused to accept my word that this one was different. When he had to, he was hurt, and I was sorry for the first time. He was a decent man, and I had loved him the best I knew how, until I learned what love really was.

Sascha told me much later that he had a steady relationship at the time he met me. He broke off with her at about the same time I did with Vitja. We both acted without saying a word to each other; what we did was clearly dictated to us by the wish to be together at the exclusion of others.

In the 1930s life in Riga was very good for nearly everybody. Jobs were easy to obtain, salaries fair, food and accommodation cheap. There were no beggars, poverty was minimal, and most luxuries were accessible to the majority of people. As most sons and daughters of Latvian farmers left the land for higher education and jobs in the city, there was a large influx of farm workers and domestics from Lithuania. Most well-to-do families in Riga had one or more domestic servants.

During my years in Riga I had several jobs; filing clerk, typist, assistant accountant and others. I did manuscript typing at home, too. I was fairly well off. I could afford good clothes, had my own dressmaker and milliner and visited the hairdresser and manicurist every week. I was a spender and never had any savings, relying on Liz to help me out when I was broke. I had the great advantage that entertainment and meals out were always paid for by my male escort, no matter how casual the relationship. As I was taken out a lot, I hardly ever had to worry about food expenses.

At the time of meeting Sascha I was secretary to a solicitor. He was a Baltic Russian, easy-going and a very good boss. His practice was small and I was his only employee. I typed his briefs, answered the phone, watched his appointments and still had time to myself. We got along very well, I did not mind extra work when necessary, and he never refused if I asked for extra time off. I was happy in this job, and the wages were good.

The only unpleasant part of it was the presence of his two Siamese cats. He adored them, but his wife did not want them in their home, so they lived in the office. My duties included feeding them and letting them out for walks. Most of the time the cats slept on top of the filing cabinet, ignoring me. As I love all animals, I tried to make friends with them at the beginning. But these were vicious cats, and every time I had to use the filing cabinet they hissed at me like snakes, their pinkish eyes glaring. In time we learned to live with each other, although I had to put up with a few scratches if I was not quick enough.

Sascha was an engineer who supervised the installation and maintenance of weaving machines for a firm of German textile makers called Schwarz, who produced woollen materials for export and local markets.

When I introduced Sascha to Liz, she was friendly and told me she found him very attractive. But she refused to believe that this last escapade was different from the previous ones. When I argued with her hotly, she patted my hand, smiling: "We will see. I have heard all this before!"

For the remaining weeks of the summer season, Liz, Sascha and I travelled to and from work by train. Sascha and I spent every available moment together, walking, swimming and sunbaking in the most secluded spots along the beaches. Seeking to be alone, we still could not avoid running occasionally into my friends or Sascha's. There were introductions, but we did not linger. We spent the nights at Sascha's flat. Wild and passionate nights, filled with rapture.

In the last days of August we returned to Riga, where I continued to share the apartment with Liz. Sascha moved back into his bachelor's apartment in a different part of the city. We did not contemplate moving in together while in town. In the 1930s it was considered shocking if a man and a woman lived openly together in sin, without being married. Not that the morals of the society of that period were any higher than they are now, but the so-called sins were better disguised and less talked about.

A large proportion of married men in Riga, especially the wealthy ones, kept mistresses. It was widely known in their circles, including by their wives. But as long as the men supported their families and paraded their wives on official occasions, it was considered acceptable, and the normal thing to do. Jokes were whispered about these *seitensprung* (side jumps), and there was constant gossip about who was with whom. Businessmen judged each other's success by the expensiveness of their mistresses, by the jewellery of their wives and by how often the wives could boast of new fur coats. Infidelity and sexual permissiveness were as common during my youth as in Victorian times or in the present generation. Only the attitude towards it differed.

While Sascha and I observed the outward appearances imposed on us by the general behaviour around us, we had no scruples about "living in sin". One of the unwritten moral rules was that a lady did not entertain a man in her apartment after, say, midnight. But no landlady objected to having a lady in a man's bedroom at any time of the day or night. Again following the ridiculous rules, Sascha always took me home to Liz's towards morning. As long as I left for work from my apartment, my reputation was intact, irrespective of where or how I spent the night.

Sascha's and my life gradually settled down to a pattern. We met every day after work, spent hours over dinner, sat in cafes, went to the theatre, opera and cinema. We both liked dancing and the city had many nightclubs to offer with good food and service, and dancing till all hours. We pursued these entertainments, finding pleasure in each other's company wherever we went. The energy of our youth was inexhaustible, and we always found time for hours of lovemaking.

Naturally Sascha and I talked about our lives and interests, to get to know each other on the intellectual level. We talked about our schools, our jobs, our former jobs, our taste in literature and sports, our preferences in food, our love of nature and animals. To our delight we found we had a great deal in common.

We also spoke of our families. I told Sascha that my parents lived in Rujen, and that Liz was my only sister. I often amused him by telling him little episodes from my childhood and about my battle with my father to get to Riga. Sascha told me he had four brothers and one sister, who was his favourite. The rest of his brothers and the sister still lived with their parents, even the oldest brother, who was married with a son. Sascha decided early to be independent and lived on his own for several years.

At the time we met, I was twenty-three years old and Sascha was twenty-six. Somehow we never got around to discussing religion or nationality. We conversed in German or Russian, as the mood took us, and neither of us had a provincial or other accent. As my surname was Hesse, I presumed that Sascha had rightly assumed me to be German. I in turn thought he was Russian or Polish, as his surname, Gruschko, indicated. (*Gruschka* in Russian means 'pear'.)

Nothing made me think that Sascha might be Jewish. His hair was brown and straight, his eyes a deep blue. His features were regular with a short straight nose and a small cleft in his strongly moulded chin. He had an endearing way of smiling with his beautifully shaped sensual lips closed, his long golden lashes half shading his eyes. When he was nervous, or embarrassed, he used to take his upper lip between this thumb and forefinger and pull on it. When he was worried, a drop of perspiration formed in the dimple of his upper lip. About four weeks after I met Sascha the fact that he was a Jew was brought home to me.

One evening we went to the Kloster Keller restaurant-nightclub, one of our favourite places in the old part of Riga. As the waiter ushered us to our table, we passed another with two couples. One of the men, who was tall and slim with a prominent nose and deepset dark eyes, rose and greeted Sascha with obvious pleasure. "Where have you been hiding? We have not seen you for ages!" He turned towards me, and Sascha said smiling, "This is Herman—Fraulein Hesse."

As we shook hands it was evident to me that Herman was Jewish. He seemed anxious to talk to Sascha, but to my amazement Sascha asked him to excuse us, and we went to our table. I noticed that Herman's companions were also Jewish in appearance, but it was of no importance to me, and I did not remark on it. Sascha seemed preoccupied that evening, and after we had our dinner he suggested we go to another night spot. I readily agreed, as I did not care where we were as long as we were together.

Before we could leave Herman came over to our table, and, excusing himself to me, turned to Sascha. "I hope you have not forgotten Joseph's wedding? David and I will be at the synagogue half an hour earlier. Will you join us there?"

Sascha was busy paying the waiter. Not looking up, he murmured, "Sorry, I had forgotten . . . sure, see you."

I was surprised at Sascha's unaccustomed curtness, but he took my arm and we left. Outside I asked innocently, "I thought only Jews can go to the synagogue?" Sascha was calling a taxi, and ignored my question. We finished the night in another club, and then as usual lay in each other's arms till sunrise.

When I got home something bothered me about the evening. I was tired, but unable to go to sleep. Herman and his friends . . . the wedding in a synagogue . . . Sascha's obvious discomfort and his desire to leave the restaurant where Herman was . . . his unusual embarrassment . . . Even making love to me that night had been somehow different, implying a sense of urgency bordering on desperation that I had never felt in him before.

All of a sudden I knew—Sascha must be Jewish! I sat up in bed, covered in perspiration. Was it possible? I knew of course that he was circumcised, but so for hygiene reasons were many Christians in Latvia, Vitja among them. Sascha a Jew! The realisation struck me like a lightning bolt, my heart was thundering in my chest, thousands of thoughts crowding my brain. Since I had met Sascha the thought of his nationality had never entered into my head. His silence on the subject and his embarrassment with Herman showed clearly his resolve to hide this fact from me. Why? It shocked me. Sascha did not trust me! What would he do if he realised I knew his secret? Would that mean the end of our relationship? He obviously must know me to be German: why did he find it necessary to keep quiet about being Jewish?

From our conversations Sascha must have known that I was not anti-Semitic, that in fact I was not against any religion, nor did I harbour any feelings of racial discrimination. But suddenly confronted with the possibility that the man I loved was a Jew, I was at a loss to accept it easily.

Of course I could not discard my upbringing. Since my early childhood my parents, particularly my father, had instilled in me that being German was a privilege, a lucky accident of birth. It was hammered into me that Germans should marry only Germans, and father made his sentiments very clear to me.

On my visits to Rujen since the rise of Hitler in Germany I had noticed a change in my father's attitude towards Jews. Prior to 1933 he had never displayed anti-Semitism; now he definitely did. He read *Mein Kampf* and spoke of the international Jewry and their bad influence on the world. Like the whole German community in Rujen, he expressed admiration for Hitler. I was not concerned with any of it and all my father's talks about Nazis and politics went into one ear and out the other. The rumbles of Nazism in Germany were certainly heard in Latvia, but it all seemed very far away and faint, and of no importance in our lives.

I had friends of various nationalities; it just happened that Jews were not among them, not because of any intentional exclusion on my part. I had a Jewish dressmaker I liked very much, and I patronised mostly Jewish shops. So did the majority of Riga's population. There was a simple reason for the popularity of the Jewish shops; the goods were cheaper than in non-Jewish shops, and the service was always excellent. Riga had whole streets with Jewish shops, selling clothes, shoes, materials, toys, jewellery and many were very exclusive. Their aim to please the customer was legendary. You could pick and choose endlessly, barter about the price and nothing was too much trouble for the person serving you. If you entered a Jewish shop a few minutes before closing time, you would still be treated as if you were their most important customer of the day. And if, after taking up an hour of their time, you bought nothing, you would still be escorted to the door with a smile and asked to come again.

Riga also had a lot of Jewish businessmen and professionals, doctors, dentists, lawyers, engineers, bankers, teachers, as well as a range of very good craftsmen.

Many Latvian Jews were wealthy and respected citizens. At times, Jews among other racial minorities occupied key positions in the Latvian Parliament.

There was a small percentage of poorer Jews, who lived on the fringes of Riga and were engaged in running small repair shops, pawnshops, and selling secondhand furniture. Many of the stalls in the *lausemarkt* or flea markets were held by Jews. It was a place similar to Petticoat Lane in London, always open, interesting, and full of bargains.

Latvian Jews were generally well educated. There were no Jewish farmhands, labourers or servants to be found. Riga had its share of Jewish schools, hospitals, synagogues, clubs, a Jewish theatre and a Jewish press. By 1935 there were about 93,000 Jews in Latvia, about 43,000 of whom were in Riga.

Outwardly Latvia treated its Jews like any other minorities. Like in most other countries there was anti-Semitism in Latvia, but it was well hidden. In spite of what was happening in Germany after Hitler's rise, there was no change in attitude by the non-Jews towards Jews. In Latvia there were no restrictions or actions against them. They enjoyed complete freedom.

Sitting alone on my crumpled bed, watching the dawn raise the curtain of night behind the window, I felt lost, unable to think rationally, my whole being thrown into a turmoil.

Not for a moment did I consider breaking off with Sascha. He was the man I loved more than anybody in the world. All my fears were concentrated on the possibility of him leaving me, if he knew I knew! I felt numb with desperation.

When Liz called out to me to get up, I crept under the blankets, claiming I was too tired and would stay home. She peered in through the door just enquiring whether I was OK, and then left for work.

There I lay for hours, sleepless, wondering what to do. I wanted to rush over to Sascha, I wanted to ring him, to hear his voice, be reassured. But fear held me in its grip. Fear of losing Sascha! In my imagination I saw his face stern, his warm blue eyes cold, his usually caressing hands pushing me away . . .

Images of my father haunted me, his anger in learning his daughter loved a Jew. My heart kept shouting to me: "I don't care if he *is* Jewish, I don't *care*! I love him, I will always love him."

But years of German upbringing, the rules I had accepted without question and some inner doubts were confusing me. Can a German really love a Jew? How can a Jew love a German? Is Sascha's love for me as deep as mine for him? Why did he conceal the truth from me? Did he intend to be with me only till I found out he was Jewish? I had never before experienced such a crisis. Questions, doubts, agony and despair tormented me till I could bear it no longer.

I got ready and went to the office. My boss took one look at me and believed my claims of being late because I was not feeling well. Somehow I got through several hours of work.

I was to meet Sascha that evening at six by the big clock on the Freedom Boulevard, a very popular meeting place. I took a tram and walked up to the rendezvous slowly, about ten minutes late. I saw Sascha looking around for me, and tears shot into my eyes. Seeing me, his face lit up with the familiar slow smile. He kissed my hand, as was the custom, and took my arm, saying cheerfully that he had tickets for the circus that night.

I made a supreme effort to control my emotions. Just being with Sascha, feeling his arm in mine, listening to his voice calmed me, and the evening passed normally.

Sascha did not display any unusual uneasiness as he had on the previous evening, and he did not mention Herman.

Sitting at dinner across the table from Sascha, I was ready to believe I was wrong and that all my doubts were only in my stupid imagination. Looking into his deep blue eyes, searching his face, I was telling myself I must be mad, thinking him to be a Jew.

The circus performance was good, and I was delighted when Sascha caught a little harmonica for me that a clown had thrown into the audience.

About midnight we were in Sascha's apartment. He undressed me slowly, kissing me as was his way, tracing the outlines of my face and body with his lips until all my clothes lay in a heap at my feet. His arms were around me, and he kissed me tenderly and lingeringly on the lips. Responding gladly, I wound my arms around his neck. After a blissful moment Sascha took my arms from his neck, holding them below the shoulders, his face inches from mine, his eyes burning blue fires.

"Inochka, would you love me if you knew I was a Jew?"

It was too much for my frayed nerves, and I burst into tears. Clinging to Sascha, I stammered that I knew he was Jewish. It made no difference, I loved him, would love him for ever and ever. I became quite hysterical, kissing his face frantically. Crying and laughing, I kept assuring him again and again of my love for him. In my desperation I even asked him to forgive me for being German and offered to embrace the Jewish religion, do anything at all as long as he would keep loving me.

I was incoherent, distraught, not comprehending what Sascha was saying to me. It took him quite a while to calm me. He put me on his bed, and covered me up with blankets as I was shivering violently. Then he sat next to me and took my hands into his. His face was pale, his eyes tormented. "Dusik," he said, the endearment he spoke more often than my name, "I love you very much. I don't care about your being German, I want to be with you always, but we must talk about our future now." He stopped the protest before I could voice it. "Listen to me, please. I did not tell you I am Jewish for fear of losing you. That was foolish and cowardly. But I honestly did not expect to fall in love with you so deeply and permanently."

How could I ever forget that fateful night? We talked, that is, mostly Sascha talked, sensibly, honestly, tenderly. I listened and knew—this Jew was a beautiful person in every respect. Never before or since in my life have I met anyone so close to being a perfect human being. I feel with all my heart I was privileged to know, to love, be loved, and be part of his life.

Sascha spoke about the Nazis in Germany, their persecution of the Jews, about the anti-Semitism always present in the world, including Latvia. He pointed out what we would have to overcome with my family as well as his. He told me that his parents would never consent to him marrying a Christian. He assured me his love for me was strong enough to face any hurdles, but I had to be sure mine was, too. He was extremely serious, and was probably more aware of the dangers ahead than I was.

Hours passed. We talked, kissed, cried made vows never to part, and came out of this baring our inner souls as one being, never to be two again. That night we crossed our Rubicon. It had been our last chance to part, to look soberly ahead, to draw back from the unknown but real danger. We scorned that chance, surrendering to our love. This magic, deep and passionate force, that permitted no hesitation, no escape; the all-consuming fire that was to burn in us literally till death did us part.

Exchanging our vows of love that night we were happy, full of hope of more happiness. We were young, strong, idealistic, our love a golden chain binding us, holding us. We did not know then how much strength we would need in the coming years to hold on to that golden chain. Nor could we know how strong would be the evil forces that would try to break it.

After that unforgettable night Sascha and I had no secrets from each other. We decided not to involve our parents for the time being and at the same time determined to marry.

I told Liz that Sascha was Jewish, making light of it. Although she liked him, she was shocked and immediately pointed out to me that marriage to a Jew was surely out of the question for me and she hoped I would realise it soon. By then Liz believed me that my feeling for Sascha was not merely infatuation, though she honestly hoped I would break it off before I got hurt.

5

The Happy Years

As TIME WENT on Sascha and I included other people into our lives. Sascha introduced me to his best friend, a Latvian named Eddy. They had been friends since childhood, and I immediately took a liking to him. He looked like Sascha; regular features, blue eyes and a good physique. But where Sascha's hair was dark, Eddy's was blond, and where Sascha was outgoing, Eddy was very shy.

Another of Sascha's friends was Kolja, a Baltic Russian, who was a tailor who ran a large business with his mother, making suits to order. Kolja was small and dark with an infectious smile. His mother was a lovely woman with a heart of gold. Herman reappeared and I met another Jewish friend, Jacob (Cobby). Cobby was an intern in the Jewish hospital. He was towering, about six foot two, very thin, with a pair of gentle, dark eyes, covered by heavy-rimmed glasses. I welcomed them all as my friends too.

But the most beautiful person of all Sascha introduced me to, was Tante, or Aunty, Paschy. She was not related to him, and the 'Aunty' was an endearment, used by Sascha and consequently by me, for this remarkable German lady. She was an accomplished pianist who made her living by giving piano lessons. During Sascha's student years he took lessons from her. After a while he lost interest in the piano, but they retained a warm and lasting friendship.

Tante Paschy was a spinster in her sixties. Her grey hair was twisted into a tight bun on the top of her head, her large mouth and narrow grey eyes were always smiling, keeping the corners of her mouth permanently up, and her eyes were surrounded by hundreds of mirth lines. In her youth Tante Paschy had suffered a severe back injury, and as a result she had a slight hunchback. What her body lacked in beauty, she made up tenfold by her wonderful nature.

On our first meeting Tante Paschy and Sascha embraced with obvious mutual fondness. Then she pressed me to her ample bosom. "Inge? German? Well my boy, you are showing good sense. From now on I will love you even more!" Her laughter rang clear, like a young girl's. I loved her from that first meeting, and the close relationship between the three of us endured.

Tante Paschy lived by herself in a small cottage in Pardaugava, the Riga suburb across the Daugava river. As she found it difficult to travel, we always visited her. She played the piano for us, fed us homemade cookies, and generally made a fuss over us. She read cards and tea leaves for us, always predicting happiness. Sometimes she would tease us. Making a solemn face she would shake her head and say she could see a little blonde coming into Sascha's life, or wagging her finger at me, she announced there was a dark man in my life whom Sascha knew nothing about.

On these occasions Sascha and I would launch a mock attack on her until she laughingly capitulated, and pointed to the ten of hearts. "That is the card of love. See? It is between you. You poor kids, you are sick with love! What will I do with you?"

God blessed Sascha and me with many true friends, and Tante Paschy was one of the best. We owed her a lot, and I remember her with love and gratitude.

I, in turn, introduced Sascha into the circle of my friends. Borgi, my old school friend had married and lived in Liepaja, on the west coast of Latvia, and we kept in touch only by letter. But over the years in Riga I had made new friends with girls I had worked with. There was Melitta, a Baltic German divorcee, older than me, a very attractive woman with dark eyes and high cheekbones. Nina, my Baltic Russian friend, was a honey blonde, full of fun, changing her boyfriends like gloves.

With my friend Nina.

There was also the latest addition to my girl friends—a gorgeous warmhearted Swedish girl, Anna Britta. She had come to Latvia to study at Riga University, spoke German with a cute accent, was tall, blond and very beautiful. Her parents in Stockholm were wealthy, and she lived in a luxurious apartment and dressed exquisitely. After being introduced to me at a ball, Anna Britta had invited me to her apartment, and our relationship developed from there.

All of us made a colourful crowd, different nationalities, different natures, but we all got along famously.

Eddy was always alone, shy and reserved. He had to be often prompted by Sascha to take part in our activities. Kolja was engaged to a homely-looking, very nice girl named Marusja.

Cobby and Anna Britta developed an interest in each other which lasted till she went back to Sweden, just before the outbreak of the war. Melitta had mostly casual boyfriends, whom she brought along. She was cynical about men in general after the breakup of her marriage. Herman seldom came and after a while dropped out.

We were a happy group and often went out together. In winter we spent a lot of time skating and skiing, both very popular sports. There are no high slopes or mountains around Riga, so we used to go by tram to the outskirts and enjoy long cross-country skiing expeditions. Large skating rinks were formed in several parks during the winter. Level clearings were heavily watered and then left to freeze over, becoming perfect rinks. From ten in the morning till ten at night music was played on gramophones, calling children and adults irresistibly to the graceful pleasure of skating. In summer Sascha rented a cottage at the seaside and during the months there we dropped any pretence and lived together. These months were more restful than when we lived in the city.

The Baltic Sea is usually calm in summer, and one can swim along the shoreline from one resort to the next. There is golden sand, fine and soft to walk on. Multicoloured deckchairs were placed all along the shore. There were also big cane baskets with draped fronts for hire to change in. Several large wooden platforms for dancing, where live music was provided at night, attracted young and old.

We swam, sunbaked, went for long walks, danced, mixed with our friends, enjoying life to the full. Returning to our 'summerhouse' we indulged in our passionate love-making.

Naturally we had our lover's quarrels. Although Sascha was tender, generous and good-natured, he had a strong character. If he felt he was right in a decision, he saw it through, and no amount of arguing or persuasion would sway him. Used to getting my own way too easily with my previous boyfriends, I respected Sascha's strength, and on many occasions, after first resisting, I had to admit that his judgment was better than mine. None of our disagreements lasted for long.

Our biggest problem was that we were insanely jealous of

each other. Since I had met Sascha, I stopped being interested in other men. But I was an unconscious flirt, and the habit was hard to overcome. Sascha took it very badly if he caught me casting a roving eye at some man. I in turn was quick to accuse him of being a Casanova if he so much as looked in the direction of some pretty girl. The making up, though, was always wonderful . . .

On one of these unreasonable occasions Sascha gave me a real scare. He was sitting on a deckchair, while I was in the water. Kurt, a casual acquaintance of ours, waded in after me. He splashed me playfully, I did the same to him, and we carried on, laughing for a while, getting farther away from where Sascha was. When I got out of the water Kurt chased me along the beach. I saw Sascha get up and walk away before we reached him.

I dried myself, collected my things and went to our cottage, feeling uneasy. The door was locked, Sascha not there, and I could not get in, as he had the only key. Baffled and worried, I walked up and down the long promenade looking for him. But he was nowhere to be found, although I checked every roadside cafe. Returning to the cottage I sat leaning against the locked door. I knew Sascha was angry with me and my heart fluttered like a frightened bird. The sun set, I was cold and miserable.

He returned late. He looked at me huddling on the floor, shivering in my swimming costume, the towel over my shoulders, and opening the door said coldly: "Had a good time with Kurt?" A silly scene followed, my tears flowing while Sascha declared sternly he was not going to tolerate me "playing around with other men" . . .

I was just as unreasonable. One day in winter I had my periods and a severe headache. Sascha had rung me about going skating that evening, and when I told him the reason why I did not feel like going, he suggested I have a rest after work and he would call on me later in the evening.

I came home early, rested for several hours and then felt better. Not knowing when Sascha intended to come, I decided to go over to his place. He was not home. I knocked at the next-door neighbour's, a young married couple, who we occasionally met at the skating rink. He was a musician and she a singer, strikingly beautiful.

I walked up and down the street in front of the apartment house, it must have been for an hour. Where was Sascha? People passed jostling me, my head ached again, I was cold . . .

Then I saw him! Sascha was walking towards me, smiling, his boots with attached skates over his shoulder, his face rosy from the frost. He looked very handsome with the colourful sweater and the woollen beanie pushed back on his head jauntily. He was walking between the couple from next door. They also had their skates over their shoulders.

On seeing me Sascha hurried over: "Dusik, how long have you been waiting? How do you feel? Why didn't you ring before coming over? You must be cold. I thought you would be still resting, so I went for a bit of skating and met the D—s there."

I could feel my face setting into a cold mask. He went skating without me! He came back with them, *she* was walking next to him! We went inside.

Sascha took off my rubber overshoes, my boots, and rubbed my feet, showing a lot of concern. I did not take in what he was saying, my mind a jungle of jealousy.

Sascha made me sit in an armchair, covered me with a woollen rug, made hot coffee and gave me an aspirin. He was fussing over me tenderly but all I could see was an effort on his part to cover up his 'guilt'. Eventually Sascha sat down opposite me, telling me about his day and making jokes to cheer me up.

Everything he said sounded logical. He did not ring me on coming home, as he did not want to disturb me in case I had been asleep. As the weather was perfect he had decided to go skating alone to kill the time until he called for me later. He had brought some delicacies and cakes, as he did not think I would feel like going out to eat.

I listened, not hearing the logic, misconstruing every word. I hardly opened my mouth to reply to all his questions. Claiming no appetite, I refused to eat anything, and finally choking on tears, asked Sascha to take me home. While he went into the hall to get my overcoat and to put on his, I went into the bathroom and closed the door.

Everything was finished! Sascha did not love me any more! He had fallen for *that woman*. I had seen her making eyes at him before. What should I do? I sat on the edge of the bath trying to think. My temples throbbed. I opened the medicine cabinet. Sascha's razor-knife lay long and shining, folded carelessly into the black handle.

That was the answer! I would slash my wrists! I would die, rather than lose Sascha! And dying I would make him suffer so he would never be able to look at another woman without thinking of me.

I turned on the hot water tap and let the water run over my wrists, my sleeves pushed up, the razor in my hand reflecting the electric light, tears streaming down my face. That is how Sascha found me when, after knocking repeatedly and not getting a reply from me, he had opened the bathroom door. I had already cut my wrists, reaching the blood vessels, and the blood was oozing out slowly.

The predictable melodrama followed. Sascha was incredulous when I blurted out my thoughts and feelings, and my wish to die. It was the worst attack of jealousy on my part and I refused to calm down. Sascha was frantic and called a doctor, who said the cuts were not serious, but advised Sascha to send me to a psychiatrist. He gave me a sedative and put a bandage on my wrists. I was in Sascha's bed feeling spent and drowsy, my eyes shut, my hands in Sascha's. He spoke to me softly and his voice shook with emotion. Eventually I let him 'convince' me that he still loved me 'more than ever'. He begged me to believe that he had never noticed that 'that woman' was pretty; in fact, compared to me she was really plain. He loved only me, no other woman would ever interest him.

To reinforce his assurances he said he would look for another apartment immediately.

After I got back to normal, I was ashamed of the scene I had caused and asked Sascha to stay in the apartment. But my extreme behaviour had made him weary, and after a week he moved out. At work and to friends, I explained that my wrists were bandaged because I had cut them with broken glass.

There were several other jealous outbursts on both our parts, although less dramatic. No doubt our irrational behaviour on such occasions expressed our subconscious insecurity. Our love was built on precarious foundations. As our relationship continued, intense and ever-deepening, we became more secure, and these outbursts of jealousy gradually faded from our lives to be replaced by complete trust.

Life was wonderful, full of excitement, and being absorbed in each other, Sascha and I drank from the cup of happiness hungrily during those dreamlike years. Looking back it seems only a dream. A bright and happy dream, from which we were to wake to brutal reality.

We saw in the year 1938 with a party, and also 1939. There were still no clouds in our sky.

The pact between Hitler and Stalin in August 1939 was the prelude to the German attack on Poland on 1 September. Poland was partitioned, and Hitler sold out the Baltics to the Russians. This secured his rear while he planned to gulp up the rest of Europe.

Planning the Nazis' eventual attack on Russia, which would make a mockery of the pact, Hitler asked all Baltic Germans to come 'home' to Germany. It was a way of checking that those who accepted this invitation were Nazis already, or friendly towards Nazism. In the second half of 1939 about 50,000 Latvian citizens of German origin responded to Hitler's call. They were mostly resettled in the newly created German provinces in Poland. A compensation system was worked out for them, as many left property behind in Latvia, some of considerable value. My grandmother, who was a *Reichsdeutsche* (a German from Germany) decided to go back to Germany, where she was promised to be looked after in a home for old people. Since grandfather's death she had been financially fairly insecure.

In 1939 she was eighty years of age, a highly intelligent and fascinating old lady.

Since I came to live in Riga, I visited her once a week. So did Liz, for after all grandmother had brought her up from the time she was eight. We brought her chocolates and boxes of candy, as she was partial to sweets. Liz loved our grandmother, and as I got to know her, so did I.

Apart from Liz, my grandmother was the only other member of my family I told about my love for a Jewish man. She did not wring her hands, scold me or condemn me. Instead she discussed the situation with me sensibly, and gave me a better understanding of the problems of anti-Semitism in the world. She had witnessed pogroms against Jews in Tsarist Russia. She did not try to persuade me to leave Sascha, but she declined to meet him, saying it would accomplish nothing, as my parents were the ones to approach. Grandmother made me very aware that Sascha and I would need an enormous amount of courage if we were serious about staying together. She was widely read and surprised me with her knowledge of Nazism. I listened to her, whilst I ignored my father's opinions.

When I learned about my grandmother's decision to go to Germany, I was disturbed and upset about losing her. My relationship with her was important to me, as she always treated me as an adult and her equal, and also because to some extent she had filled the gap in my life left by a mother not capable of fulfilling her role.

Before leaving, grandmother had a long talk with Liz and then with me. She advised me to confide in my parents about Sascha, and not to rush into a marriage with him. She also predicted that the Nazi persecution of Jews would spill over from Germany.

Our parents had come from Rujen to say goodbye to her and they, Liz and I saw her off on the ship. It was a sad parting for many other people too, and we saw many faces streaked with tears. I wept openly.

Liz had booked our parents into an hotel, and after the ship departed we all went to the hotel's dining room for dinner. When I said how sad it was that we would not see grandmother again, father said bluntly: "It won't be for long, so cheer up." A silence descended at the table as Liz and I looked at father questioningly. He cleared his throat, then declared he and mother wanted to go home too, and they naturally expected us to join

My parents in Rujen, summer 1939.

them. The Führer had called his people, and we should be grateful for the opportunity to join the Third Reich, which was leading the world into a better future.

Liz and I exchanged glances. At that time Liz was in love with a Latvian who had no intention of going to Germany, and neither had Liz. She informed father quite calmly about her decision to stay, and that her decision was final. Father got very agitated arguing with Liz, but when he saw that she was adamant, he turned to me: "At least we have *one* daughter who has not forgotten she is German!" I looked at Liz in panic. She signalled: this is it, tell them.

I knew the moment of truth had come, and I jumped headlong into it. My face was burning, my hands cold, but I was ready to be defiant. No matter how I phrased it, the facts came out. I was not going either, and, oh horror of horrors, I declared I loved a Jew!

The expected storm followed. Disregarding the people around us, father ranted with fury, calling me a monstrosity of German blood, and wishing I had never been born to disgrace him. Hitler was right about the Jews polluting German blood, he said.

My mother was crying, and we all left the table with people staring after us. Liz tried to calm father, but to no avail. He pushed me out of the way, declaring I was no longer a daughter of his, and grabbing my mother's arm stormed to their room, followed by a distressed Liz.

I left also, feeling low in spirits but unbending. Nobody would tear me from Sascha, he was more important to me than father, mother and the world.

The following morning our parents left for Rujen, seen off by Liz. Before departing father had dressed Liz down for not protecting me from the evils of an association with a Jew. He reminded her of his trust in her by letting me come to Riga, a trust she had betrayed. As my older sister he held her responsible for permitting the unspeakable to have happened to me.

Liz had never been afraid of father and stood her ground, reminding him that I was twenty-five and responsible for my own life. But she was very upset about it all, and once again pointed out to me how impossible my situation was with Sascha. She firmly believed marriage between us could lead only to a disaster, and not only because of the opposition of our parents. Her warning fell on deaf ears.

I did not contact my parents after that scene, but Liz stayed in touch with them. From her I learned that they had finally decided not to go to Germany without us, but they had lost their German friends in Rujen, who had answered the Führer's call and all left. As a result our parents became very lonely and isolated. In early 1940, prompted by Liz, they decided to move to Riga.

There was still no communication between them and me, but Liz assured me that mother often enquired after me, and father seemed to have mellowed.

After hearing of my parents' intention to move to Riga, Sascha and I found a little cottage for them in Pardaugava, the same suburb Tante Paschy lived in. Sascha paid six months' rent in advance and we made it cosy with curtains, carpets and some furnishings. I had told Sascha about my encounter with my parents, although I had omitted father's rudest remarks. He knew I was very sad about the deep rift between my parents and me, and encouraged my wish to do something for them.

Liz met them when they finally arrived in Riga and took them to their new home. We had agreed that she would not mention Sascha's and my involvement with the cottage, to avoid any problems. Thinking it was Liz's effort, they gratefully accepted, finding the new surroundings quite agreeable.

After the distressing experience with my parents Sascha and I decided not to tackle his parents for the moment.

Sascha always went home for the important Jewish festivities. He told me he had not mentioned me to his family, but he knew they had some information concerning their son's *shiksa* girlfriend. From time to time there had been pointed remarks from his mother, leaving no doubt about her feelings on that subject. Once both parents and his older brother even attempted to take Sascha to task about his obligations as a Jew. He mentioned it to me in passing, making light of it. But I knew of course it worried him; he loved his family, as I did mine.

In spring 1940 we had decided to get married soon. Sascha thought it was now time to find out where his parents stood, and he wanted to take me to meet them. I knew once he had made up his mind, he would go through with it. I had strong reservations and prepared myself for some hostility, but I understood Sascha's wish to get the meeting over.

It turned out to be worse than I had expected. They had a large apartment, and when we walked in at dinner time the whole family was seated around the table.

Sascha was holding my arm tightly and said in German: "Good evening. I would like you to met Inge, my fiance."

There was dead silence. Everybody stared at me for what to me seemed an eternity. Then all hell broke loose. Everybody seemed to be shouting or screaming, though all the noise came from Sascha's parents and the eldest brother and his wife. The rest sat immobile and in silence, avoiding looking at me. Antagonism vibrated around me like something tangible.

All the screaming went on in Yiddish, but I could follow the meaning, and the word *goyim* was repeatedly shouted with venom. Sascha kept hold of my arm, and replying to his mother's last outburst, said in a very quiet, icy voice, "It is my life. Inge will be my wife. If she is not welcome here, you will not see me in this house either."

I had not had the chance to say a word, and the whole ugly scene made me feel sick.

Sascha ushered me out. At the door his mother grabbed at him, trying to pull him back, but he shook her off. Before we reached the street the eldest brother called after us, obviously for my benefit, in German, "How dare you bring *her* into our home?"

Walking towards the taxi, I glanced at Sascha. His face bore a pained expression, his lips pressed together hard, and a drop of perspiration glistened on his upper lip. I could not help the tears running down my cheeks. We did not speak. In the taxi Sascha took off my glove and pressed his lips to my palm.

This storm also left us undeterred and unrelenting in our resolve to stay together. It was just us and our love against, it seemed, the rest of the world.

We were planning to marry in autumn when we returned from the seaside. These were troubled times, and we did not delude ourselves that our future would be as easy as our past three years of carefree happiness. We both agreed that an engagement was a formality we did not need, but Sascha was going to give me the engagement ring when we set the date of our wedding.

It was the custom for the bride to wear a plain gold ring on the third finger of her left hand while engaged. The same ring was placed by the groom onto the third finger of her right hand at the marriage ceremony.

As it happened we had an engagement party after all. In May 1940 Sascha and I again moved into a cottage at the seaside. It was an exceptionally hot day, unusual for the season. On this particular morning we had been swimming for hours, and later, tired, dropped onto deckchairs in the little garden of our cottage. The sun was really beating down, and Sascha suggested we get out of it and rest indoors. I murmured sleepily I would follow him in a minute, and he disappeared inside. It was very pleasant to just lie there with my eyes closed. I did not notice that I drifted into sound sleep.

The next thing I knew, Sascha was shaking me by the shoulders and saying something in an agitated and concerned tone of voice. I opened, no, I tried to open my eyes, and found I could not unstick my lids. My face felt on fire, my head ached terribly. Sascha lifted me into his arms, carried me inside, and put me on the bed. He told me to lie still, then rushed out. I felt dizzy and nauseated, unable to move. Sascha was back, and something cool and soothing covered my face. "You are badly sunburnt, I am putting some sour cream on your face. Lie still, don't try to open your eyes yet." The cold thick cream melted immediately on my burning skin and Sascha kept applying more and more.

I still felt terrible, but the burning gradually eased, and Sascha suggested I try to open my eyes. With difficulty I managed to pry the lids open a slit, but my vision was blurred. Then I began to shiver and Sascha decided to call a doctor.

The verdict was as expected—sunstroke. Luckily I had had a towel covering my body while I slept, so my face was the only affected area. The doctor approved of the sour cream treatment as first aid and scolded me for exposing myself so carelessly to the midday sun. He applied some ointment, gave me tablets for my splitting headache and ordered me to rest for several hours.

While Sascha was seeing the doctor to the door, I took a mirror from the dresser and peered at my face. The sight of the purple, swollen image shocked me and a few tears tried to squeeze between the sausage-like lids. Sascha sent me sternly back to bed, making me take the tablets, and drawing the curtains. He sat with me, coaxing me into relaxing and going to sleep. Whimpering and miserable, I let him console me until sleep dropped its healing cloak over me.

I woke refreshed and realised it was dark outside, and that Sascha was not in the house. I got up, grateful that my eyes opened more easily and stared into the mirror again. My face was still very red, the eyelids puffed, my nose shiny as a lantern. Disgusted, I decided to stay behind closed doors until I looked human again. Feeling sorry for myself, I sat in the dark room, and a few minutes later I heard Sascha come in.

My headache was gone. I was hungry and wondered if he had brought some food. Sascha flew into the room like a gust of fresh wind, switched on the light, and lifting me out of the chair, whirled me around.

"Get dressed! We are going out to dinner. Enough lazing around!"

I protested vehemently, appalled at the thought of being seen with that face. But Sascha would not relent; he had booked a table in my favourite local nightclub, the Jolly Mosquito, and he would not take no for an answer.

After his persuasions failed to convince me, Sascha said with the familiar determination to get his way, "If you persist in being silly over a bit of sunburn, you can stay here and sulk. I will go alone."

I knew when I was beaten, and that no complaints or tears would work. So I set about to do what I could with makeup to repair my face. Sascha assured me that the damage was well covered, and insisted I wore an elegant black and white cocktail dress. He looked very handsome in a light grey suit, freshly shaven, his blue silk shirt reflecting his blue eyes.

Arriving at the club, we were taken to a table for six. I looked at Sascha, raising my eyebrows, and he hurried to explain that he had 'by chance' run into Nina and her boyfriend and had asked them to join us. Eddy and Cobby were also coming to cheer me up.

I protested and called him cruel, not sparing my feelings concerning my terrible looks. Sascha brushed off my lamenting and asked how I liked the flowers he had ordered for me. In the middle of the table was an enormous bunch of dark-red roses. The card attached to it said in Sascha's handwriting: 'To my only love.' My spirits rose, and I thanked him, smiling, the effort making my skin hurt around the mouth. The soft candlelight and the dark sunglasses covering my eyes made me relax. The waiter brought champagne, and suddenly I was glad

Sascha had made me come. When our glasses were filled, he said this toast would be special.

We sat across the table facing each other, the roses and candles moved to the side. Taking my left hand, Sascha kissed each finger separately. Smiling he opened his other hand, palm up. A plain gold band was glittering in the candlelight! I cried, "Oh!" with delight, and he slipped it onto my third finger.

"To our engagement, my darling!" Our glasses clinked. Our friends arrived, greeting us noisily. Our group had thinned out; Melitta had been repatriated to Germany in 1939, Anna Britta had gone home to Sweden, leaving Cobby, who promised to follow her, but he never did. Kolja and Marusja got married, and as she was expecting their first baby, they kept to themselves.

Everybody was joking about my red face, but I did not mind it at all. The glasses were filled again. I flashed my ring. There were many toasts and congratulations and the night was full of music, laughter and the warmth of friendship.

Dancing in Sascha's arms, my hot cheek resting against his shoulder, I silently thanked God for giving me this man. As if by magic, he had turned an upsetting incident into a festive occasion, my pain into joy, my tears into laughter. I would forget the sunburn, but not the red roses or the gold band on my finger.

6

The Russian Occupation

IN EARLY JUNE 1940, we in Latvia were still ignorant of the impending occupation of our country by the Soviet Union. The outbreak of World War II and the rape of Poland by the Nazis shocked the world deeply, but the Baltic people refused to believe that the war would affect them.

At the outbreak of the war all three Baltic countries declared themselves neutral. In September 1939 Estonia, threatened by Moscow, was the first to sign an Estonian-Soviet mutual assistance pact for ten years, giving the Soviets lease of considerable parts of Estonia. Latvia's foreign minister was the next to be 'invited' to Moscow. On 1 October 1939 he signed a similar pact. Lithuania followed. The Baltic countries had no alternative; they were left to face the Russian colossus alone. Europe was facing Hitler.

At that time Latvia had a population close to two million and an army of twenty thousand men.

After signing the pact with the Soviets the Latvian public at large was optimistic and Latvian-Soviet relations remained harmonious until June 1940. But the conspiracy between the two criminals, Hitler and Stalin, had wider consequences for the Baltics. Assured that the Nazis would not interfere, the Soviets made the next move.

They occupied Lithuania on 15 June 1940. The following day Estonia and Latvia were issued an ultimatum to allow Soviet troops to enter.

Karlis Ulmanis, the Latvian prime minister and president since

1936, addressed the Assembly over the radio. The Latvian national anthem, 'God Bless Latvia', was sung in unison over and over again.

It was the last time it was sung in freedom. On 17 June 1940 Soviet troops moved into Latvia, without a shot being fired. Ulmanis drove through the streets of Riga, asking through a loudspeaker that the population remain calm. He was not seen again in public.

On that memorable day, Nina and I sat in the Cafe Luna overlooking the Freedom Boulevard. We silently watched column after column of Russian soldiers marching down the Boulevard. Artillery and tanks followed. A number of people greeted them with flowers and shouted welcome. The majority stayed indoors. The future was very uncertain. People were at a loss as to what to expect from this occupation that had descended on them out of the blue, abruptly ending nineteen years of prosperity and freedom.

On 20 June Vyshinsky, an emissary of the Soviet government, came to Riga to 'assist' in the forming of the new Latvian government.

On 21 June Karlis Ulmanis was deported to Russia. The new Latvian Government was headed by Professor Kirchenstein, a left-wing liberal. The Communist Party was legalised. Elections were held the following month and the result was a foregone conclusion. The Working People's Party held the power, and was Communist-controlled. Latvia was proclaimed a Soviet republic, and the liquidation of the Latvian army and home guard began. Many officers were arrested and killed.

After the initial arrests and deportations, life settled down to an uneasy calm, everybody trying to adjust to the unfamiliar Communist regime as well as possible.

Luckily Latvia was so rich that it would take a lot of plundering by the Russians before we would feel any painful effects. The farmers, as always in wartime, fared the best.

Several of our acquaintances disappeared. Among them was one of my former boyfriends, a Russian, who was a member of the Sokoli (Falcons), an anti-Communist organisation. Taken also was a college friend of Sascha's, a Latvian and a distant relative of Eddy. He belonged to Daugavas Vanagi (the Eagles of Daugava), a widespread Latvian nationalistic organisation. Many years later I learned that the Russian had lived, married and died in Siberia and the Latvian had returned to Riga in the 1960s.

Sascha, Liz and I kept a suitcase packed with warm clothing, as most people did. Nobody knew if, or when, or for what reason, there would be a knock on their door from the Russian secret police. Arrest could result from a casual remark, or more likely from denunciation for personal revenge.

After the arrival of the Russians jails were emptied of political prisoners, and in the process a lot of undesirables surfaced. The human scum that thrives on the misery of others presented itself to the new masters, eager to serve, denounce, inform. They were given red armbands and went about terrorising the population, glorying in their power to bring suffering. These thugs, mostly Latvians, uneducated, cruel and without scruples, were as much feared as the Russians themselves.

One day my solicitor boss disappeared, and his distraught wife told me he had been arrested in the middle of the night, no reason given. Fearing some reflection on me, being his employee, I rushed to Sascha with the bad news. He wanted me to take another job immediately, as unobtrusively as possible. Nina was working in the cosmetic department of a large co-op store. On Sascha's advice I contacted her, and as she had worked there for several years and was well liked, she promised to help me by approaching the 'comrade', with whom she had flirted. As a result I was accepted, after a lot of questioning, and put in the department of men's hats. The girl who worked with me on that counter was nice, but I did not like the job at all. It was boring, we all had to wear dark blue uniforms and the rules were strict. We constantly had to attend meetings where some 'comrade' or other would talk a lot of rubbish about the achievements of the work-plan, and of how lucky the Latvians were to have the 'privilege' now to be part of 'glorious Russia'.

As well as listening to all these speeches, we had to do physical work for the new regime, which included helping the farmers dig potatoes. I didn't have the right clothes; the commissar came

With a workmate in the co-op store where I worked for a few months in 1940.

up and told me I had to wear sensible clothes and boots. I wasn't going to do what they wanted and protested, "But I don't *have* any sensible boots! I only wear high heels!" No matter, I still had to obey. I had always been rebellious against rules and restrictions and found it hard to keep my mouth shut. Sascha had to caution me constantly.

Because the Russians were officially 'friends' with the Nazis they left Sascha's German firm alone, after making some changes to the management. One of the risks of being arrested or liquidated by the Communists was to be in a leading or important position of some responsibility. Any underling reprimanded for a mistake or laziness could inform on the boss as being against the new regime. Sascha's position in the firm brought that danger with it. But with his winning ways, Sascha became friendly with the commissar who unofficially ran the firm, and so remained safe during the Russian occupation.

Sascha and I set the date of our marriage for 31 August. We were going into it with open eyes; Sascha was still a Jew, I was still a German. The Nazi hounds were sniffing at the borders and rumours of the persecution of Jews in Germany, Poland and other occupied countries persisted. There was no telling whether the Nazi curse, so close behind our borders, would reach us one day.

But we had made our decision three years previously—the golden chain of love held as strongly as ever. We simply could not imagine a life apart, so we had to have a life together, come what may. We decided on a civil ceremony in the registry office.

A few weeks before our wedding, while we still lived in Bulduri by the sea, Sascha and I rented a three-room apartment in Woldemar Street, Riga. It was a very long and wide street, with young trees planted on both sides. Most of the apartment houses were fairly new, this area of Riga still being in a developmental stage. Our house was a new three-storey building, our apartment one flight up. The rooms were large with windows facing the street, letting in a lot of light and sunshine. The house porter lived in the basement apartment. Showing us around he seemed friendly and accommodating, although he wore a red armband.

We were both excited about our new home, and I in particular felt like Cinderella whose fairy godmother had granted her wishes, because Sascha had taken me on a wonderful shopping spree.

He told me he had some savings, and we could use them to furnish our new apartment. I knew he had a good income but I did not expect the extravagance he offered me. I was free to choose whatever I wanted in the way of furniture and everything to go with it. We ordered beautiful furniture made to order, with designs and materials picked by me. There was a bedroom suite, dining room suite and lounge room furniture, all chosen out of marvellous glossy magazines. It was wonderful to sit in elegant surroundings, with salesmen fussing over us, and be able to make choices without regard to the cost.

Sascha and I took our time. We leafed through the magazines, choosing then consulting each other, discarding, altering and finally deciding. Part of the living room furniture was a wall unit with shelves, a pullout desk and a cocktail bar. There was also an exquisite standing lamp with attached coffee table. I still vividly remember the lampshade, because I never saw one like it again, or one more beautiful. It consisted of eight panels, four of pleated peach-coloured silk, interspersed with four panels of white silk, on which were handpainted a dancer in black and gold, each figure in a different dance pose.

I picked crockery, cutlery, curtains, linen, a lace bedspread and many, many other beautiful items to make a home. I was like a child at Christmas, and kept asking Sascha whether this was all right, whether what I picked was not too expensive.

Sascha knew about my humble circumstances during my childhood and adolescence. He laughed at my questions and said he enjoyed seeing me so happy and so overwhelmed by the funds he could put at my disposal. He assured me that if I reached the limit, he would stop me. After days of this sheer pleasure we did reach the limit. We were heading in a droshky for our new home, where the furniture had already been delivered, but we still had not moved in. The horse trotted along. Sascha's arm was around my shoulders and I was hugging my last purchases; some ornaments and several colourful cushions. It was getting dark, the streetlights coming to life one by one. Sascha laughed, saying we must hurry to be home before midnight, or our droshky would turn into a pumpkin, and I would turn from a princess into poor Cinderella.

I was blissfully, unbelievably happy, our wedding only days away, the man I loved next to me . . .

The last day in August was cool but sunny. I wore a pale-blue silk dress trimmed with white, carrying a large bunch of white lilies Sascha had sent in the morning.

He and Eddy picked me up for the last time from Liz's apartment, where I had officially lived. Eddy and Liz were our witnesses to the ceremony. Liz had long since given up trying to talk me out of marrying Sascha. I knew she was still concerned for my future but she did not show it, remaining warm and loving towards me.

Liz fussed over me as I dressed for this important occasion. The dressmaker as usual had made my dress very fashionable, flattering for my figure and tiny waist. I wore very little makeup, my cheeks were flushed naturally by the excitement, my hair fell in thick curls to my shoulders. I wore silk stockings and high-heeled blue shoes made from sharkskin. No hat, no coat. I carried only the lilies.

Liz wore an elegant grey tailored suit, her hair as usual in a heavy plait like a crown around her head. Sascha wore a dark blue suit, a white silk shirt and a tie striped in shades of dark red and blue. Eddy was in a dark grey suit and white shirt.

On our wedding day, 31 August 1940.

All four of us drove in a taxi to the registry office. The ceremony was brief, we exchanged our vows and signed the registry. It was over in a few minutes. We were husband and wife!

After the ceremony we went to the Rome Keller restaurant for a wedding breakfast. It was intimate, in a separate room with excellent service and food for which that restaurant was famous.

At eight that evening we had invited about twenty friends into our new home. Everything was ordered from the fine caterers Otto Schwartz, including the setting of the table. Champagne bottles cooled in silver ice buckets. Shortly before eight o'clock the caterers left and Sascha and I hurried to change. Sascha put on a lighter-coloured suit, while I changed into my other wedding outfit; a peach-coloured taffeta cocktail dress.

A last inspection of everything, then my husband and I were ready to welcome our guests proudly into our home.

Liz was the first to arrive, and she had tears in her eyes when she embraced me and then Sascha. She wished us luck, and we knew she meant it.

Eddy had gone with a taxi to pick up Tante Paschy. She was our only elderly guest, apart from Kolja's mother. Needless to say, neither my parents nor Sascha's were present. That was the only bitter drop in our cup of happiness. We celebrated till late into the night. For our honeymoon we booked into a guesthouse in Kokness for two weeks. It was a resort not far from Riga in a quiet wooded and hilly countryside, ideal for lovers.

Months of undiminished happiness followed. Sascha had been a perfect lover and friend and he proved to be a perfect husband as well.

Our sexual desire for each other did not diminish after our marriage. If anything it became stronger, as if we knew our time together was limited and we could not get enough of each other. Living legally and openly together added another novel and pleasant feeling. I know that words in any language are too poor to express what it means to love completely, sincerely, unselfishly, to share joy and sorrow, and be truly one with another person, physically, emotionally and spiritually. To have been blessed with such a relationship, even for a short time, is truly a gift from God Himself.

Between our wedding and Christmas 1940, two pleasant things happened.

Since the scene in spring at his parents' home, Sascha had not been in touch with his family. He did not talk about them to me, and I knew very little about them, apart from their names, ages and occupations. Sascha's eldest brother Aron was married and had a son, then four years old. Aron ran a fur business with his father. Jacob, younger than Sascha, was studying medicine, and Abrascha, in his early twenties, was a teacher in a Jewish school. The two youngest, Mischa aged seventeen and the only sister Karina, sixteen, were still at school.

One day towards the end of 1940 Sascha came home accompanied by a young man of slight build, with dark hair and brown eyes behind heavily rimmed glasses.

"Dusik, meet my brother Abrascha!" Sascha was beaming. I had seen Abrascha only once at his parents' home that evening and I did not recognise him, but I did not ask any questions. When he kissed me on the cheek and said he was happy to meet me, I was overjoyed. From then on Abrascha became a frequent guest, and I came to know him as an intelligent, quiet and pleasant young man.

About a month after his first visit, he turned up unannounced with Mischa and Karina, who were obviously very ill at ease. They were both extremely good looking; both had brown hair and Sascha's dark blue eyes. Mischa was very tall, Karina dainty and slim, her face full of changing expressions, reflecting her thoughts. Her eyebrows were dark arches, her lashes long and curving.

On seeing the pair behind Abrascha at the door, Sascha's face lit up, and he pulled them inside. After the introductions it did not take long for them to relax, and soon we chatted as if we had known each other for a long time.

Sascha did not conceal his happiness in having part of his family accepting me, and the prospect of seeing them from now on. We knew of course their visits were clandestine and would remain so; their parents and the other two brothers were not to know about them.

We used the familiar term *du*, as relatives and close friends do. It was obvious that Sascha loved Karina dearly, and she adored him. I quickly developed a deep affection for this charming girl, and was delighted when she showed an attachment for me too.

After a few visits she told me she had an admirer, a young Latvian. He was a greengrocer whom she had met when doing the daily shopping for her mother. She obviously liked him, as her eyes sparkled when she spoke of him.

Mischa knew about his sister's admirer and kept teasing her about him. Abrascha jokingly remarked that one *goyim* in the family was enough. We laughed, but we all knew it was a serious matter, and Karina was very unlikely to stand up to her parents as Sascha had done.

About the time that Sascha's three siblings joined us, Liz told me that I could expect a change in father's attitude. She had worked to heal the rift between our parents and me whenever she got a chance. She had told them that I was now married to Sascha and very happy. Mother and I had exchanged letters through Liz for some time. She said she missed me, and was prepared to 'forgive'. Liz told me that mother was nagging father, blaming him for depriving her of me. Sascha and I had offered the first olive branch of peace by sending my parents one of our wedding photos with greetings and both our signatures. According to Liz, father was ready to capitulate, and they eventually arranged to come to our apartment on a Sunday afternoon.

I was very nervous, not wanting anything to go wrong, pacing the apartment an hour before they were due. Sascha suggested going out, as it might be better for the first meeting to be just between me and my parents; he was understandably apprehensive about their attitude towards their Jewish son-in-law. But I would not hear of it. They had to see both of us, or they could leave again. I had set the table; a plate with the best cakes, flowers, a welcoming card I had written and decorated myself, on each of their plates.

At the arranged time, not a minute later, the doorbell rang, and we opened the door together. Hot tears burned my eyes when I saw my parents standing there. Somehow they both seemed older than I remembered them only about twelve months previously. Our greetings were unnecessarily loud, and they entered awkwardly, making a big performance of wiping their feet on the entrance mat.

At that moment, my control disappeared and I threw my arms around father's neck. He hugged me tightly, and our tears met and mingled on our cheeks. I could not speak but after a moment I put one arm around Sascha and pulled him against my father. It was an extremely emotional moment when father, without hesitation, included Sascha into his hug. Mother seemed momentarily left out, but then we embraced her and she broke the spell by remarking admiringly that our apartment was beautiful, although we were still all standing in the vestibule.

Father was very sentimental, and easily moved to tears when his heart was touched. He was much more affected than my mother by this meeting, and had probably suffered much more than she had in being parted from me, although he had engineered it, being convinced he was right at the time.

I helped him out of his overcoat, and gave him a tour of the three rooms, taking my time, to enable both of us to unwind. Sascha did the same with mother.

We sat down to coffee and cakes, and slowly the conversation developed. We talked about many things, but politics, Hitler and the Nazis were not mentioned.

My parents stayed for several hours, and we relaxed more and more. When they left, we escorted them to their tram, and on parting we all knew that the past was past, and a new relationship would develop. It promised to be a good one and most importantly for me it would include Sascha.

For, strange as it might seem, my father, the anti-Semite, developed a sincere and deep affection for Sascha. Mother was less affected one way or the other. She was pleased that I was married, that I was well off financially, and that I was happy. She was not capable of thinking deeply or far ahead, preferring as always to rely on father's decisions and his guidance. She knew she could sway him if she wished, as she had done in my case, simply because she missed me and wanted to see me again. The reason for our fight had in her mind become father's fault, and now that we had made up she did not seem to care about Sascha being a Jew. Regrettably my mother was a fairly shallow person, although affectionate and incapable of doing harm to anybody.

These family reconciliations added enormously to Sascha's and my happiness. We were no longer entirely alone. Having good friends is one thing, but a family means so much more.

A few months after our wedding, Liz married too. Sascha and I were not invited to attend. I knew her husband had never approved of my relationship with Sascha, but I was hurt at being excluded. I knew she loved the man very much, so I did not blame her, as I understood only too well what love could make us do or not do. I was hoping Liz would find happiness. After her marriage we saw Liz less and less often, on fleeting visits. We were never invited to her home, and I never saw it.

By Christmas 1940 I was pregnant. Returning from my doctor with the confirmation, I flew into Sascha's arms: "I want a boy with your blue eyes!" He laughed happily: "No, a girl with your black eyes first!" When told the news, father and Tante Paschy voiced their concern that it might not be the right time to have a baby. But the fact was accepted gracefully and no more well-founded warnings were aimed at our cocoon of happiness. Tante Paschy started knitting dainty little white things, and Eddy turned up one day with a lovely pram.

We spent a wonderful Christmas in 1940, with a big tree in our cosy apartment glowing with candles and gaily wrapped presents under the tree. Father had brought his guitar, and I was so strongly reminded of the Christmases of my childhood. As well as my parents, Tante Paschy and Eddy had come. We drank to everybody's health in champagne, toasting our happiness, our future baby.

I was only too happy to use my pregnancy as an excuse to quit my boring job. I wanted to quit when we got married, but the Communists looked with displeasure at anybody who

Sascha and me photographed in a Riga street early in 1941. I was then pregnant with our daughter.

did not want to work for their 'glorious regime'. So I stayed on until my doctor agreed to give me a false statement declaring I was in danger of losing the baby if I continued to work. In fact nothing was wrong with me. I was strong and healthy and apart from morning sickness for a month, I felt marvellous.

After leaving my job I had a lot of time to myself, while Sascha was at work. My father gradually got into the habit of visiting me every second day, usually without mother. In a few short months father and I developed a new and gratifying relationship. It was no longer a case of a stern father and his unruly daughter whose virginity he strove to preserve. We found friendship and understanding between two adults, underlaid with deep affection.

We sat in two easy chairs, my charming lamp illuminating my hands busily crocheting or knitting some baby things. Father usually brought along some of his unfinished wood carvings to occupy him. We spent wonderful hours talking and I learned more about my father in the few months than I had known during the many years of living with him.

He spoke freely about his life as a young man in Russia. I heard with surprise for the first time about the fact that he had been married and divorced before he met and married my mother. We discussed sex like equals, and I came to understand father's frustration with a cold and indifferent wife, who considered sex relations an ordeal. He admitted to me that he had been unfaithful to my mother, driven to it by the need to feel that he could give a woman pleasure. I felt for him, having experienced the height of pleasure in the sex act with Sascha, and being a passionate person myself.

We talked about politics. Father persisted in his opinion that international Jewry were mostly responsible for the Nazi persecution of the European Jews. We argued hotly about it, but father always made it clear that he did not blame all Jews at all, and he assured me he thought the world of Sascha. As far as I was concerned Sascha was the only Jew who really mattered. I had no opinion of Jews in general, though I was quick to defend them because of Sascha.

My father never frightened me with any speculations about what could happen in Latvia if the Nazis did not stop their advance. He believed they would win the war very soon, and all would be back to normal in the world. He insisted the Führer had to restrain the Jews temporarily during the war, but once it was won, he would restore them to their former positions. It was a very naive assumption, but I liked to believe it too.

When I was a very young girl, father had taught me to play chess, as he loved the game and needed a partner. Now, during his visits, we often played several games. Father was an excellent player and I constantly lost to him. Normally I accepted defeat as the natural result of his being a much superior player.

In general I was not too easy to handle in the second half of my pregnancy. As it progressed I became easily upset, and

losing in chess caused me some distress. Father did not notice
it, as I did not let my tears flow till after he had left. Then
I would kick the chess figures all over the room, and promise
myself never to play another game. I had become unreasonable
in many other ways, cry for the most ridiculous reasons and
throw tantrums, which I would normally not do.

I also had unusual food preferences, and particularly desired
cakes with a lot of fresh cream. Sascha brought some home
each day, but often I wanted some more late at night, and
he endeavoured to get them, even if it meant getting out of
bed to walk a long distance.

I particularly remember one occasion when I was about five
months pregnant. My waist was noticeably expanding by then,
and there was a rounding to my lovely flat stomach.

That day father had arrived about eleven, had lunch with
me, and then we settled down to play chess. By the time I
was losing my queen for a bishop in our third game, I dissolved
into tears. Father was first amused, then alarmed. I made some
lame excuse of wanting to be left alone, and he left after some
persuasion. I collapsed into an armchair and wept like a spoiled
child, all self-control evaporated.

Sascha was due home soon, and we had planned to go out
for dinner. Still crying, I dragged out some dresses to choose
from for that evening. To my profound dismay, not one of
them would fit me! A new flood of tears followed. When Sascha
came home I was sitting broodily in my underwear, tears still
wet on my cheeks. Having experienced several of my tantrums
lately, Sascha did not make any remark. Taking one look at
the discarded dresses on the floor, my miserable appearance and
the chess pieces flung into a corner, he got the picture. He
sat down in the other armchair and stretched out his arms
to me: "Come to me, Dusik!"

I did, and placing me on his knees, Sascha rocked me gently,
my head resting on his chest, without words. It had the desired
calming effect, and between sobs and hiccups, I unburdened
to him all my sorrows. The terrible fact that father always beat
me in chess; that none of my dresses fitted me; that I had
no waist left, my figure spoiled forever. And of course I knew,

soon I would become so fat and ugly that Sascha would stop loving me.

He let me go on, stroking my hair and drying my tears with his handkerchief. Then, bending his face into my dishevelled curls, he spent the next hour talking to me in the deep soft voice I had loved since first hearing it on that distant summer day on the beach. I am sure every pregnant woman yearns to hear similar words of reassurance from her husband. Magic words Sascha found for me, words I wanted to hear. Instead of telling me how silly I was, how childish my tears, how unjust of me to doubt his love, he patiently built up my pride and self-assurance. He told me how much he looked forward to our child, how proud he was to become a father. How he cherished me beyond words because I was bearing his child. To him my bulging body was more beautiful than ever. He spoke of the special beauty of a woman approaching motherhood and how he basked in it with me. Had I forgotten that this child was created by our love, was the fruit of our love?

Sascha's words fell like dewdrops on a parched flower.

Later we bathed, and I laughed happily when Sascha sponged my rounded belly. All sorrow was forgotten. We dressed, and true to himself Sascha coaxed me into wearing a dress that still just fitted me, exposing my condition. My fitted spring coat did the same. But it was April, and too warm for my fur coat, which was loose and which, until now, I had hidden in.

Then women disguised their pregnancies with clothing as long as possible, and were seldom seen in public during the last months. I had the same reluctance to be open about my condition. But that evening, strolling with Sascha arm-in-arm along brightly lit Reinis Boulevard, I let go of this uncalled-for feeling of embarrassment of being an expectant mother, replacing it with pride.

The following weeks passed pleasantly, as I was much better adjusted and relaxed about my pregnancy. Sascha put in a word with my father about my chess problem, and suddenly father claimed he preferred to play cards with me instead of chess. I guessed the reason behind his change of mind, but did not care and kept winning shamelessly at cards.

In the spring of 1941, disquieting rumours persisted. There was talk about Jews being 'resettled' in Germany and other European countries that had fallen under the Nazi regime. There were vague speculations about some 'racial laws' in Germany concerning Jews, about Hitler's plan to conquer the whole world. But these rumours were not taken seriously in Latvia, as officially Germany and Russia were 'friends'.

Because in their incredible stupidity, Stalin and his advisers believed that Hitler would honour their pact, there was no anti-Nazi propaganda in Latvia during the Russian occupation. The Soviets concentrated on indoctrinating the Baltic population with their Communist ideas and, failing, they often resorted to arrests and deportations. The NKVD arrested and deported to Siberia about 15,000 people of all nationalities from Latvia. Among the deported were about 5000 Jews. About 6000 people were rounded up in one action on 13 and 14 June 1941. All these unfortunates were dragged from their homes, mostly during the night and put in goods trains bound for Russia, without any explanations given or charges made. At that point the Soviets must have had some idea that an attack on them by Hitler was imminent. The deportees were most likely regarded as 'enemies' of the Soviets, and some kind of fifth column for the Nazis.

Thousands of friends and relatives of the people crammed into the goods trains, milled around them, desperately seeking their loved ones. Warm clothing and food parcels were passed through the windows, while grim-faced Russian soldiers with machine guns looked on. Nobody was allowed in or out of the trains until they slowly puffed out of the station. Last handshakes, last unconvincing encouragements were called out, children were lifted to the windows for a last kiss from father, handkerchiefs fluttering, tears flowing—a sad sight, a tragic parting, in many cases forever . . .

On 22 June 1941, Germany attacked the Soviet Union without provocation. Marching first into Kaunas and Wilno in Lithuania, the Nazi hordes poured over the borders. The horrible news spread like wildfire, bringing fear and panic with it that could not be stopped or controlled by the Russians. Their army was in complete disarray, obviously not prepared for the attack. There was no order of any kind in Riga. The population was stunned, as they had been at the time of the Russian occupation a year earlier.

Offices, businesses, shops and schools closed, without being directed to do so. People filled the streets, like sheep streaming in different directions, looking for some leadership or instructions. Soldiers and civilians alike grabbed any transport they could find, with the one purpose of getting away from the rapidly advancing Nazis. There were thousands of Latvians who were either Communists by conviction or who had collaborated with the Soviets for their personal gain. There were the thugs and hoodlums who had donned the red armbands, to get the privilege of venting their hostility on innocent people and of experiencing power they had never had under normal circumstances. There were also the families of Russian military and civilian personnel who had enjoyed the good life in Latvia.

All this mass of people desperately tried to put some distance between themselves and the Nazis. Their only wish was to get into Russia proper, knowing very well that tiny Latvia would present no obstacle to the Nazi armies. Although we did not know the whole, terrible truth about the Nazi horrors, Sascha and I knew and guessed enough to become very alarmed at the prospect of being under their rule.

As usual, we had our summer cottage at the seashore, but towards the end of June, Sascha felt it safer for me to stay in Riga. In the last days of June several of our friends gathered in our apartment. Opinions and fears were exchanged, possibilities discussed. Anna, a Swiss woman and her Jewish husband David, thought it would be best to stay and see what happened. So did Lee, a Baltic German, whose wife Erna was Jewish. But Eddy, Cobby and Nina joined me in expressing the feeling that the east offered more security for Jews than could be expected from the Nazis. When I suggested fleeing with the Russians for Sascha's sake, Eddy supported me. Cobby felt that was the right course to take, but he said he could not leave his family, who did not want to go, leaving their large business behind. Nina, who was fiercely anti-Nazi, was undecided what to do. She had no family, and her latest boyfriend was away from Riga. Sascha did not say much, just cautioned me to take it easy, and not to succumb to the general panic.

After our friends had left, I insisted we go and investigate the possibilities of leaving by any transport. Sascha agreed, but he was adamant that as I was seven months pregnant he would consider travel only if it was comfortable for me.

We walked to the central station, a very long walk. All trams had stopped operating. Nobody went to work, the streets were crowded. The sight at the station was almost incredible. Screaming masses of people fought to get into several stationary trains; Russian soldiers forcibly removed civilians already on the trains; some were beaten, others trampled. People, mostly Russian soldiers, were hanging out of the train windows, balancing on the steps, and even sitting on the train roofs. As well as the trains, buses, trucks and horse-drawn vehicles of every description were at the station and the surrounding streets and boulevards. People were struggling with animal ferocity to board any of these transport facilities. Screams and curses filled the air, the chaos and panic were frightening beyond description.

Sascha led me away without a word, and I knew he would never agree to expose me to any attempt to run. The transport available was only for a fraction of the frantic, milling crowds. For most of them there would be no chance of escape.

When we got home, my father was waiting. He was seventy-two and had walked eight kilometres, from across the Daugava. He expressed concern for Sascha's safety, telling us that the latest rumours stated that the Nazis had 'walked' through Lithuania without opposition and had crossed the borders of Latvia in the south. Nobody expected the Russians to put up a show of defence for the Baltics. He suggested that Sascha should try to flee to the east without me. Calmly and logically he pointed out that as a German I would be perfectly safe; it was only a question of Sascha's safety. He was sure our separation would not be for long, as now the war surely would be over very soon. Again and again he stressed his conviction that things would be 'normal' for everybody, including Jews, once Hitler had won the war.

After the first shock at the thought of being parted from Sascha, I joined my father in his suggestion. Alone Sascha could easily find a way to get out of Latvia, if necessary on foot. He was strong and healthy and his chances were very good without being burdened with me in my condition. All I wanted was for him to be safe. He did not have to worry about me; father would look after me and our baby till he could return.

Sascha listened to us in silence. His head was bowed, a drop of perspiration glistening in the dimple of his upper lip. His white-knuckled hands were gripping a wooden figurine father had carved for us. I pleaded with him to listen to us; I could not bear the thought of him facing the danger of the Nazis because I held him back, not being able to go myself. Father and I used up all our arguments, hoping Sascha could be persuaded.

But my husband wore the stern expression he showed when he had made up his mind and was not to be moved. He said he would *not* part from me and our child. That was final.

My father left—a worried, tired old man.

Eddy returned that evening and stayed with us late into the night. I appealed to him to persuade Sascha to change his mind, but Eddy just shook his head at me. On leaving, Eddy gripped Sascha's hand with both of his, saying, "I will be there, if and when you need me."

All through the next days truckloads of Russian soldiers, columns on foot, and all kinds of horse-drawn vehicles overflowing with them passed our house, as our street was one of the main routes to the east. By the end of the day only stragglers in ones and twos were hurrying past. Then the street grew quiet—the ominous stillness before a storm.

The night was long. Sleep eluded us. Sascha cuddled me, talking softly, pretending to be calm. I willed my fears into the background. Once again we would face together whatever was to come.

On the morning of 1 July 1941, Nazi troops entered Riga unopposed. From our window we now watched endless columns of the German Wehrmacht marching by. They embodied order, discipline and confidence. Well dressed, boots shining, singing loudly, they marched in perfect unison—the conquerors.

7

The Nazis

SOME OF THE Latvian population greeted the German soldiers with flowers, seeing in them their liberators from the Russians. They expected their country to be free and independent again, but soon realised their mistake: in terms of the ferocity of their rule, the Nazis were worthy successors to the Soviets.

Latvia became part of the Reich area called Ostland, with Otto Heinrich Drechsler in charge. His headquarters were in Riga. The Reich Commissioner for Ostland was Heinrich Lohse. The chief of the Gestapo was Strauch, later replaced by Dr Lange.

Germany refused to accept the sovereignty of the Baltic states.

The black, impenetrable cloud of terror and death called Nazism had descended on my country.

Countless people were arrested, and now the jails were filled with the 'enemies of the Reich'. Shooting, torture and deportation to concentration camps became common. Nazi friends and collaborators surfaced quickly, like scum on muddy waters. The Nazis were joined by Latvian pogrom bands. To those who considered the Baltic population civilised prior to the war, the news of the massacres was barely credible.

The new masters were busy, letting the population know who was boss. The new order of things became clear very quickly. Germans were the master race, with all the privileges and no restrictions. All other Aryans, including Latvians, were second-class citizens, not comparable to the Germans, but acceptable to them. All Jews and Communists and their sympathisers were sub-human, deserving only contempt, punishment and finally extermination.

German became the official language. The swastika flag and Hitler's picture had to be displayed in all official places, and having them was 'advisable' in private homes. Riga's streets were renamed. Any attempt at asserting Latvian nationalism was squashed: the national anthem was forbidden, as was wearing the Latvian army and National Guard uniforms.

One of the first orders the Nazis gave was the surrender of all weapons, including firearms. Then came the order to surrender all bicycles and skis. Sascha and I had no bicycles, and we burned our skis.

In common with other countries conquered by the Nazis, Latvia was stripped of metals, raw materials and stored goods. Livestock was decimated. Deliveries of farm produce to the Germans became compulsory.

Some Baltic Germans who had gone to Germany in 1939 were recalled to take up various leading positions in administering Latvia.

It is historical fact that the Baltic Nazi sympathisers helped to destroy their own people. During the Nazi occupation, which lasted three years, about 25,000 Balts were killed by the Nazis and their helpers.

This figure represents human lives: people living, breathing, laughing and hoping prior to 1 July 1941.

But these happenings pale compared to the endless suffering imposed by the Nazis on the Jews of Latvia. Contrary to Nazi propaganda that the Jews collaborated with the Soviets, only a small number fled to the interior of the Soviet Union. About 75,000 Latvian Jews fell into Nazi hands, and it is estimated that 60,000 of those were murdered. Information obtained from reports made by Stahlecker, commander of Einsatzgruppe (action group) A, put the number of Jews killed in Latvia between July and 15 October 1941 as 35,025. Furthermore, he stated that *eight Balts served in his firing squads to every one German.*

In the first days of the occupation, a call went out from the Germans to Latvians to fight the 'inside enemy'. The Jews.

The response to this call for murder was enormous. Apart

from criminals and hoodlums, many prominent Latvians responded. Some were members of the *Perkonkrust* (swastika) organisation, others belonged to Latvian student groups. These were formed into bands, and issued guns. While the Germans were involved in sorting out their military position in Latvia, all power to persecute and kill Jews was handed over to Latvians.

The bloody murder of Jews began, all over Latvia, with speed and incredible cruelty. Jews were thrown into rivers to drown, locked into synagogues that were then set alight, shot in their homes and on the streets. Thousands perished in Riga during the first few days of Nazi occupation. In a matter of weeks after they entered Riga, all businesses owned by Jews, all their capital, was confiscated. All Jews had to register as such under punishment of death. Army, SS and Gestapo officers were billeted in Jewish homes and apartments; the occupants were ordered to leave at a few minutes' notice, leaving all their possessions except minimal clothing behind. Synagogues were burned, Jewish schools closed. One Jewish hospital, some Jewish doctors and several Jewish shops were permitted to function, for Jews only; Jews were forbidden to enter any other shops, theatres, cafes or restaurants, nor could they use public parks or public toilets. All public transport was forbidden to them and they had to walk in the gutters of streets, not on the footpaths. Anybody assisting or employing a Jew faced severe punishment. Every Jew had to wear a yellow star of David. The country towns fared worst. In these places, including Rujen, all the Jews were murdered. Signs were erected, proudly declaring the towns *Judenfrei* (free of Jews).

In August, Latvia's first ghetto was established in Liepaja on the west coast. A little later the Riga ghetto was set up. It was created in a part of the city where many minority groups lived, mainly Russians and Lithuanians. The non-Jews were ordered out of the area, and the Jews were ordered in. More than 30,000 Jews were confined in a very small area.

While this was being organised, constant streams of Jews walked slowly in the gutters, carrying bundles or pushing carts with their few belongings.

Children clutched toys, mothers clutched their children. Most

non-Jewish passers-by averted their faces, pretending not to
notice this evidence of human misery shuffling along with bowed
heads to an unknown fate.

Sascha did not go back to his job at Schwartz after the fateful
1 July. He registered with the other Jews and was given a yellow
ration card. This had the letter 'J' stamped on it allowing half
the portions of rations given to non-Jews, and obtainable only
in the few shops marked 'Jews only', and only during specified
hours of the day. Sascha and I refused to submit to this first
degradation. We did not use his card, depending only on mine.

On 18 July, the law came into force requiring all Jews to
wear a yellow star of David. Not wearing this outdoors was
punishable by death. The star was to be sewn to the front of
all coats, on the left side. I cut one out of some yellow material
and pinned it to one of Sascha's sports jackets. He immediately
decided to disobey the law, and I agreed wholeheartedly. We
were not beaten into submission yet; our spirit was strong, and
we were prepared to take chances.

Sascha did not look in the least Jewish, so there was little
danger of him being detected and detained on the street. We
continued our walks each day, as we had always done, for my
benefit during my pregnancy. I understood and fully shared my
husband's resentment, humiliation and frustration, and urged
him to resist the regime as much as possible. But no matter
how much we loathed the Nazis, they had the power of life
and death over everyone.

While taking chances in going out with Sascha, I rarely let
him go out alone, and I always answered the door myself. What
only a month before had seemed far away, not touching us,
had now become our horrible reality. I withdrew all our money
from the bank and we kept it at home. We weren't rich, but
we did have some assets. During the years at Schwartz, especially
during the Russian occupation, Sascha bought woollen cloth
at cost price, and brought it home. Our wardrobes were full
of woollen outfits, and we also had a trunk full of woollen cloth.
We also had a fair bit of money as he was on a good wage
so we were very well off. I also had some jewellery and furs.

Like many other people, we turned to the black market, which quickly sprang up and flourished. Money was worthless there but any items such as jewellery, clothing or shoes—things that had disappeared from the shops in Riga to the benefit of the Fatherland—were in great demand.

One of Sascha's friends, Lee, had very good black market connections. A solidly built man in his mid-forties, he had greying dark hair. His grey eyes were slightly protruding, his mouth, which was always moist, was a darkish red. He was wonderfully helpful to us, being able to obtain almost anything from the black marketeers. We did not suffer from any food shortages or indeed want for anything much at that stage.

Lee, whose wife Erna was Jewish, told us that the Jewish partner of a German citizen was safe, provided that the gentile partner stayed with him or her. We knew that in September 1935 the Nuremberg Law had forbidden mixed marriages, but in existing unions being married to a gentile in Germany apparently gave a Jew a special status; he or she was called a 'privileged Jew'. The Nazis had therefore avoided confronting the problem of mixed marriages at home, and the same system seemed to prevail in the occupied countries, including Latvia. Lee was confident that Sascha and I were relatively safe, provided we kept a low profile. He had not even registered Erna, though she never left their apartment.

Lee advised us to give our Telefunken radio to somebody for safekeeping; it was definitely dangerous, because every day people were arrested for listening to the 'enemy' broadcast. And so when my father called on us again, he took our radio with him.

Of course Lee was not our only source of moral support. Though he looked after our food requirements and kept us informed about any new developments, Eddy and Tante Paschy boosted our morale. Eddy called in every day. Our friends and my father helped us to bear the strain. My mother, however, did not visit us after the Nazi takeover because father said she was too nervous. Liz also stayed away.

July passed, and so far we were standing up to the ordeal reasonably well.

In the first days of August a truck stopped in front of our house. There was a knock at our door, and as we always did, Sascha went to our bedroom, closing the door, before I answered the knock. Not knowing what danger lurked outside, I opened the door, forcing myself to look calm. A soldier in SS uniform, two Wehrmacht soldiers and several civilians with swastika armbands faced me. Without any greeting, the SS man shoved a paper into my face, pushing past me into the flat. It was a document in German with some official stamp, stating our name and address and ordering the confiscation of all the furniture on our premises.

Controlling my anxiety, I tried to sound outraged, while the rest of the men stamped into the hallway. "It must be some mistake. I am German. Why would you confiscate my furniture? Here, see for yourselves!" I found my passport in the desk and handed it to the SS man. He looked at me, hesitated, read the order again. Then with typical Nazi logic he declared his decision; he was prepared to consider the bedroom and dining-room as mine (German). But the living-room he pronounced Jewish, and consequently its furniture could be confiscated.

I knew arguing was pointless. I stood by helpless while the men dragged out the beautiful furniture I had so lovingly picked out only a year ago. Tears of impotent anger burned my eyes as my exquisite lamp went out the door, too! I was grateful they did not enter our bedroom, where Sascha was, feeling, like me, helpless.

Now we both stood at the window watching the truck drive away. I could not help crying, but Sascha, pale but calm, hugged me comfortingly: "Let us thank God we are still together. Don't cry, Dusik, they are not worth your tears. Come, show me your fighting spirit!"

An hour after this robbery, we had another visitor. In the apartment above us lived a young man. We only knew that he was a ballet dancer and a homosexual. On meeting us he had showed an undisguised attraction to Sascha, and I used to tease Sascha about it. Now he (I don't remember his name) came to offer his help. He had seen the furniture being taken from our apartment and suggested we give him whatever we wanted to save in case the Nazis decided to take the rest.

I was apprehensive. These offers of 'help' from non-Jews to Jewish neighbours were very common, mostly accepted by desperate, haunted Jews. This 'help' proved very profitable to the 'helpers'. But I let Sascha persuade me, and he and the young dancer transported our dining room furniture upstairs. At Sascha's urging I also gave the man some silver, crystal and other valuable items, many of them wedding presents. Now we only had our bedroom furniture, and a table and chairs in the kitchen.

The dancer assured us of his sympathy and promised to look after our property until times were 'normal' again. After he departed our caretaker arrived at our door, offering the same 'help'. We thanked him and told him we had nothing of value left. Our caretaker was a Communist sympathiser, real or fake, who had worn the red armband during the Russian occupation. Now he had exchanged it for the swastika band. He was bound to be anxious to prove worthy of the Nazis and therefore we considered him dangerous. His extreme friendliness towards us made us doubly suspicious. As it happened, our suspicions were probably justified.

8

Sylvia Enters Our World

On the morning of 16 August 1941, two men in civilian clothes called on us. Some inner voice told me there was real danger when I saw them at the door.

"Gestapo," one of them said curtly, "you and your Jewish husband will come with us."

I called on my reserves of courage, and asked politely why and where we would be going. In reply I got another growl: "Get the Jew." I opened the door to our bedroom, knowing Sascha had heard the exchange of words. "*Mach schnell, Jude,*" barked one of the hoodlums, giving Sascha a push, with the arrogant '*du*' they used for addressing Jews. Sascha took his sports jacket with the star from the hook in the hallway and helped me down the stairs. A car was parked in front of the house. One of the men sat next to the driver, the other placed himself in the back between Sascha and me. We were driven in silence to the Gestapo headquarters in Reinis Boulevard. Everybody in Riga knew where that feared establishment was. On arrival we heard a rude '*Heraus!*' then we were marched by both men through several rooms, filled with many obviously drunk men, most of them young. They were all in civilian clothes, wearing the swastika armband, and had machine guns on their laps or over their shoulders. We entered a large room, without windows, the air grey with tobacco smoke. It was filled with uniformed SS men, sitting and standing around. Nobody said a word. We were taken to a double door, and the two men who had brought us disappeared through it, leaving us standing outside.

Panic had constricted my throat, I felt I would never be able to make a sound again. Who had informed on us? The young man upstairs? Our caretaker? I made a movement to touch Sascha's hand, but he put it in his pocket and took out a handkerchief. His eyes signalled 'Careful!', his just detectable smile said 'Courage!' We stood there like condemned criminals. I felt dizzy, and desperately wanted to sit down.

After what seemed an eternity, the door opened and one of the men gestured to me to come in. That room was small and very hot. Several young men, some in SS uniforms, others in civilian clothes, stared at me. One sitting behind a large desk was elderly. He looked up, eyeing me up and down. I was in my ninth month of pregnancy and near collapse with terror.

"Do you realise that listening to the enemy radio broadcast is punishable by death?" he said. His tone of voice was threatening, his stare icy. Relieved by the remark about a radio we did not have, I managed to find my voice and replied with some confidence. If that was the charge, I said, it was easy to establish that we had no radio in our possession. Besides why should I, a German, be accused of such a crime? While talking, I handed the man my passport. My name or my reply had some effect, as the interrogator asked me to sit down.

He studied the passport, then handing it back to me, managed a frosty smile. "You may go. We will check out about your not having a radio."

"Can my husband go with me? I don't feel well." I tried to keep the fear out of my question. There was no reply, and I was led by the arm out of the room.

Sascha and I could only exchange a glance before he disappeared into the same room I had left. The man led me back to the outside door, where he left me without a further word.

Noticing a bench across the street, I fell on to it, numb with fear. I had no way of knowing what they would do to Sascha. They might need a real reason or proof to detain me, a German, but no such rules applied to Jews, who lived and died by Nazi whim alone. I wanted to stay close to the horrible building where my beloved husband was. I knew I could do nothing against the monsters who now held him in their power, but I could not make myself go away. Deep despair gripped my heart. It was our first encounter with real danger.

A sudden sharp pain made me catch my breath. My stomach was contracting in spasms and I realised with a shock that I was prematurely in labour. A second and third spasm of pain came and went before I got up and started to walk towards home. It was at least one kilometre away.

Doubling up with each new pain, I looked back towards the sinister building, hoping to see Sascha emerging from it. I couldn't believe all this was really happening. Hardly aware of what I was doing, I hailed a passing horse buggy and, tears streaming down my face, gave my address. The coachman was a friendly old soul, who seeing my distress tried to comfort me. He waited at our house while I stumbled upstairs and got my case, packed for the hospital.

At the beginning of my pregnancy I had been booked into one of the large hospitals in Riga. After the Nazi occupation I was told by my doctor there that we had a 'problem'. It was an Aryan hospital and I could have my child there, but my Jewish husband would not be allowed to enter it. Outraged, I immediately went to the only Jewish hospital operating. I was told that being a German I could not be admitted as they were forbidden to treat Aryans.

Thanks to the intervention of a Jewish doctor friend, as well as Sascha himself, the hospital administration relented and gave permission for me to come for the birth of the baby only. For the regular checkups and any medication, I still had to consult my Aryan doctor. Now I was on my way to the Jewish hospital, labour pains racking my body, while my agony and helplessness over Sascha had twisted together into an iron band crushing my heart.

The street was nearly empty. Suddenly I saw through my tears Sascha running down the street towards our home. I screamed to the coachman to stop. "Saschinka, here, I am here!" I cried. He stopped, saw me and jumped in. Clinging to him, I fainted with relief.

The next contraction brought me back to reality. Sascha was

cradling me. In response to my frantic questions, he told me not to worry. He had been freed after questioning by the man behind the desk, and he had not been mistreated or threatened. But on the way out he was made to wait for a long time in the room filled with the drunken thugs with guns.

It was a long ride to the hospital. The coachman turned and smiled at me. Pointing at the star on Sascha's chest, he said, not in an unfriendly way, "You get me into trouble with this. How about covering it up?" I put my head on the star, and left it there till we arrived at the hospital. Sascha was concerned that my labour had started about two weeks prematurely, but now that he was with me, I calmed down, and the regular spasms of pain did not seem too bad. After a sister in the hospital questioned me about the frequency of my contractions, she said I would be admitted, then she left.

It was time to say goodbye for the next ten days. The hospital rules did not permit husbands to visit their wives during that time, though they could see their babies through a glass window. They were allowed only to leave flowers and messages.

Our arrest had made me terribly nervous, and I implored Sascha not to remain in our apartment by himself, but to stay with our friends, changing the place frequently. He promised to do as I asked, and said he would come each day, even though we could not see each other. The sister returned to say that my bed was ready. Sascha asked permission to stay till the baby was born. She gave him a sarcastic smile. "The baby will not come today, and maybe not tomorrow," she said. "You cannot stay. Husbands are not welcome here."

Sascha embraced me tenderly. We kissed.

"Please be careful!"

"God bless you, Dusik! I will be back tonight." I was led away into a room with four beds, two occupied by women.

A nurse helped me undress, gave me a drink, and left. The two women conversed in whispers, having already had their babies.

A doctor came, examined me, and when I asked if the baby was due soon, he shrugged. "First baby? Not today, maybe tomorrow." Semi-conscious, I floated in a mist of pain. Nobody seemed to care about me. The doctor, the sisters and the nurses were all businesslike and very cold. Not a word of reassurance or comfort. I wondered if it was because they knew me to be a German. I desperately missed my husband, I needed him so much! Feeling very alone, I cried.

The hours dragged on, the intervals between the contractions getting shorter. I could not help moaning. I registered through a haze that it grew dark, the lights went on, there was some clatter of dishes.

A nurse touched my shoulder: "Your husband is here, this is a note from him." I came alive. A page torn from a small notebook, Sascha's familiar handwriting! Words of love, comfort and courage!

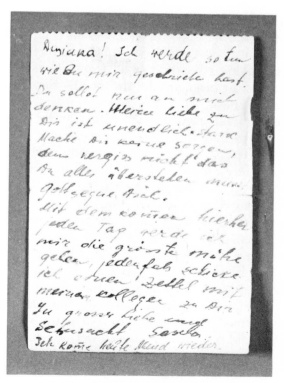

The original of Sascha's note to me in hospital. This first of his notes has somehow survived with me for fifty years.

Dusinka!

I will do as you asked.

Just think of me. My love for you is boundless and strong.

Do not worry. Don't forget you have to cope with everything.

God bless you!

I will try very hard to come here every day. In any case I will send a note to you with my colleague.

With all my love and longing, Sascha.

I will come back this evening.

Hastily I scribbled a reply: "I am fine. The pain is not bad. Be careful. I love you . . . !"

By eleven o'clock that night the labour pains began in earnest. I was taken to the labour ward and placed on a wide bed. Another woman was in labour opposite me. We both moaned, nurses came and went. I lost track of time as the pain became excruciating, taking possession of my whole body. My hands were put behind my head, around the iron bars of the bedstead, and I was told to push.

I screamed and screamed as I felt my body being cruelly ripped apart. I begged to be given something to relieve the pain, just for a moment. The faces of the doctors and sisters floated past, unemotional. "Push! There is nothing we can give you. Push." Sweat and tears dripped into my mouth. "O God, help me . . . !"

On 17 August 1941 at 11 am our daughter was born. Exhausted and barely conscious I had a glimpse of a red body, a red face with closed eyes, some dark tufts of hair on the scalp. Then I was in the other room again, and I slept and slept.

Twenty-four hours after the birth, my baby was brought to me for the first time. I unwrapped the rug and nappy and examined her, marvelling at the incredibly tiny fingers and toes so perfectly formed. Her red colour was gone, replaced by a rosy glow. She did not cry, but moved her tiny hands and feet constantly, as if in a struggle against an invisible restraint.

For the first time I got a smile from the nurse as she put the baby's mouth to my nipple. The tiny puckered lips parted, and then closed and suckled. An indescribable feeling of peace, well-being and tenderness flooded my whole body. Holding this precious new life in my arms, I became a mother. A small fist pressed against my breast, the little mouth released the nipple, the slightly puffed lids parted. A pair of enormous dark eyes looked into mine . . .

According to the rules of that time, a woman after giving birth had to remain in hospital and in bed for ten days. After a week I was allowed to sit up, after nine days stand up and walk. My baby was brought to me only at feeding times, otherwise she was looked after by the nurses.

Sascha came each day, sometimes twice, often accompanied by Eddy. We exchanged notes of affection and happiness over the birth of our baby daughter. Sascha was permitted to look at her through the glass and he assured me he thought she was beautiful. (I complained that she did not have his blue eyes as I had wished.) We both could hardly wait for the ten days to pass. I tried to make conversation with the other women but they, as well as the staff of the hospital, remained cold and unfriendly towards me.

One of the beds in my room was occupied by the woman who had been in the labour ward with me. She had a very difficult birth with instruments, and her baby girl was refusing to take any nourishment. After a few days the husband was allowed to visit his wife and baby. A doctor held a hushed conversation with them, and it was evident the baby was seriously ill. The woman cried a lot, especially when the baby was brought to her, and the sister made vain attempts to coax her to feed.

I could see from my bed the pitiful little bundle, the shrunken head, the yellow skin, the face contorted into a mask of suffering. In a few days the baby was dead from yellow jaundice. I remembered that pathetic little face for a long time. It seemed to express all the suffering of her race.

At last the ten days passed, and I stood at the door with our baby in my arms. My anxiety over Sascha's safety had never eased while I was in hospital. I had lived from one of his calls to the next, never sure there would be a next one.

Now we were together again, all three of us! Sascha held our child for the first time and the tenderness of his touch, the love in his eyes confirmed my belief that he would be a wonderful father.

We arrived home and found that our apartment had not been interfered with, as I had feared.

We slipped into our new role of being parents with ease. Friends started to arrive. My parents came, my mother for the first time since the Nazi occupation. We discussed names, and settled for my choice, Sylvia, and Sascha's, Ingrid.

Our little daughter was a good healthy baby; ate and slept well and seldom cried. Life for our little family had acquired a new meaning and brightness again.

But there was much trauma to come.

A month after I got home, a Wehrmacht officer presented himself with a billeting order to take over our apartment, which he said was listed as Jewish. I used my argument of being a German, and produced my passport. The officer seemed sympathetic, but said he had his orders. He pointed out that if he did not take over our apartment, it still had to be vacated for the Wehrmacht. He suggested coming back in two days, to give us time to find other accommodation. When I agreed, he asked to see the bedroom, where Sascha sat by the window, holding Sylvia. The officer nodded to him, and said he had no objections if we took our furniture with us. He did not remark on the lack of it in the other two rooms.

When he left Sascha and I discussed the new problem confronting us.

After the Nazis marched into Latvia, Sascha put aside his anger and resumed contact with his family. They still did not accept me, but I was more than willing to overlook this, understanding Sascha's desire to keep in touch in these troubled and dangerous times. His family had suffered: his father's business had been taken from him, their bank account confiscated. Abrascha was very disturbed, all Jewish schools were closed, Jacob had been kicked out of the university.

Abrascha told us that the greengrocer whom Karina had jokingly called her 'admirer' had seriously offered to marry her. Karina had told Abrascha about the proposal, and he had gone to see the young Latvian. He loved Karina and wanted to help her, pointing out that in marrying a Christian (an Aryan), she had a better chance of survival. Abrascha was in favour of it, seeing safety for his only sister, and he had come to get Sascha's support in convincing their parents. Both brothers tried. Sascha told me later they spent hours begging them to give Karina at least a chance, as it was known that Jews in mixed marriages were treated better. But Karina's parents flatly refused even to consider the matter, abused the sons and scolded Karina severely.

It was hard to say what Karina herself felt. We saw her several times during July and August. She still went every day to the greengrocer, who supplied the family with vegetables free of charge. Her parents accepted his kindness, sure of their daughter's obedience. Karina said she was very fond of the young man, and she knew he was decent and well-meaning, but she could not and would not go against her parents' wishes. I was deeply sorry for this lovely girl, who was being denied her chance of survival.

When the Riga ghetto area was decided on and the transition began, Sascha's parents and family moved into the area. It was a long distance from where we lived, and I worried when Sascha visited them, running risks by taking off his star and using the tram, which was forbidden to Jews.

Now that we had to vacate our apartment we had to decide where to go. It was unlikely we would obtain another apartment in the Aryan area, on account of Sascha. All accommodation was supervised and regulated by the TODT organisation. Not feeling comfortable about the ghetto area, Sascha suggested I look for accommodation for me and our baby in the Aryan sector, or move in with my parents or Tante Paschy. He was prepared to move in with his family till 'things settle down'.

But I refused to be parted from him. There were no restrictions yet on people's movements in and out of the ghetto area, so I insisted we move there while we looked for a better solution, as we had only two days at our disposal. After considering all possibilities Sascha agreed, but he made me promise that at the slightest sign of danger I would take our baby and leave.

For Sascha's sake I was willing to move into the same house

as his family was living in now. But even under these dramatic circumstances Sascha's parents, especially his mother, wanted no part of his *goy* wife. They even refused to see Sascha's child, and never did. It was odd how savagely Sascha's mother resented, almost hated, all non-Jews, especially considering her own background. Her mother had been a Christian, a Russian who married a moderate Jew and, retaining her own religion, had christened Sascha's mother in the Russian Orthodox Church. When Sascha's mother met his father, she converted to Judaism before they married. Sascha had told me her story, and we often discussed the paradox of her behaviour. It was hard to understand why she, a half-Jew herself, was the most orthodox Jew in the family and the most implacable towards me.

Eventually Sascha and I moved with our baby into a tiny flat in the ghetto area, several streets away from his family. We had brought our bedroom furniture and our clothing with us. Eddy had hired a truck and helped us move.

The next weeks were uneventful. We devoted ourselves to our beautiful baby and kept in touch with the 'outside'. Eddy, Lee, Nina and Tante Paschy visited us, but my father and many others stayed away. We tried to remain confident that the situation would improve, but we could hardly overlook the depressing atmosphere around us, the uncertainty, fear and enormous tension. Endless rumours circulated, all bad. Some new order or decree was issued daily, further restricting the lives, rights and movements of the Jews.

Eddy and Lee had been trying to find some accommodation for us 'outside' without success. One day Eddy arrived very agitated. He had it from a reliable source that the ghetto area was to be closed off from the outside world on 25 October; nobody would be permitted to enter or leave without a pass issued by the ghetto commandant. The ghetto was to be watched by armed guards, some German, but the majority Latvians. Only Jews selected for 'working parties' (slave labour) would be allowed to leave the ghetto, accompanied by guards.

We sat in silence for a while, stunned by this news. Sascha asked Eddy to take me and our baby out of the ghetto immediately. When I objected, he reminded me of my promise.

He was very upset, and begged me to understand how deeply unhappy he was at the thought that he might jeopardise Sylvia's and my safety. He assured me that he could face his fate in the ghetto if he knew we were safe. Lee had told us of several mixed marriages where the Jewish men were living now in the ghetto while their families remained 'outside'.

I was terrified at the prospect of being locked in, but not willing to abandon my husband. Eddy offered to take all of us in for a while. He lived in the suburb of Sarkandaugava with his mother and sister, and was willing to try to persuade them to let us stay until we found something else. We knew Eddy's mother did like Sascha, but harbouring a Jew now was a dangerous thing to do, and Eddy was not sure of her reaction. Apartments 'outside' were scarce, any new tenants screened. Nothing was decided, and Eddy left.

Looking at the barbed-wire fence encircling the ghetto area sent shivers down my spine. We spent a sleepless night, each wanting the best for the other and arguing bitterly in the process. Sascha's argument about the safety of our baby as our most important consideration won out. I promised again to leave with her before the ghetto was closed.

Next morning I fed the baby, and then put her into Sascha's arms. "I will go to Nina and ring Eddy, see what his mother said," I told him.

Sascha looked worried. "Don't put it off for too long. You promised. We have to face the reality." I kissed them both.

Without saying a word to Sascha, I had formed a plan of my own. It was a bluff, my last effort before leaving Sascha behind in the ghetto alone.

A Latvian passport bore the Christian name and surname of each person applicable at the time of the passport being issued (at twenty-one). In my case it was my maiden name: Ingeborg Erika Hesse. The date of my marriage and the new name were entered in the back pages. So were Sylvia's name and her date of birth. These facts were crucial for me now, if I was to succeed.

I went to the German Kommandatur opposite the opera house, and, walking up the wide steps, said a silent prayer. Finding the appropriate office, I approached the TODT man behind a desk. Desperation gave me strength, and I spoke out with a show of confidence I did not feel. Presenting my passport opened on the front page to him, I actually succeeded in sounding arrogant: "As you can see I am a German. I have been living in . . . street and as this area has now been allotted to Jews, I have to get out. I cannot find an apartment in the Aryan area, so could you please help me? It is urgent, as I have been asked to leave today."

Lucky for me the TODT man was obviously harassed by the many people lining up behind me. Glancing at the name in my passport and registering my sweet smile, he pulled out a list and scribbled something on official-looking paper. "There you are. Next!"

I thanked him with another sweet smile, and taking the paper left in a hurry. Going down the steps I looked at it. The irony! It was exactly the same kind of order that a month previously had forced us to surrender our apartment to the German officer. The order stated that a three-room confiscated Jewish apartment without furniture was at my disposal as of that day.

Pocketing the precious document, I hired a large horse-drawn vehicle, big enough for the remnants of our furniture. When I returned home I hurriedly told Sascha what I had done. He hugged me without words.

Sascha and the coachman loaded the furniture, while I packed our other belongings into suitcases. I turned Sascha's jacket with the star inside out and carried it over my arm and, climbing in behind the coachman, Sascha sat next to me with our baby in his arms. There was no time for him to say goodbye to his family.

The coachman lifted his whip, the horse trotted briskly. It was just getting dark when we passed through the gates of the ghetto, still unguarded. People passing glanced at us, some with curiosity, most with apathy.

We were leaving the ghetto practically at the eleventh hour. Only days later on 25 October the large gates were shut and locked, the thousands inside doomed.

When we arrived at our new destination Sascha went to see the house caretaker and showed him the document from the

TODT man. The caretaker did not show any surprise and took us upstairs to the apartment that was to be our new home. He apparently remained, then and during the months we lived there, ignorant of the fact that one of his tenants was Jewish. He helped with the furniture and Sascha gave him and the coachman generous tips. We had three large, empty rooms enveloping us with the autumn chill. But we were 'outside' again and for the moment we were safe.

9

Torn Apart

DURING THE NEXT few weeks we relaxed. With Lee's help we acquired a few pieces of furniture to make our place more livable. Lee assured us there was still no danger for 'mixed marriages' when the couples remained outside the ghetto. Nobody had been harassed by the Nazis and the general mood was optimistic.

We kept constantly in touch with friends and family, visiting each other, exchanging news and giving moral and practical support where needed.

Since we lived 'outside' again my father resumed his visits but mother kept away. She sent me letters with father, imploring me to think of myself and the baby's safety, and let Sascha, being a man, take his chances. Father, on the contrary, being capable of strong emotions and great loyalty, understood and approved of my loyalty to the man I loved. Eddy, Lee and Nina were our constant visitors; when Kolja sought us out again, we were overjoyed. We had not seen him since the Nazi occupation and had assumed that he had fled with the Russians. But it turned out he had gone into hiding with his family to some relations in the country. As things settled down, he returned to his tailoring business and had not encountered any problems. In fact Kolja told us, laughing, that quite a few members of the 'master race' had become his satisfied customers, some showing their appreciation of his excellent workmanship by bringing him cigarettes and chocolates. Kolja's mother never failed to send us something tasty she had cooked or baked. Even Liz dropped in for a few minutes, concerned, but so nervous and ill at ease that it left no doubt this visit had been made unbeknown to her husband.

Our most favoured visitor was Tante Paschy. In spite of her frailty, she braved the long tram journey. Nobody could console, encourage and make life look so wonderful as she could. She invariably took Sascha into her arms, pressed his head to her bosom and stroked his hair, like a child's, telling him all would be well, she just knew it! She always arrived laden with the most delicately knitted and crocheted baby jackets, bootees and dresses.

We came to know several new couples of mixed marriages. One of them was a Russian girl, Katja, and her Jewish husband Felix, the son of a very prominent jeweller. His father had managed to hide many precious stones and gold before the Nazis took his exclusive shop on Chalk Street. He and his wife went into the ghetto, giving their son part of the saved jewellery. Katja and Felix had a five-year-old son and seemed to be devoted to each other. They lived in a luxurious apartment and Felix spoke self-assuredly of their plans to go to Sweden. Lee was trying to obtain false documents for them. Lee had exceptional connections to the black market and it seemed he also knew the 'right' people among the feared Gestapo. We never asked him any questions, and trusted him completely. After all he was 'one of us', his own wife being Jewish and his daughter a 'Mischling'.

Another couple we knew were Anna and David. Being Swiss, Anna had retained her Swiss passport. David was a Jew and a Latvian citizen. Anna constantly enquired in the Swiss embassy about their chances of entering Switzerland. They had no children and believed Anna's Swiss citizenship provided them with some protection. Among us they feared the Nazis the least, and had even kept their radio set, which none of us had dared to do.

Our group consisted of six 'mixed' couples. We all had our plans and hopes, and we encouraged each other.

After the Riga ghetto was secured behind locked gates, little news reached us on the outside. Rumours, the shadow of the facts, circulated strongly. As anticipated, after closure nobody could enter or leave the ghetto without a special pass. Groups of 'working Jews' were taken out of the ghetto, escorted by guards, mostly Latvians, with the swastika armband. These slave labourers (among them women) were forced to perform heavy manual work, loading and unloading trucks, repairing roads and railways. Non-Jews passing these unfortunate human beings looked away and hurried on.

The inmates of the ghetto wore their own clothes, no uniforms. A few German policemen were in charge in the ghetto, but the guards were all Latvians. They wore green armbands. There was a puppet Jewish police force inside the ghetto to keep order among their own people. Guarding the Jewish working columns were usually one Latvian man, sometimes a woman, or even a youth. It was obvious nobody expected any trouble from the 'slaves'.

I was terrified to let Sascha go near the ghetto, even to visit his family. He respected and complied with my wish that we remain together at all times, and not take any unnecessary risks.

Eddy, our wonderful friend, undertook to find out what he could about Sascha's family. Somehow he did contact Mischa while he was out with a working party. The family was all right, the boys mostly outside in working parties, while Karina worked in the ghetto kitchen. Mischa said they could use some food and cigarettes for barter. From then on we sent them parcels, which Eddy or Lee smuggled in by bribing the guard. Some of the Latvian guards were not averse to money, cigarettes or bottles of vodka. But caution was imperative, as many of the hoodlums used as guards at the gate and along the fence were more deadly and cruel than the Nazis themselves. They would not hesitate to denounce anybody trying to help a Jew. But once the channels through bribery were established our group and others who had relatives behind the walls of the ghetto used these channels to help their dear ones.

In November 1941 we started to hear rumours of an order to liquidate the Riga ghetto. But before they could be confirmed, the Nazis struck.

Like thousands of people in Riga, Sascha and I heard that something unusual was happening in the ghetto. Mostly it was

rumoured that the Jews were being relocated to other places.
Some said they were destined to go to Germany to work in
the factories. Others, more pessimistic, spoke of shootings.
Everybody knew the city's buses were used to transport Jews,
but nobody knew where. The belief that something terrible was
happening in the ghetto gradually prevailed in everybody's minds.
No Jewish working parties were seen in the streets.

Sascha was very worried about his family. Lee and Eddy who
tried to find out what was going on, were turned back, long
before they reached the ghetto, by armed guards.

We learned the horrible truth about what happened in the
ghetto between 29 November and 9 December gradually over
the next few months.

On 29 November orders were posted all through the ghetto
for the inmates to be ready for transport to other destinations.
At that time there were about 32,000 Latvian Jews in the ghetto.
On that day additional guards were brought in. Then a group
of SA men in brown uniforms arrived. Late that night Germans
and Latvians, all drunk, stormed into the houses, shooting men,
women and children. About a thousand Jews perished on that
one night in the Riga ghetto. The panic was enormous.

On the morning of 30 November thousands of terrified Jews
were formed into columns, each surrounded by Latvian guards
with one German in charge of each column. Rows of the town's
blue buses were drawn up outside the ghetto gates. The
announcement came over the loudspeaker that transport to
other destinations had been arranged and would proceed. To
keep up this pretence, everybody was marched or driven to
the Rumbuli railway station. From there they were taken in
small, heavily guarded groups to the nearby forest, where they
were massacred.

Actions on a similar scale followed on 8 and 9 December.
Some victims of these actions were murdered in Birkenwald
(birch forest). The remaining Latvian Jews (about 4000 men
and 300 women) were put into a section of the ghetto named
the Little Ghetto. Women were separated from the men. No
children remained. The large, now empty section was named
the Large Ghetto and was intended to house Jews brought in

from the west. It is estimated that about 50,000 Jews from Germany, Austria, Bohemia and Czechoslovakia were deported to the east, principally to Riga and Minsk. The first transport of these Jews arrived in Riga in the middle of December.

When the first group of Jewish slave workers appeared again on the Riga streets, the news spread and Sascha hoped to hear from his family.

But then Lee brought us the hideous news. In the 30 November action his whole family had been murdered.

There was no way of softening the blow. Sascha stared at Lee, deathly white. "*All* of them? Karina too?"

Lee could only nod. He had checked and rechecked with his sources, before coming to us. He had known for several days, trying to find the courage to tell Sascha.

We sat in silence, death standing among us. The death of nine innocent people!

I saw a mental picture of Mischa laughing, while trying on a new sports coat, a present from us, Karina's sparkling eyes as she talked about the greengrocer's compliments. An unwarranted and inexplicable guilt stopped me from uttering words of comfort to Sascha. What could anyone say at that moment? What could Lee say? A German. What could *I* say? A German.

We seemed to be frozen into silent statues for ever. At last Sascha got up and walked to the door, moving his legs as if his feet were glued to the floor and it took a great effort to move them. He shut the door quietly behind him and we heard the front door click shut just as quietly. I made no attempt to hold him back, though I guessed he had left without a coat and without his star of David, and I had no idea what he intended to do or where he would go.

Lee put his arm around my shoulders and said, "There is nothing you or anyone can do. Leave him be."

I was shaking all over. Lee poured us a brandy, and after we continued to sit in silence a while longer, he left. I went into the bedroom and sat down by the pram. Our baby daughter slept, little fists clenched, cheeks rosy, dark eyebrows slightly puckered.

God in heaven, *why?* Why Sascha's family? Why all of them? Lovely Karina, only seventeen.

I was not a churchgoer but I believed in God, and had prayed since childhood. I had never liked learning prescribed prayers, which had no meaning for me. But I did pray in my own words, always addressing Christ, not God, in my prayers. Now, folding my trembling hands, I asked Christ to give Sascha strength to bear the unbearable. To keep him safe. To help me help him. To bring him back to me and our child.

Hours passed and it grew dark. Sylvia awoke, I bathed and fed her and walked up and down through the rooms, holding her in my arms. Eventually I put her back into the pram, and seated next to it I moved coloured rings hanging on a string in front of her. She grabbed at them and gurgled in delight.

I heard the front door open and shut. Sascha was back. I rushed into the living room, my mouth dry. Would I find the right words? Sascha stood there, stooped, his face drawn, aged, his eyes dry, burning with a strange cold fire.

He fell into a chair and I knelt before him. "My beloved," was all I could manage to whisper. I wished he would cry, or shout, or smash something. His calmness was so unnatural it froze my heart.

The night dragged on. I handed Sascha a coffee, he drank it. I gave him a brandy, he drank it too, all without a word. I attended to the baby, then took a bath and changed into my dressing gown. Sascha had not moved from the chair, had not said a word since his return. Later I sat on the floor next to him, and taking his hand held it to my lips. He stroked my hair and, leaning back in the chair, closed his eyes.

Neither Sascha nor I slept all night. Dawn broke, the baby awoke, as she did each morning at about six, loudly demanding to be fed. I went into the bedroom, changed her, and put her to my breast. The beautiful dark, innocent eyes looked at me, and her crying stopped when the little mouth found the source of nourishment. The familiar feeling of peace surged through me, while my baby suckled until she was content.

Suddenly I knew what I had to do. I wiped the traces of milk from the little face, ran my fingers gently through the dark fluff on her head, and entered the other room. Without a word I put the child on Sascha's lap. His arms went at once to hold her, and he lifted her to his chest. The dam broke . . . Sascha sobbed and sobbed, and eventually he slept.

Gradually we resumed our life. When our friends visited us, nobody mentioned Sascha's family. So far, his was the only loss among us.

The bad news continued to reach us. We absorbed what we could in horror.

Whole regiments of Lithuanian police were sent to Latvia, where they joined Latvians to guard the camps and ghettos and to take part in the murder actions.

At the end of 1941 the Salaspils concentration camp was set up. Foreign as well as Latvian Jews were interned there. Political and criminal offenders who were Aryans were also sent there. It gained a reputation as the worst in Latvia.

Krause was put in charge of the Salaspils camp and was also the commandant of both Riga ghettos. He was extremely cruel and sadistic. The Jews called him 'cannibal'. His assistant was Max Gimmlich. Krause ordered any Jew caught smuggling anything into the ghetto shot on the spot.

The areas where the mass murders were carried out during the Nazi occupation of Latvia were heavily guarded and off limits to the civilian population. But the veil of secrecy was sometimes torn, and horror stories leaked out: stories of mass graves with layer upon layer of corpses. Hundreds of terrified Jews were pushed at rifle point to the edge of the grave. Then they were machine-gunned, and fell into the mass grave, some dead, some wounded, on top of the corpses already there. There were whispered stories of men putting their hands over the eyes of their children and mothers begging on their knees for their babies to be spared. There were heart-tearing tales of little children who, shivering in the cold, asked their mothers whether they could keep their singlet or a favoured toy. The victims were ordered to shed all their clothing before they were shot. Truckloads of clothing, shoes and other last possessions, including many children's toys, left after the deed was done.

The orders to kill, when and how many, in Latvia as in all occupied countries were issued by the Nazis. They were the decisionmakers, the supervisors, to make sure the murders were done in an orderly way, with the minimum of resistance and a maximum of secrecy. Many records testify to that fact.

The actual killing was done by selected locals. In Latvia these were Latvians, Lithuanians and some Ukrainians. These monsters proved worthy of the honour bestowed on them by their masters. The murderers were kept in a constant drunken stupor, and no doubt rewarded well. But even to these creatures the bloodbath proved occasionally too much; one of the killers went berserk and on coming home shot his wife and two children. Another shot himself. Some of these Nazi lackeys were actually arrested by the ever-watchful Gestapo for disobedience if they showed some humanity towards Jews.

All these stories circulated among the population by *Mundfunk* (word of mouth). Fear hung in the air like a heavy cloud; nobody dared to speak out. Confidences were exchanged with the utmost caution, and suspicion of everybody flourished. It took the opening of the concentration camps after the war, films taken by the Allies, and films and documents by the Nazis themselves, to confirm the Nazi genocide. But it is undeniable that rumours of most of their atrocities circulated for years, although many were not believed, because people did not want to credit them.

As Leon Uris put it so bluntly: "The world committed the unforgivable crime of conspiracy of silence, and all the moralists in the world have condoned genocide by the conspiracy of silence." No amount of whitewashing, excusing, denying or minimising the enormous Nazi crimes, which has been attempted since the war, will ever remove the shameful stain from the history of many nations.

Lee, the oldest and wisest among us, made the suggestion that our Jewish partners should convert to Christianity. Although the Nazis refused to recognise any religion, Lee thought that the church still had some influence. Unfortunately no church had voiced objections about the treatment of the Jews, but it did not lend support to the persecutions either. Being

one of their flock could possibly lend some measure of security
to the Jewish partner of an Aryan.

We discussed the question at length. David had already been
christened, Lee had obtained a certificate of baptism for his
wife. The Jewish partners of the other two couples did not find
acceptable the idea of becoming Christians. Jews who converted
to Christianity were called *Geschmad* and despised by other Jews.
It was decided that Katja and I try our respective churches.
Katja's Russian Orthodox Church refused to see Felix, using
lame excuses. Our Lutheran pastor was helpful, provided Sascha
was prepared to come to him every day for two weeks to be
taught about Christianity, like a child would be before being
confirmed.

Sascha had no objections. He has always been a 'modern'
Jew, not observing the kosher dishes, eating everything, including
pork. He celebrated Christmas with me and helped me colour
Easter eggs, often teased by Cobby, who was not orthodox either.

As arranged Sascha went to see the pastor every day. We
were planning to have his and Sylvia's christenings together.
My father offered to be Sascha's godfather, and Tante Paschy
was to be his godmother. She was also to be Sylvia's godmother
while Eddy wanted to be her godfather.

The big day arrived just before Christmas 1941. Father arrived
in a dark suit, and showed me a cross he had carved from rosewood
for Sascha, embossed with tiny copper roses and leaves. Eddy
had brought a silver cup for Sylvia. Tante Paschy gave Sascha
a small gold cross, and for Sylvia she had made a gorgeous
christening dress, crocheted from white wool in delicate flowers
and trimmed with pink bows. Mother and Liz were absent. We
had not invited anybody else.

In the living room Tante Paschy and I had constructed an
altar from several suitcases covered with a white damask
tablecloth. On it stood a vase of gladioli that Eddy had somehow
managed to get.

The pastor came and was introduced to everybody. He placed
a golden crucifix and a Bible on the makeshift altar and we
assembled in front of it. The ceremony was very solemn, as
it could only be in these dramatic times.

Sascha knelt with father and Tante Paschy and they said the '*Vater Unser*' (Lord's Prayer) together. Then Sascha declared in a steady voice: "*Ich glaube an den Vater, den Sohn und den Heiligen Gheist . . .*" (I believe in the Father, the Son and the Holy Ghost . . .).

The pastor gave Sascha and the godparents Communion, and then they all embraced. Father held Sascha tightly in his arms, and tears coasted unashamedly down his face. Being very religious he felt that by becoming a Christian Sascha had ceased to be a Jew, and had become truly one of us.

When Sylvia's turn came, Tante Paschy held her in her arms, Eddy next to her. Our four-months-old daughter smiled happily all through the ceremony.

We had some wine and snacks. The pastor was a young and very pleasant man. He stayed after the others had left and talked with Sascha and me about many things. Leaving, he expressed the sincere hope that our little family would weather all storms, and he offered his help and advice if we should need it.

The pastor had issued official baptism documents for Sascha and Sylvia. We hoped this might add another brick to the wall of defence we were trying to build against the Nazi monster confronting us.

Sascha did not discuss his conversion with me, and I avoided talking about it. I never knew whether he had become a Christian in his heart, and I did not care. All I cared about was to shield and protect my beloved husband, to the limits of any power at our disposal.

Christmas 1941 arrived. We bought and decorated a small Christmas tree, putting little presents under it. It was our baby's first Christmas. She was a very happy baby, our delight. Sascha held her in his arms, letting her touch the shiny decorations and blow at the candles. On Christmas Eve my parents, Tante Paschy and Eddy sat around the tree with us.

Sharing the food and wine, we tried hard to appear cheerful. But I am sure Sascha thought of his dead family and none of us could help remembering with melancholy Christmas 1940, when we had been so very happy.

During January 1942, a Latvian and his Jewish wife were

arrested by the Gestapo and accused of listening to the enemy radio broadcast. Like us, they had no radio, and like us they were released after an interrogation at the Gestapo headquarters. David was arrested in the street by Latvian police. He was without Anna, but wore the stars (by then Latvian Jews had to wear two—one on the front, the other on the back) and had his Jewish registration card. After several hours of detention without explanation, he was allowed to go. There were several similar cases of arrests of the Jewish partner of a mixed marriage in all instances, they were shortly released.

The Nazis seemed uncertain how to deal with mixed marriages. But by February 1942 they found a way of getting hold of the last Jews still living in freedom in Riga, under the protection of their Aryan partners.

Anna raised the alarm among us. She was summoned to Gestapo headquarters, where she was told that her marriage to a Jew was not recognised by German law, and was therefore invalid. She was required to sign a document of annulment of her marriage as 'a pure formality'. She protested vehemently, pointing out her Swiss nationality and the fact that David was a Christian. She got the sarcastic reply that religion did not change anything, and a Jew was always a Jew. Her refusal to sign the annulment would result in her being considered a *Geltungs-Jude* (a Jew by conviction) and consequently she would be treated like one.

Anna could not see that she had a choice, and had signed the document. Then she went straight to the Swiss embassy and, explaining the situation, pleaded with them to help her and David to get to Switzerland. They offered her an immediate entry, but refused to intervene on behalf of her husband. All her pleading fell on deaf ears. The day after Anna's visit to the Gestapo, David was picked up from their apartment and taken to the ghetto.

Anna was heartbroken, and we all gathered around her to try and give some comfort. But we knew, now, what was in store for the rest of us.

After this first case of annulment, others followed, there was no escaping. When Katja's turn came, the Gestapo added a new threat; in case of her refusal to sign the abhorrent document, her son, a *Mischling* (half-Jew) would be taken from her and sent to an institution to be trained as a servant for the master race. Katja signed and Felix was taken to the ghetto.

Sascha and I spent days and nights in utter desperation. We could see no way out this time. The fact that I was a German and Sascha a Christian could not lend us any protection in the face of this new, treacherous 'law' the Nazis confronted us with. It was out of the question that we would expose our child to the monsters by refusing the marriage annulment. We knew that a few days later, Sascha would be taken to the ghetto. We knew a number of young Jewish men and women used for forced labour still lived there. Cobby was among them, although his family had been murdered. Since the mass murders of November and December 1941 similar events had not occurred. We thought that Sascha would be relatively safe there; he was young and strong and determined to survive. We clung to the hope that he would survive in the ghetto for as long as it took the Nazis to lose the war. At the time there were encouraging rumours that the Russians had stopped the Nazi advance in the east. Besides, America had entered the war about two months before.

Sascha showed no weakness, but unceasingly tried to instil strength and confidence in me. He kept reminding me that I alone now had to care for and protect our daughter, and I could not be found wanting. "Dusinka, please be strong, for Bubuly, for me!" He must have said that a thousand times in the days and nights of waiting for the inevitable.

I alternated between helpless tears and assuring Sascha I would not cave in. We planned ways of keeping in touch 'after', aided by Eddy, Lee and Kolja; none of us even considered submitting meekly to the enforced separation.

I received a letter, ordering me to present myself at Gestapo headquarters on 16 February. Our hour had come! The news spread, and our friends arrived; the pastor, sad and humiliated that he and his church could not help, Eddy, Kolja, Lee, Nina, Tante Paschy, Katja, Anna and my father. They all came to give us courage, but they also knew it could be the last goodbye.

It was decided that Lee would escort me to my ordeal. When
the time came only Eddy, father and Tante Paschy remained
with Sascha to await my return. The others had left after a
handshake, a kiss, a few words. Sascha was nursing our baby
and smiled at me encouragingly as I left to denounce him. I
had no tears left, and I agreed with my proud husband that
I must not show these monsters how deep the pain was.

My interview turned out to be worse than I had expected,
lasting longer than the others' had done. Maybe the fact that
I was German gave the sadists special pleasure.

There were five of them, young clowns, sneering at me. They
took my passport, pretended to study some papers in front of
them, and took turns addressing me. "You are a pretty woman,
it is a shame you were misguided by the Communists. After
all, you have superior German blood in you. If you are very
lucky, you could even find an Aryan who could forgive you
and marry you."

"You must be grateful that our Führer is prepared to forgive
misguided creatures like you."

"You must have been confused because your country was
occupied by the Communists when you married that dirty Jew."

"We know the Jews want to pollute German blood."

"We are glad to see that you have come to your senses now
and want this despicable union dissolved. We can help you."

"Of course this so-called marriage is invalid anyhow, but
signing this annulment will make you feel better."

They went on in this fashion till I felt I could not take any
more without screaming into their stupid faces. I was aching
to tell these hoodlums that they were not worthy to lick my
Jewish husband's boots. But my lips remained pressed together,
and I endured the humiliation till they had finished with me.

At last I was allowed to sign my consent to the annulment.
I was handed a volume of *Mein Kampf* and told to read it.
The one who gave it to me looked stern, when he added; "You
realise, Frau *Hesse* [he used my maiden name with emphasis]
that any contact with your former Jewish husband will be
considered from now on as a direct violation on your part of
the German Racial Law. You are an Aryan, do not forget it

again. I must warn you, we know how to deal with *Judenknechte* [Jew-serfs]."

Somehow I got outside, where Lee was waiting for me. The blazing rage in me prevented me from crying, but I felt dirty, helpless and above all a traitor to Sascha. On our way home Lee went into a public toilet and left *Mein Kampf* there. It was the only appropriate place for it.

On our return, father and Tante Paschy made a fuss with coffee and snacks. Sascha did not ask any questions, I did not volunteer any information.

After a while, Lee and Eddy left. Lee was oozing confidence and assured Sascha everything would work out. Eddy and Sascha hugged each other. "Thanks, my friend, for everything. I know you will look after them for me."

"I will, till you come back. See you tomorrow, or the day after for sure." They both tried to sound casual, not quite succeeding. I looked at these two men, one a Jew, one a Latvian. So different and so alike, and both such beautiful human beings.

On leaving Tante Paschy wept, which made it easier for Sascha to say goodbye, because he was able to comfort her.

The parting with my father was laden with emotion, as we expected. Father shook hands, embraced Sascha, clapped him on the back, hugged him again, *"Kopf hoch, mein Sohn!* Remember, it will soon be all over, and we will have you home again."* Another hug. And all the time heavy tears were rolling down his cheeks into his white beard. We felt relief when he left.

I will not attempt to describe the remaining hours Sascha and I spent together . . .

Next morning, 17 February 1942 at eleven in the morning (exactly six months since our daughter had been born) a German SS man and a Latvian policeman called to pick up my husband. They were polite, produced the document, and then silently waited in the lounge room while we said goodbye in the bedroom, behind closed doors.

There were no words, no tears left. We clung to each other, we kissed. Then Sascha picked up his child and pressed her to him. That picture is engraved on my mind forever.

The innocent baby touches her father's face with her little chubby hands, showing her two new bottom teeth in a broad smile. The agony in the beloved face of my husband, forcing a smile in return, his blue eyes dark with burning tears. "My Bubuly, my darling, precious daughter! God be with you, and watch over you!"

He buries his face in her fluffy hair, and then hands her to me.

When Sascha enters the other room, he appears calm and composed. In the hallway he pulls on his winter coat with the yellow stars I have sewn on it the night before, while the two men look on in silence. All three walk to the door. Sascha does not look back as he goes through it carrying the suitcase he has been allowed to take, which I have packed with clothes.

I rush over to the window, our baby in my arms. I watch the beloved figure walking in the gutter, being led away, out of my life, into uncertainty and danger.

I do not know how long I stand there at the window after Sascha and his escorts have disappeared from view.

Sylvia is snuggled into my neck. I am experiencing the deepest feeling of loss in my life, and am learning the meaning of profound and helpless suffering imposed by the most cruel and ruthless regime in the world.

10

The Golden Chain of Love Holds Fast

I WILL NEVER KNOW how I found the strength to go on after Sascha was taken from me. But I did. The first few weeks I lived in a fog of despair, unable to accept what the Nazis had done in depriving Sascha of the little protection I was able to give him as his Aryan wife.

My father was very sympathetic. He spent many hours with Sylvia while I occupied myself in exploiting every possible opportunity of staying in touch with Sascha. Eddy was the first to find a way. He went to the area of the ghetto and invented reasons to talk to the guards. Somehow he found out what working groups of Jews were used, where they were sent, and how many guards were usually with them. Most of the men guarding the ghetto and escorting the Jews to their slave work were Latvians and Lithuanians. Later Ukrainians were added.

Eddy, pretending to be anti-Semitic, found out a lot of useful information. Thanks to his efforts I was able to see Sascha, for the first time since his departure, on 4 March, his birthday. I had made a small parcel containing a tiny cake I had baked and three cigarettes. We knew the Jews were searched at random on returning to the ghetto, and at that stage I did not take any chances. Eddy found out that Sascha would be shovelling snow from the footpath with several other Jews in one of the main streets on that day.

Father was minding Sylvia, while Eddy went with me. We walked down the particular street arm in arm, talking in Latvian and laughing like a carefree couple. There they were! About ten men with shovels were clearing the thick layer of snow from the wide footpath. Among the figures with yellow stars was my Sascha. My heart missed several beats and I felt dizzy. Eddy squeezed my arm till it hurt. "Don't panic now, come, you want to see Sascha." He steered me across the street to the footpath where the men were working and pulled me into the open double door of an apartment house. It seemed really dark after the bright sunlight outside. Eddy pushed me behind the stairs: "Don't keep him long, there will be other times." With a reassuring smile, he left and I stood there, shaking all over.

Time stood still. My eyes adjusted to the darkness of the vestibule. A figure slipped through the doorway and I was in Sascha's arms. He covered my face with kisses, my arms were squeezing his neck, I was stammering, "Happy birthday, Saschinka!" His laugh sounded like a sob. My handbag and the parcel were on the floor. There was so much I wanted to say, so little time.

"Take care!"

"Don't worry."

"I'll see you again soon."

"You look fine."

"I love you."

"O God, I miss you!"

"I must go." Our lips met in a last feverish kiss. Sascha was at the door when I remembered the parcel. I stuffed it into his coat pocket before he slipped outside.

After this first meeting there were many more. We were taking enormous chances. There were times of complete despair, times when it was impossible to have contact. But there were also the hours of wonderful togetherness, thanks to our true friends.

Bribery played an important part in our meetings.

Running terrible risks, Eddy discovered which guards would accept bribes, and he had no qualms about using them. Parcels could be smuggled in, messages passed on.

After a while, Eddy discovered an old Latvian guard who liked his drink even more than the others did. For two bottles of vodka, he could be persuaded to leave Sascha behind after the rest of the working party had gone, picking him up later. Eventually Sascha bribed the old man himself.

I came to these meetings alone, leaving Sylvia in the care of father or a friend. Sascha didn't tell me what life was like in the ghetto. I never, never stopped worrying about him, from one day to the next, from one meeting to the next.

To let Sascha see his daughter at least, I would walk the streets of Riga for hours when the weather was fine, wheeling Sylvia sitting up in her pram. Often I knew where Sascha would

Taking Sylvia for a walk, hoping to see Sascha from a distance. This photograph was taken in the spring of 1942 when Sylvia was about ten months old.

be forced to work, but sometimes I would come upon his group by chance. At other times, I completely failed to locate him.

Reaching the working group, who were usually shovelling snow, cleaning the-gutters or collecting rubbish, I would stop and look at the display in a nearby shop window. I took my time, turning the pram so that Sylvia would face the workers. Then I walked slowly past, talking to the baby, never looking towards the Jews.

All the people who walked past the work gangs studiously avoided looking at them; many averted their faces and some made loud, unpleasant remarks about how slave labour 'served the cursed Jews right'.

By the time I reached the closest point I could find to where Sascha was, I would stop. Bending over Sylvia, I pretended to adjust her bonnet or jacket, taking as long as I dared. I knew Sascha used every minute to feast his eyes on his daughter.

Months passed. I had nothing to do, except look after Sylvia. We still lived in the large apartment from which Sascha had been taken to the ghetto. I was very unhappy. But my love for our little girl filled my heart. She was beautiful. Caring for her helped me cope with the empty rooms in the apartment and my constant longing for Sascha.

Sylvia was very healthy and always slept well. Although I cuddled, kissed and carried her in my arms a great deal, she was not spoiled. She had the sweetest nature, did not throw tantrums or cry, and was easily potty trained.

She always made me laugh because when she wet her nappy, she always sneezed. She would make a sound to attract my attention then, looking at me with her huge dark eyes, she sneezed loudly and gave me a wide grin. She was not shy, and would cheerfully let all my friends cuddle her. But she showed a marked preference for my father, Eddy and Tante Paschy.

Naturally, when Sascha and I met, our child was the main topic of conversation. He wanted to know everything about her, every detail. I brought photos of her constantly, told him which tooth had now come through, how many sounds like words she uttered and what they were, what food she liked and what she disliked, and when she took her first tottering steps at the age of ten months.

Tante Paschy with Sylvia and me in the spring of 1942, a few months after my marriage to Sascha was annulled by the Nazis.

For six months we were afraid to expose Sylvia to the dangers of our meetings. But as her first birthday approached, I asked Eddy and Lee whether there was any chance of arranging something that would enable Sascha to see his child on her birthday. Lee came up with the idea of somehow bringing Sascha to our apartment. Eddy saw the old Latvian guard personally and gave him money for a lot of vodka, and he agreed to bring Sascha to our apartment on the morning of 17 August. He was to tell the house janitor that my bathroom needed fixing and 'the Jew' was a plumber. Lee offered to stay outside the house keeping watch. We would have about one hour.

To start the plot operating, I told the janitor that the taps in my bathroom were leaking. When he offered to have a look

I said I was going out, and would call him later. He was a Latvian, reason enough for me to be suspicious of him. While Sascha had been living with me, the man had never made any anti-Semitic remarks and had been polite to both of us. After Sascha was taken in February 1942 the fellow seemed to avoid me, but I had no problem with him.

I was very nervous, and spent a sleepless night. Early on the 17th I fed Sylvia, dressed her in a pretty dress, and prepared to wait. Flowers, a cake and other food was on the table.

At eleven o'clock (one hour later than arranged) there was a knock on my door. When I opened it, the guard, whom I knew from many previous meetings, grinned at me and, sidestepping, let Sascha enter. He followed and shut the door. Sascha and I did not talk or touch while I led the guard into the kitchen. I had prepared a plate with ham and several sausages for him and, of course, there was a full bottle of vodka and a glass. He sat down, and I shut the door on him.

Sascha and I embraced, clinging to each other for a few minutes, then he took the jacket with the stars off and we entered our living room. Sylvia was sitting on a mat on the floor with some toys. She looked up at us and smiled. Sascha bent down and very gently lifted her into his arms. She looked at him curiously, and then turned to me, as if to ask, "Who is this new uncle?" I smiled at her through tears, as I watched Sascha pressing his child to his chest. He cradled her head in one hand, touching her short dark curls. "My Bubuly, my darling, happy birthday. God bless you and keep you!" He tenderly kissed her eyes, her rosy cheeks, her face, her chubby arms and legs. He had not touched his child for six months, and the deep emotion was written on his haggard face. For several minutes he sat on the floor, just holding her close. We cut the cake. Sascha helped Sylvia to blow out the candle. She showed him her toys and walked around the room for him, proudly if not steadily. Then she pointed to me and said clearly, "Mama." I pointed at Sascha: "Pappy." The word was unfamiliar to her, and she did not repeat it.

I looked at the two human beings I loved most in the world. Why, oh why had we been torn apart? My love for my husband

and my determination to stand by him never wavered. No cost, be it monetary, physical or emotional, would be too high for me to pay to enable Sascha to retain contact with his wife and child.

It was a pathetic way to try to keep the dream of a family alive. But this occasional togetherness was all that was possible to us, and I knew it gave Sascha strength to bear the unbearable.

Sascha had displayed a lot of moral courage during these terrible months. Often his strength helped me to fight despair, rebellion, hatred and helplessness. He helped me, who was free, while he was a prisoner, reduced to the level of a slave. He discussed the terrible present only if necessary; persistently he brought up our happy past, dismissing the possibility that the present situation would last. His favourite sentence began: "When all this is over . . ."

I walked to the window several times. Across the street Lee had the bonnet of his Volkswagen open, pretending to do something to the car.

After an hour and a half the guard staggered into our room. He was noticeably drunk and declared it was time to go. Lee came up and stayed with me a while, helping me to relax. He was always so confident, and he inspired confidence and trust among us, the remaining partners of the mixed marriages.

When Lee had left, the janitor called on me. For the first time in my dealings with him, he displayed an unpleasant arrogance. He said he knew no 'plumber' had come, but my Jewish husband, who had no right to come here. "I should report the lot of you," he growled.

I did some quick thinking. There was no point in denying anything, as this man knew Sascha's face. I just said the guard had not known Sascha's relationship with me, and had brought him to fix the taps. It had taken so long because the guard had been drinking and talking to me while he waited. It was obvious to me that the janitor did not swallow my story.

After this encounter, the wretched man frequently asked me for large amounts of money, claiming my apartment needed fixing. But no repairs were carried out. It was blackmail, and I could see no end to it. I decided to move to another apartment.

I found an advertisement in the paper. Somebody wanted to exchange their two-room apartment for a three-room one. I contacted the people, and we quickly came to a mutual agreement. But before I could carry out my decision to move, I came down with pneumonia. Eddy was helping me pack when I collapsed with a high fever and was very ill for several weeks. Eddy nursed me through it, with help from my father, Nina and Tante Paschy.

Eddy was a special friend. He was the first to establish contact with Sascha after 17 February; he was fearless in dealing with guards in tricky situations. His help and moral support for his best friend Sascha and for me were immeasurable. After Sascha went to the ghetto, Eddy always found the time to be with me when I needed him. We talked about the good times of the past, made plans for the future, Sascha always part of them. Often I cried helplessly in Eddy's comforting arms.

Eddy looked very like Sascha, and I would make him sit against the window of the darkened room. In profile, in the twilight, I could make myself imagine Sascha was there. Eddy knew about my fantasies and submitted to them willingly.

There is a beautiful saying in Russian: "You do not discover your friends in happy times. When disaster strikes and tears flow, the true friend is the one who cries with you."

Sascha and I were especially blessed with true friends. My gratitude to them will die only with me.

Kolja and his lovely mother remained fiercely loyal to us after Sascha was taken from me. Without hesitation, they offered their workplace as somewhere for us to meet. Kolja's tailor's shop was at street level, where he took his customer's measurements and they could choose from the shelves full of materials. Underneath that room was a large cellar room where several tailors did the sewing. There was a divan where Kolja's mother took her afternoon rest, a table, some chairs and a hotplate. Behind a door a spiral staircase led from the front room to the cellar room.

This cellar room became a heaven for Sascha and me. A key was hidden in a certain place, and on the rare evenings when it was possible, we spent exquisite hours together. For

Eddy early in 1943. His strong resemblance to Sascha is obvious from this photograph.

these meetings very heavy bribery was required; only a few guards would take the chance of letting a Jew out of the ghetto and being there to let him back in. Once outside the ghetto Sascha walked a long distance to Kolja's. He removed the stars and had to make sure not to arouse any suspicion by hurrying unduly. His Aryan appearance was a big help. Besides, the Nazis were used to Jews being submissive; they would hardly expect one of their 'subhumans' to dare to walk among them.

Tante Paschy continued to visit me, bringing beautiful knitted and crocheted things for Sylvia, and often babysat for me. Nina refused to be depressed and, remaining her old bubbly self, was always ready to help.

I was still meeting the other mixed marriage partners. But I did not confide in them, my parents, Nina or even Tante Paschy about the fact that I was in touch with Sascha after he was taken from me. Everybody involved with us was at risk, and we did not dare to think of the penalty to our helpers if we were caught. Nobody except Eddy, Lee, Kolja and his mother knew that I met Sascha after 17 February, the fateful day when according to the Nazis he had ceased to be my husband.

After I recovered from my illness, I moved to the smaller apartment. The janitor in the new apartment house was a woman. She was a Latvian, robust and sour-looking. But she was friendly enough towards me when I moved in with the help of Eddy and Lee.

My new apartment was two flights up, and consisted of a large bedroom, a small lounge, kitchen and bathroom. It was sunny and had a nice large vestibule. I had my bedroom suite and two small armchairs and odds and ends. I asked Lee to make some enquiries about some furniture, specially a table, for my lounge, as he was the man who could obtain anything.

Before I saw Lee about it again I had a surprise visitor. One evening I answered my door and there was Vitja, to whom I had been engaged when I met Sascha.

During the five years since we had parted we had run into each other often, always acknowledging each other. Later we had had several casual conversations, and exchanged news about our lives. Vitja knew about my marriage and that I was very happy. He had married a Latvian girl in early 1941. The last time I had spoken to Vitja was after the Nazi occupation, when I was out shopping without Sascha. We sat by the canal and talked about the situation. Vitja had been concerned about me, but at that stage it had looked as if partners of a mixed marriage could still stay together.

Now, over a year later Vitja was standing at my door. Entering, he took me gently in his arms. He stroked my hair, then lifting my head from his shoulder, he looked into my eyes. "I know what you must have been through, Inochka. I have been away on a big job in Liepaja and just returned. I came as soon as I found out where you lived. How can I help?"

My dear, goodhearted Vitja! We sat down and I told him everything, knowing I could trust him implicitly. He was glad I had so much help and support, although I mentioned no names. He gave me his phone number at his office, and then said he would see the young dancer from our former apartment about returning the furniture he had stored for us.

Sylvia was asleep, but I took Vitja to her cot. I knew he loved children, but he told me he had none yet. He wound one of Sylvia's dark curls around his finger, as he had loved to do with me. "She is a beautiful baby, Inochka. The best reason for you to fight on."

A few days later, Vitja was back with the dining room table and chairs and the buffet we had given the ballet dancer for 'safekeeping'. When I asked about him Vitja said he denied having our things, grew abusive and threatened to call the police. There was an ugly scene, but Vitja was not intimidated, and in turn threatened to beat him up if he did not produce the furniture. There was no way Vitja could get the porcelain and crystal we had entrusted to the cheat, though. The only item Vitja saw on the fellow's table was a dusky grey Swedish crystal fruit bowl, a wedding present to us from Anna Britta. Vitja recognised it by my description of the items which were supposed to be there, apart from our furniture. There was another argument but Vitja won again and brought the bowl back to me.

After that, I kept in touch with Vitja but did not involve him in my dangerous life. He said his own marriage was not happy, but when in early 1943 he told me he had a daughter, he was ecstatic.

Another unexpected visitor to that little flat was my cousin Helmut. Helmut was a second cousin on my father's side, and I had met him after arriving in Riga and settling down with Liz. Helmut and I always stayed in touch, and he came skating with us during the winter. Shortly before I met Sascha, Helmut's parents moved from Riga to Wolmar, and he went with them. We exchanged cards, but did not see each other. In 1939, Helmut and his mother (his father had died) went to Germany, as many other Baltic Germans had done.

Now Helmut told me that he was a private in the Wehrmacht

With my cousin Helmut while he was on leave in Riga.

and on his way through to the Eastern front. Though I was
very glad to see him, having always been fond of him, I did
not know how he would react to the news that I had married
a Jew. But he had seen Liz before calling on me and she had
tactfully informed him of my situation. I was pleasantly surprised
to find him both sympathetic and understanding. He told me
that by no means all members of the Wehrmacht were in
agreement with Hitler's policy concerning the Jews. Apparently,
he had heard only that they had been stripped of their property
in Germany and resettled in the east; if he knew more than
that, he did not say so. I told him only that my former husband
was in a ghetto and that I was not in touch with him.

While he was in Riga, Helmut visited me several times. He

told me that he had been conscripted in 1940 at the age of twenty-three and had seen action on the western front, then spent some time in the occupation forces of France, Holland and Denmark. While on leave he had married an old girlfriend, and he proudly showed me photographs of his wife and his baby son.

Helmut and I got on famously, and Sylvia approved of him too. We went for walks, and he generously offered us some of his rations. From him I learned that many Baltic Germans were settled in the occupied Polish territory and were given shops and businesses and houses. The previous owners, who were probably Jewish, were not there to object; the new ones did not ask any questions. Helmut and his mother had been allotted a fully furnished apartment and a newsagency to run.

When the day came for his departure, I was sad to see him go into the hell known as the eastern front.

I received two letters from him, and after that, nothing. Later his mother wrote to my father, saying that her beloved only son had died a hero for the fatherland.

My cousin Helmut was not the only member of the German armed forces who proved more sympathetic than I had anticipated.

One day in September 1942, I found out from Eddy that Sascha would be taken with a group of about thirty Jews to a site outside the city to work on a new aerodrome. On this occasion they would be escorted by members of the Luftwaffe, not the usual guards.

I was weary. The site was most likely off limits to civilians, and I was not sure about my chances of coming anywhere near it. But I could not let pass an opportunity of seeing Sascha, even from a distance, and of giving him a glimpse of us.

I took the tram to the last stop in the direction I needed. Then pushing the stroller, while Sylvia tore apart some field flowers I had given her, I walked on along a dirt road towards the woods. Though the day was warm and sunny, some yellow and red leaves on the ground reminded me that the autumn had arrived.

I had planned my journey right; I now saw a column of men

marching ahead of me. Their yellow stars were clearly visible, and so were several German uniforms alongside and in the rear of the column.

I left the dusty road and entered the woods. Making sure there were enough trees for cover from the road, I moved forward slowly, parallel and behind the group of men, till they came to a halt. Loud commands broke the silence, and the men wearing the stars scattered over the large gravel field carrying picks and shovels.

I sank to the soft, mossy ground among the pine forest, spread a rug out, sat down and placed Sylvia next to me. I talked softly to her, trying to judge whether a laugh, or cry, or shriek from her would be heard by the men. My mind was searching for a way to get closer, while at the same time I avoided appearing interested in the Jews or the aerodrome site.

Sylvia was gurgling happily as I tickled her with a leaf. I strained my eyes in vain to make out Sascha among the men, but they were too far away. Agonising about what I could do, I shifted my attention to the men in uniforms, standing together. There were about ten of them.

Suddenly one of them detached himself from the others and moved to the woods. He walked casually, stopped to light a cigarette, seemed to hesitate, and then came towards me. I could see he was wearing the uniform of a Luftwaffe officer.

Always prepared for emergencies, I suppressed the panic rising within me as a hundred possible explanations for my presence in these woods flashed through my mind. Before the man reached me, I had fixed a smile on my face, deciding to flirt and play dumb.

The German gave no sign of surprise as he stopped and looked down at me. The expression on his face told me nothing. Tossing my hair, I asked boldly for a cigarette. He offered me one, and lit it for me.

"Are you not a bit far from town with your baby? What made you take such a long walk?" The question sounded casual, but I knew better than to relax. Laughing provocatively, I crossed my legs, making sure my skirt rode up above my knees. Hoping I looked cheap and harmless, I said flippantly, "I like long walks,

I like forests, and I like German officers who give me cigarettes."

While the words left my lips, I felt inside like a tightly coiled spring. My brain was working feverishly; had he noticed me following on the road? Had he spotted me by chance? Was his suspicion aroused?

He sat down next to me smoking in silence, his head bent. I waited. He reached out and stroked Sylvia's dark curls. She smiled at him, and his serious face lit up momentarily with a friendly smile. "I have a wife and a baby son at home, I have not seen my boy yet. He was six months old yesterday."

I remained silent, watchful, sensing something unusual. He looked me full in the face: "Which one is the father of your child? I will send him over to you."

My heart missed a beat, all the blood drained from my face. He had guessed! Was it a trap? Was he genuine? Dare I take a chance? While I hesitated, he rose and said, "I understand. But you also must understand that I am Luftwaffe, not Gestapo. I do not like what is happening here." He gestured towards the field, his face grim.

Following my instinct, as I so often did, I grabbed his sleeve, preventing him from leaving. Hastily I described Sascha, giving his first name, as I could not point him out from where we were.

He threw his packet of cigarettes on the ground. His voice sounded gruff. "Tell him he can stay fifteen minutes. Then you must leave at once. Go back through the woods, and do *not* come here again."

As he turned to go, I whispered: "Thank you!" Shaking like a leaf, my eyes followed the man who had turned out to be a human being. I watched him walk among the working men, stop briefly and point towards the woods. Moments of suspense!

A figure with a star walked away from the others, paused by a truck then walked on towards the woods. The next instant I knew who it was. He was carrying a saw over his shoulder and he entered the woods, quite a distance from where we were. I realised the officer had sent him on some pretence, and that he was oblivious of the presence of his wife and child so close by.

I rose and softly called his name, afraid to shock him too much. "We have fifteen minutes!"

Walking back through the silent forest, I was dwelling on the wonder of a German officer actually helping me and my Jewish husband! The darkness in our lives seemed pierced by a tiny speck of light. Its glimmer, no matter how feeble, must sustain our will to endure, our courage to fight on, and to hope.

I lifted my head, blinking away the tears. As long as that speck of light was there, in the distance, beyond the darkness surrounding us—all was not lost . . .

The year 1942 was nearing its end. From January 1942 till the summer of 1943, the survivors in the Riga ghetto had a period of relative peace. There were incidents but nothing on the former scale. Only small murder actions occurred. There were wilful killings in the ghetto itself by trigger-happy guards. The Nazis allowed the Latvians, Lithuanians and Ukrainians an absolute free hand with the helpless Jews there. This scum of humanity gave way to their cruelty and wielding of power by shooting any Jew in the ghetto, when they choose. The Nazis demanded no explanations for such killings.

Though Sascha never talked to me about the conditions and horrors of the ghetto, I heard a lot from others. I never stopped worrying that one day Sascha could arouse the wish in one of these cretins to kill him for the 'fun' of it.

When Christmas 1942 approached I bought a few gifts, with the help of Lee's black market connections. I told him, Eddy and Kolja how much I wished to find a way to spend some time with Sascha at Christmas. But the chances were slim as most guards would take time off and the Jews would be locked up inside the ghetto. Lee suggested that Sascha should come to my apartment if a suitable guard and a large bribe could be arranged.

We had one advantage: nobody in my new apartment house knew about my past. I was listed under my maiden name, and the janitor had never seen Sascha.

The plan was put in motion. Eddy took my pearl ring and a large amount of money and after several days of sounding out the situation found one young Ukrainian who for that high price agreed to let Sascha out of the ghetto on Christmas Eve after dark, when he was alone on duty at the gates. But he would be replaced by another guard at midnight, so Sascha had to be back before then.

Eddy clinched the deal, giving the man the ring and promising the money at the time Sascha would slip out. Eddy would be outside the gates, and would walk with Sascha to my place, pretending all the way to be two drunks, and talk loudly in Latvian about women.

Christmas Eve. How many wonderful memories I harboured from the twenty-seven I had celebrated so far! I had loved it as a child, loved spending it in Riga with friends, with Liz, and the last five years with Sascha. Now it was Christmas Eve 1942. I had put a small Christmas tree in the corner of the lounge, decorated it brightly and put gift packages under it. As soon as it grew dark, about half past four, I began to wait. Would everything go right? I paced the floor, peered through the curtains at the deserted street, listening to any sound from the stairs.

Sylvia was toddling around quite steadily by now, and had many words in her vocabulary. She was fascinated by the tree, and I picked her up again and again to let her touch the colourful decorations. As it neared six o'clock, I expected Eddy to come alone and tell me Sascha could not make it. Lee had not arrived either as promised. I had no phone. Holding Sylvia in my arms I lit all the candles on the tree. As she laughed and tried to touch the flames, a soft knock at the door made me jump.

Sascha and Eddy, covered in snowflakes and smiling, enter and whirl me and Sylvia in their arms.
    "Everything is all right."
    "Thank God you are here!"
    "How long?"
    "Happy Christmas!"
    "Come to me, Bubuly!"
    "The tree is beautiful."

Three short knocks, followed by one. Lee's signal. "Happy Christmas, sorry I am late, Here, Sylvia, a gift for you."

We stand around nervously for a while. I offer some wine and we clink glasses in a toast to a better coming year.

Eddy hugs us in turn and leaves. He will be back at 11.15 to walk with Sascha back to the ghetto. Lee will sit in his Volkswagen just outside the next house to mine, until Eddy comes back. Before he goes Sascha shakes his hand. "You know, Lee, how grateful I am to you! I have no words."

"I am glad I can help. We have to stick together."

Now it is just our little family! It really is Christmas!

Hours of happiness! Sascha gives Sylvia a little doll and a wide red ribbon for her hair. For me he has a silk scarf (I still have it).

Naturally all this was bought by Lee on the black market, probably with the money I had given Sascha to obtain food for himself. I had noticed Lee thrusting a parcel into Sascha's hand while greeting him. The abnormal circumstances were just part of our lives.

All three of us admired our presents and then it was time to eat all the good food I had prepared.

Sascha was feeding Sylvia, who was quite happy to sit on his lap, letting him put tasty morsels into her mouth. Sascha had not seen her since the brief meeting at the aerodrome. He admired how much she had grown, more teeth, the curls much longer and thicker, and she could say so much already and walk so well. Several times she stretched her arms towards me, expressing the wish to come to me, but I managed to distract her, or Sascha changed their position and she remained on his lap or in his arms.

My heart was filled with joy, and ached at the same time watching them. How many fathers hardly spend time with their children? Here was one deprived of his right to see or touch his child. His face was alight with happiness, every caress a sensation, and every minute had to be counted.

We could not prolong their togetherness past eight o'clock. Sylvia got tired and restless, and Sascha kept looking at me in dismay.

I made her bath, and for the first time in ten months, Sascha undressed his Bubuly, bathed and put her to bed. We both sat on the bed next to the cot and watched Sylvia close her big dark eyes and fall immediately asleep.

To her another nice day had ended, another 'uncle' had played with her. Thank God no Nazi evil had ever touched her directly.

The loving, gentle father became a loving, passionate husband . . .

Knock, knock, knock . . . knock! Lee's signal. Was it already time? Lee looked frozen. My apartment was warm and I poured him a hot cup of coffee. Ten minutes later Eddy arrived. Sascha went into the bedroom for a few more moments with his baby. Then he put on his overcoat. I put my Christmas present of a thick blue woollen scarf around his neck and smiled at him, holding back the tears.

All three men had a large glass of brandy. Nobody spoke. A last kiss for Sascha. I pressed Lee's arm: "Thank you!" Putting my hand to Eddy's cheek: "Take him back safely."

The door closed softly behind them. I stood at the window watching them get into Lee's car. He was driving them part of the way, then going home, while Eddy took Sascha back to the ghetto gates. I had given Eddy a bottle of vodka to give to the guard in addition to the previous bribe, just in case he decided to be difficult.

I pressed my forehead against the iced-over window pane. It was snowing heavily. A real white Christmas! I remained motionless, reliving the past hours.

We all had taken such an enormous risk, although none of us said a word referring to it. While I was in Sascha's arms, his heart beating against mine, I could not help straining my ears for any unfamiliar noises. I could sense Sascha had done the same all evening. My apartment had no other exit than the front door. It was too high to jump out the window. Lee might not have had enough time to warn us.

I tore myself from the window. Kneeling down on the floor between Sylvia's cot and the bed, I prayed. I did that often. I did not form any words, it was a plea inside me, a plea for help from any higher power. My religious beliefs were all mixed up.

I asked God for help, but felt he was cruel and unjust, letting so many innocent people suffer. Why? What was his purpose? Why should we, the persecuted, turn the other cheek and be forgiving? I could not forgive. I hated the Nazis and all they stood for. I wanted revenge for the humiliation we suffered.

Still on my knees, I put my head on the edge of the bed and cried bitterly.

My clock showed 12.30 am. If anything had gone wrong, Eddy would have come back to me. I took a deep shuddering sigh and got off my knees. Sascha was 'safely' back in the ghetto.

Among rumours of German retreats and Russian victories along the eastern front, we prepared to face 1943.

In April 1943 about 140,000 Latvian men were drafted for service as volunteers. Some of them were actually keen to fight the Communists, and had tried to join the Wehrmacht but were refused. But now, suffering one defeat after another at the hands of the Russians, the Nazis 'consented' to use young Latvian men to help stem or delay the Russian advance.

A Latvian SS Legion was formed and put under the command of the Latvian General Bangerski. The men wore a badge with the Latvian colours and the inscription 'Latvia' on the arm. They were sent to the eastern front, where no doubt most of them perished.

It was a shock when Eddy suddenly told me he had joined this newly formed section of the German army. I was at a loss to explain his decision and to my shame was quick to condemn him. I knew he hated the Nazis, he was Sascha's and my best friend. How could he desert us? I was deeply hurt by his action, and said accusing and nasty things to him. He did not justify himself, remaining determined and grim-faced. He said he would write to me and asked me to reply, but to be careful what I said, as the Feldpost (army mail service) was screened.

While I stood speechless, Eddy cuddled and kissed Sylvia goodbye. Then he took me by the shoulders and kissed me hard on my mouth. It was the first time he touched my lips in the nearly six years I knew him. The door shut with a loud bang behind him. I was not to see Eddy again for nearly a year.

When I next saw Sascha, he said Eddy had come to say goodbye, telling him he had been drafted against his will and did not want to go. Sascha was very sad and I thought it best not to share my negative feelings about our friend with him.

I missed Eddy greatly but I was very angry with him. Then, after ignoring his Feldpost letters for some time, I started to write to him.

Time passed. Rumours about the Germans retreating persisted, although the official news continued to boast German victories on all fronts. But their defeat in Africa and General Paulus' Stalingrad surrender could not be kept secret for long.

We, the Aryan partners of Jews, desperately needed to believe that salvation was near. When meeting, we each had some good news and kept clinging to hope.

David had died late in 1942; Anna could not find out the circumstances. Soon after, she left for Switzerland.

We Aryan wives did not tell each other whether and how we helped our husbands, and whether we met. But we knew we all did, using our own means and resources.

Once when I visited Katja she seemed ill at ease. I asked whether she had had bad news about Felix, but she said he was all right. We chatted over a cup of coffee, real coffee at that. Katja seemed to have good resources.

A young man of about twenty entered the room without knocking. Katja put her hand to her mouth and shot me a guarded look. How hard it was for us to trust anybody!

The boy wore a bathrobe. His face looked familiar to me. Katja put her hand on mine. "This is Jonny Press. Remember Press Men's Fashions on Chalk Street? Come here, Jonny. This is a friend." The boy approached me and we shook hands. "I am glad you are all right."

Katja gave him a cup of coffee. "He comes to me whenever he can, to have a hot bath. You know his parents are dead?"

I nodded. I knew. "My husband was a friend of your father's. You look like him."

I remembered the exclusive fashion store. The handsome, elegant Herr Press and his attractive wife. Their other son had died of a tumour before the Russian occupation. The parents

SASCHA

158

had taken him overseas in hope of a cure. But it was a hopeless case and I remember well how broken-hearted the parents had been at the funeral.

I also remembered the last occasion when I saw Herr Press (I do not remember his first name). It was on the steps of the German Kommandatur, on the day I successfully applied for an apartment outside the ghetto under my maiden name. Clutching the precious paper, I had been hurrying down the wide stairs. Approaching me were three men; two in uniforms were half leading, half dragging a third between them. This man was hatless, his clothes in disarray, and his nose was bleeding, blood dripping onto the front of his white shirt. This man was Press. As I passed the group, I looked down. I don't know whether he saw or recognised me.

For a long time after this encounter I was filled with shame for not at least having looked at him. I knew there was nothing at all I could have done to help the poor man. But the feeling of guilt stayed with me, a feeling of having somehow betrayed him.

Soon after our encounter on the steps I learned that Herr and Frau Press had been murdered in one of the actions. I heard that Frau Press had been selected to be transported for extermination, her husband being left as a working Jew. But he pushed himself into the vehicle to be with his wife.

Now I was looking at his young son, the only survivor of a once happy and prosperous family.

In March 1943 came a change of ghetto commandants. The new commandant was Eduard Roschmann.

Roschmann was an Austrian and a lawyer by profession. (Or so we heard—we later heard that he was a partner or an employee in a Graz brewery.) His rank was low, but this made no difference to the power he wielded as the commandant of a Jewish ghetto, which was absolute. All the same, the Jews were relieved to see Krause go; commandant since 1941, he was known as a bloody tyrant. They hoped that a well educated man such as Roschmann could not be as bloodthirsty as Krause had been. Krause was a former Berlin policeman, with a poor education, apparently. Roschmann's adjutant was Max Gimmlich. After the change of power, Krause, however, still appeared in the ghetto often and spent hours with Roschmann.

It seemed at first that the Jews were right; the ghetto was quiet for some time under Roschmann's rule. He spent most of his time in the office.

And then one day he sentenced seven Jews to death for some misdemeanour. In front of the other ghetto inmates, he shot them himself.

I doubt that the execution of the seven unfortunate Jews marked the first time Roschmann had killed; it so happened that these were the first he executed in the Riga ghetto.

The hope of the ghetto Jews was shattered when Roschmann became another Krause. With Gimmlich and a large German Shepherd dog, he would walk through the ghetto, shooting at dogs and cats. More than once, he used Jews for target practice.

As Krause had done, Roschmann appeared at the gates to check the working parties as they returned. If the smallest item had been smuggled in, the unfortunate culprit was shot on the spot. Roschmann did the shooting.

It was not long before Roschmann became known as the Butcher of Riga.

So far, Sascha and I had been very fortunate in our meetings. Bribing the guards still went smoothly, Sascha remained in good health and good spirits, at least to me. We had several close calls when we met, but somehow we always survived them.

Janis, the old Latvian guard who liked his vodka, had become quite chummy with Sascha. We never let him run out of money, even if he could not arrange meetings. There were weeks when this was not possible because of work rosters or guard changes at the ghetto.

In the spring, Sascha, together with several other Jews, was taken by Janis to a timber yard to load or unload trucks. The job was timed to last for several weeks. Three times Janis arranged another guard to take the rest of the Jews to another job, and brought Sascha to the timber yard alone, picking him up after several hours. So we were able to meet in the little shed in the corner of the yard. Everything had gone well, and on a beautiful spring day I decided to bring Sylvia along.

I put a frilly dress on her, but my hands were unsteady. No matter how safe we thought we were, the place remained risky.

Sylvia's big, innocent eyes looked up at me. Thank God at twenty months of age my baby knew nothing of Nazi persecution, or the chance I was taking again. I pushed the stroller along several streets, not risking going straight to the timber yard. I had learned to be alert on the streets, making sure I was not followed. I had also learned to look at ease and relaxed, like other mothers who were taking their babies for a stroll. I walked when I would have liked to run. My inner tension was well hidden behind a perpetual mask of calm. I knew how to look out of the corner of my eyes, cross streets, avoid anyone who knew me and *never* show fear or insecurity.

The awareness that keeping in touch with Sascha was extremely dangerous for all of us never left me, especially when Sylvia was involved. But love, like faith, can move mountains. In our case the mountains were the Nazis standing in our way. They had made a mockery of our happy marriage. They had put barbed wire between us. They had filled our hearts with fear and despair. They had humiliated us and had made us suffer to the very limits of endurance. But our love kept overcoming fear, disregarding orders, and it found holes in the barbed wire fence. We managed to go on, managed to hope. I knew I would never abandon Sascha, as long as there was breath in me . . .

Fragments of these thoughts flashed through my mind as I approached our rendezvous. On the last corner I stopped and bent over Sylvia. Fumbling with her dress gave me time to check my surroundings once more. Reassured, I straightened up and taking a few more quick steps, I pushed the little side gate open.

The yard was half full of all kinds of boards and pieces of timber. My eyes shot to the old workshed in the far corner. The door was shut, the window covered with brown paper. The familiar sickening fear tied my stomach into knots. Had something gone wrong? But as I hurried towards the shed, the door opened and Sascha pulled us inside.

He lifted his daughter into his arms, a happy smile lighting up his face. My eyes were blurred with tears as I watched the little chubby hands pat his cheek: "Uncle Pappy, Bubuly has a flower for you." Sascha took the squashed daisy, and kissed the rosy cheeks, the dark eyes.

At last he put the child back into the stroller (there were no chairs in the small square room) and took me into his arms.

"We have three hours, Dusik, before old Janis picks me up!"

"That is wonderful!"

Slowly the excitement died down, and sitting on boxes, we hurried to tell each other what had happened since we last met. Then I unpacked the food I brought along, spreading it on the rickety table by the window. Sascha was bouncing Sylvia on his knee, delighting in her burst of laughter.

We were trying to act like a normal couple, out on a picnic with their child. But we both knew that our ears were strained for every sound from outside. We discussed cheerfully the latest news from the Allies; the Nazis were retreating in Russia, the tide had turned.

An hour passed and our little girl had fallen asleep in her father's arms. After he put her gently into her stroller, I took her place on Sascha's knees. Resting my head on his chest, I felt secure in his arms, all fear, all unhappiness forgotten. We kissed tenderly, then passionately . . .

Suddenly Sascha's arms tightened around me. At the same moment I heard voices, the sound of a truck, screeching gates. We were at the window, peering through the slit in the paper, and saw a truck rattle in through the open gates. Six men, including two German soldiers, spread out and started shifting some planks, loading them on to the truck.

My heart thundered. I looked at Sascha and read my thoughts in his face; if one of the men entered the shed, what? . . . Prison? Concentration camp? Torture? Who knew? Nazis could do with us as they pleased. Human rights did not apply to us. In their warped minds Sascha had none, and I had abandoned my rights by being with him.

We both turned and looked at our still sleeping child. What would happen to her? We had had many close escapes, but never when our child was with us. I had brought her only because we had both decided it would be safe.

Sascha whispered into my ear: "If they come in, forget about me, think of yourself and our baby. Beg, do anything to save her!" I could only nod, numb with fear, my hand in his. We stood hand in hand, our eyes glued to the slit in the paper on the window.

There was some coarse language, laughter, and then one of the German soldiers took off his coat and ambled towards the shed. My mouth was dry, the blood pounding in my ears, and we watched motionless every step of the approaching danger.

The soldier reached the door of the shed, stretched out his arm, and . . . hung his coat on the door handle! Lighting a cigarette, he walked back to the others.

My knees gave way. Sascha eased me onto a box, his drawn face bending over me. He desperately tried to smile: "It is all right, Dusik, we are safe, they will soon go. Breathe in deeply."

But it was not over yet. At any minute one of the men could decide to enter our sanctuary, the flimsy toolshed. I sat stiffly on the box, Sascha holding both my hands. His were cold as ice, but steady, mine were trembling. Then my mind went blank, the acute terror gone.

My eyes travelled over the remnants of our lunch on the table, various boxes on the dirt floor, the stepladder in a corner. This shabby place had been filled with our happiness only minutes before. Now danger lurked in every corner. What was happening to us? We were crouching there like trapped animals.

A new thought made me catch my breath, and I turned to look at our baby. What if she woke up and made some sound? She slept on peacefully, her cheeks rosy, her dark curls dishevelled, her pink ribbon on the floor.

Dear God, do not let the worst happen, please, dear God, protect our child! Please, dear God, please, please!

The silent prayer filled my whole being; I lost track of time. The soldier walked over to the shed again. We knew a few more agonising moments as he took his coat. Then the truck rumbled through the gates, and they were shut.

Suddenly all was very quiet.

I heard Sascha's comforting voice, the familiar endearments, his blue eyes looked at me full of concern and love. I could not talk, but reassured him with a shaky smile, feeling tears slowly rolling down my cheeks and dripping onto my folded hands, dripping, dripping . . .

The danger was over. For that time.

11

The Quest For Freedom

IN MARCH 1943 the Kaiserwald concentration camp was established in Meza Parks, formerly an exclusive area of the city containing beautiful villas belonging to the rich. It had large parks, a zoo and a restaurant. The concentration camp contained Jews from the Dagauvpils, Leipaja and Riga ghettos, as well as non-Jews, who were political prisoners or criminals.

There was a lot of unrest; rumours persisted that the Riga ghetto was to be liquidated, abolished, and all inmates transported to Meza Parks. This was part of the persistent rumour that Himmler had a definite plan to liquidate all Jewish ghettos and kill their inhabitants. The Final Solution.

Sascha and I met one day in June at Kolja's place. Somehow we always felt secure there. Kolja's kitchen was very safe, a good meeting place for us. It had three doors, one leading to a lane, another to a disused bathroom with a big window, and the third to Kolja's tailor's shop. This one was kept locked whenever Sascha was on the premises. Sascha always came in and left through the door leading to the lane.

This particular day, Kolja and his mother were very excited about an English language broadcast they had heard the previous night. The Allies were confidently predicting the collapse of the Nazi armies: the Allies were victorious in Africa and the Russians were giving the Nazis a terrible beating all along the eastern front.

Kolja hugged Sascha: "You will see. It will be over soon. The Russians can't be far from our borders."

Kolja's mother produced some food; our mood was optimistic.

Then Kolja suggested that Sascha should now consider escaping from the ghetto. Sascha could hide on his premises, passing as one of his tailors, until a more suitable place could be found. Kolja pointed out that with the Russians approaching, a number of people would be eager to prove that they were anti-Nazi; and what better way than to have helped a 'poor persecuted Jew'?

We discussed the prospect of escape eagerly. Getting out of the ghetto was no problem, but hiding for a longer period was very risky for the escapee and the helpers. There was the added risk that Kolja's employees would talk. No matter how decent they were, the more people knew, the bigger the risk for everyone. Sascha voiced his fear of what consequences his dash for freedom could have for me and our child.

Nothing was decided. We had more discussions, more heart-searching, more good news from London. I could see a new light of hope in Sascha's eyes.

As well as Kolja and his mother, we confided in Lee. He was very positive about Sascha's chances. His suggestion was for Sascha not to remain in Riga for long, but make his way through the countryside to the east. He believed the rumours that the Russians were already at the eastern border of the Baltic States. He said that once Sascha reached them, he would be safe. In fact, the Russians at that time were at our borders, advanced briefly, but were repulsed by the Nazis. (Central Latvia did not fall till August 1944, and Riga on 13 October 1944.)

June and July 1943 in many ways were most eventful months. An attempt by German generals on Hitler's life made the Nazis jumpy; German heads rolled. The propaganda against the Jews, 'the real enemies', intensified.

Many Latvian Jews escaped from the ghetto at that time. Most were recaptured and shot, some were hanged in the ghetto. To discourage would-be escapees further orders were made public: that for every Jew who escaped, three of his relatives or neighbours were to be shot.

A small resistance group of young men existed in the ghetto. They were Latvian Jews and a few Lithuanians. All their attempts to get help from outside were in vain. These men wanted to fight for their lives, but had nothing to do it with.

Then came an unexpected opportunity. The Nazis had stored a lot of guns and ammunition, captured in the wake of their victories in the east, in the Pulferturm, a tower in the old part of the city. Jews from the Riga ghetto where ordered to sort, polish and oil the weapons. It was a golden opportunity for the resistance group. Taking enormous risks, they managed to smuggle many guns into the ghetto and hide them.

That happened while Krause was still commandant of the ghetto. When rumours of guns being hidden in the ghetto reached him, he started to investigate. Houses and cellars were searched, Jews interrogated. Nothing was found and Krause lost interest.

When Roschmann came onto the scene, Krause told him about the gun affair. Roschmann became very interested. He worked thoroughly, following every lead and digging in all directions. He was relentless. The resistance group was in mortal danger.

In June 1943 Roschmann was at last successful: a cache of guns and ammunition was found in a bunker, dug in some ruins in the ghetto. There were also valuables, food and water. Many Jews were arrested, imprisoned and interrogated.

More than one hundred young Latvian Jews paid with their lives for their attempt to resist the Nazi monster.

The Jews in the ghetto knew that Roschmann was partial to jewels and gold, so they tried to bribe him to save some lives. He took the bribes but still had them all shot.

While all this was going on, the security in the ghetto was even stricter than before. I was not able to see Sascha for several weeks. After the guns were recovered and the culprits shot, the ghetto was back to 'normal'.

It was July when we next met at Kolja's and Sascha was understandably very depressed. We discussed his escape again in earnest; there was more reason than ever to leave the ghetto now. If Sascha was sent to Meza Parks concentration camp, we would not be able to meet and there would be no chance of escape.

Encouraged by everybody, especially by me, Sascha decided

to chance it. For security reasons it was important not to involve any more of our friends. Lee also advised us to leave Kolja's tailors out of it. Kolja's wife also knew nothing of possible plans, not because she was untrustworthy but for her own security.

But no matter how careful, how confident, we were, the possibility of Sascha's recapture had to be considered. Sascha said he was prepared to do anything, but he was determined not to be recaptured alive. He was afraid of breaking down under torture and endangering me, Sylvia and our friends. Once he decided to make a dash for freedom, he would not even contemplate being a Nazi slave again, even if he were allowed to live. And he was absolutely determined to put up a fight for his life, and, if he had to die, to take as many of our enemies with him as he possibly could. He would not consider any plan unless he could have the means of ending his life.

We all understood and respected the way Sascha thought about this. Kolja and Lee both promised to try to obtain a revolver or poison for him.

But what did I still have to barter with? The only items I still possessed that would have any value on the black market were a silver fox cape, a heavy gold chain and a few rings. Kolja's mother offered a beautiful pearl necklace if what I had was not enough. I was very touched by her generosity, but declined it. She and her son had helped us tremendously through the last difficult eighteen months. In any case, Lee assured us that he was pretty sure he could get a revolver using the things I had.

A week passed, without a chance of seeing Sascha. My mind was in turmoil. Could we carry it out? Would my poor, beloved husband be a free man again? What would happen if he reached the Russians—would they help? Would they turn him into a soldier who would die fighting the Nazis? To judge by the beastly Ukrainian guards, the Russians hated the Jews. Perhaps Sascha was safer in the ghetto after all? I could not sleep for torturing myself over the question of whether I was encouraging Sascha to face worse danger still.

But I could see that he was driven by new hope of avoiding the fate of slavery. He had to be given the chance for freedom, no matter what the outcome might be. I cried, and prayed, and hoped and despaired.

Then one evening Lee arrived, all smiles.

"I have good news, Inge, a soldier is tempted by your silver fox cape. He wants it for his girlfriend and is willing to give a .32 revolver for it."

"Wonderful! You are a darling, Lee!" Grateful and excited, I gave him a hug. What it meant to have such a friend!

I could not believe my eyes when Lee grabbed me by my shoulders and pulled me to him possessively. "I want my own prize—you! I have wanted you for a long time. Don't forget that I am taking a big risk, getting that revolver for Sascha. I expect some appreciation in return."

I could not believe my ears. I stared speechless at the man who was asking me to sell my body for a gun that would mean freedom for my husband.

Then rage overwhelmed me and, pushing him away, I screamed, "Get out! My God. Have you no shame? I hate you! I will tell Sascha. I will tell your wife!"

"We will see."

His pale grey eyes were now cold, his face distorted by an ugly grin. He turned from me and walked out without another word.

I collapsed on a chair. Nothing had prepared me for the insolence of his action. For more than two years, we had had no reason to doubt his camaraderie and sympathy. After all, we were in the same boat. He had managed to keep his Jewish wife and their daughter with him, although his wife never went outside their apartment. We did not know whether his marriage had not been annulled because of his Gestapo connections, or bribery, or both. He often remarked how happy he was to have his family together, and how much he loved his little 'Fräuchen'.

After the first shock wore off I cried helplessly with the hurt of being betrayed so horribly by one of our own.

My first reaction was to run to Kolja and tell him. But I knew I had to spare Sascha the horrendous truth about Lee's demand. Because the Nazis had forced him to undergo such humiliation and suffering, I felt a fierce need to protect him, in addition to the love and loyalty I always had for him. I knew that Sascha also spared my feelings by not telling me what life in the ghetto was really like, assuring me that it was not too bad. I knew better than to believe him, but appreciated his desire to protect me from worry as much as was in his limited powers. So when I next called on Kolja, I decided not to tell him about Lee. I said I had not heard from him, and asked what success Kolja had had. For once he was pessimistic, as all his efforts had been in vain. He just did not have the right connections.

Whenever Sascha was in a working party not far from Kolja's, and if it was possible, he would slip away and spend a few minutes with his devoted friends, leaving a message for me, getting one, or just enjoying some delicious snack.

Now Kolja told me that Sascha had called in the previous day for a few minutes. He said Sascha had second thoughts about the escape. He again insisted he would not consider it if he had no means of ending his life. He said again that if he was recaptured alive, the Nazis could possibly resort to torturing him. He refused to take the risk that they could break him and he would admit our involvement in his escape.

Tears filled my eyes. Kolja tried to console me, saying Lee would surely be able to help us. I desperately wanted to tell Kolja what a pig Lee had turned out to be. I sat there in their tiny kitchen feeling so alone and helpless, seeing Sascha's chance for freedom fade away. I wanted to kill Lee, wanted somebody to help us, wanted to be in Sascha's arms. I put my arms on the little table and dropped my head on them and gave way to the tears that were choking me. Kolja patted my shoulder, stroked my hair. "What is the matter, Inochka? Why are you so discouraged? I am sure Lee will get what Sascha needs. You have always been so strong. Come on, stop crying. I will call mama, she will cheer you up."

Kolja escaped from my distress to his customers, and his jolly, lovely mother fussed over me until my sobs ceased and I accepted a piece of her cabbage *pirog* (pie). Then she said Sascha had left a message for me that he could arrange to come in the evening in four days' time. He would wait in Kolja's cellar, hoping

I could make it too. The prospect of seeing Sascha so soon and alone for several hours cheered me up immensely.

After repairing my makeup I thanked and hugged Kolja's mother, leaving much happier than when I had arrived.

When I came to Kolja's four days later, the key was not in the usual place. I knocked our signal knock. The door opened immediately, and shut quickly behind me. I was in Sascha's arms.

As usual when we met like this we stood clinging to each other, our hands and lips caressing each other's faces without words. We walked down to the cellar. Sascha lifted me off my feet and carried me to the couch.

We made love. We spoke of love, we were engulfed in love. The ugly world outside ceased to exist.

When we came down to earth again, Sascha said he had wonderful news. Lee had come to see him the previous day. A guard, obviously bribed by Lee, had taken Sascha to the fence in a remote corner of the ghetto and left him. Lee was on the other side of the fence. Greeting Sascha he passed him some money and cigarettes. Then he told him he could get a revolver by the following week if I was willing to give my silver fox cape for it. Lee said he had not seen me yet, but had no doubt I would agree.

I sat up, staring at Sascha in the dim light we dared to use. Lee's audacity stunned me into silence. I watched the excitement in Sascha giving way to astonishment then embarrassment. The thought must have crossed his mind that I was sorry to lose the fur which had been a birthday present from him. While I was searching for words, Sascha said quietly that Lee could try something else, or we could wait.

I swallowed hard, my heart feeling like a rock in my chest. Lee had cut off my retreat. He had cunningly set a trap for me that he knew and I knew I could not escape. There just was no way out for me! I could not possibly tell Sascha of the real prize Lee was asking. He was counting on me not telling Sascha the truth and by going directly to Sascha he had backed me against a wall.

Exposing Lee would be cruel and would also end any escape attempt by Sascha. The bitter disappointment in Lee would hurt Sascha deeply. It would be a blow to him as a man, for his wife was being insulted, and what could he do about it? He was a prisoner without rights. Deprived of his human dignity and honour, he could not defend his wife's honour.

I knew I could not deny Sascha the gun. I knew I had to remain silent. I knew I had to pay Lee's price.

I managed to reassure Sascha, explaining my stunned silence by saying I was surprised it had all happened so fast. Of course I would gladly give the fur. The news was wonderful, now we could really make plans. I smiled and chattered, and said I would wait for Lee to bring the gun to me, and then take it to Kolja, who would hide it till Sascha could take it after leaving the ghetto for good.

In the first week of August, Lee called on me very late at night. He seemed relaxed and self-assured, as always. I did not attack him with verbal abuse, as I had intended to do. I showed my profound resentment of him in a stony silence.

I paid his price.

The ordeal amounted to rape with consent. When he left I was in possession of a .32 revolver and six bullets.

As arranged, I left the gun with Kolja. Next day, I saw Sascha briefly in the entrance to a house; he was removing furniture from the one next door. I told him about the gun; he told me all was working out well . . . We had only a few minutes. When Sascha asked me to convey his sincere gratitude to Lee 'our reliable friend', I felt sick with disgust for Lee, shame for myself, and pity for Sascha.

On 10 August we met at Kolja's for the last consultation about the escape plan. It was during the day; Sascha had slipped away from a nearby work assignment. He wore the star, and he kept touching it, anticipating the time when he would be able to take it off.

Kolja's mother was with a customer in the front room. Sascha, Kolja, Lee and I were crowding the tiny kitchen. We were all smoking nervously. Sascha was holding my hand. I was avoiding looking at Lee.

"So when is it going to be?" Kolja lit another cigarette. "The next few days are difficult, what about the fifteenth?" Sascha's troubled eyes looked at Kolja. He was taking the biggest risk by allowing Sascha to stay on his premises at the beginning. "Good, good, come after we are gone. Everything you will need will be in the cellar. I will put the gun in the basket next to the second sewing machine, under the pieces of cloth and cottons."

Lee cleared his throat. "I have an attic in mind where you can stay at least two weeks safely. So you only need to stay here about three days." Appearing his usual relaxed and friendly self, Lee put his arm around Sascha's shoulders. "I don't want you to worry about Inge and Bubuly, you will have enough on your mind." Smiling, Lee proceeded to tell us that he had rented a small cottage about ten kilometres out of Riga from a farmer he knew. He said it would be the best and safest for me to be out of Riga while Sascha was making his escape. The cottage was ideal, and Sylvia and I could stay there for a month or longer.

"God knows, that takes a load off my mind. Thank you Lee, from the bottom of my heart." Sascha shook his hand, Kolja patted his back. I clenched my hands into fists under the table. With an enormous effort I smiled and reassured Sascha that I would do what he and our friends considered best for all of us. I asked Lee for the name and location of the cottage and promised to leave the next day unobtrusively with little luggage.

I said firmly I did not want 'anybody' to accompany me and Sylvia. Lee shrugged his shoulders, and instructed me about the best way to get to the farm, telling me I should change forms of transport several times.

Sascha shook hands once more with the men and they left the kitchen. Sascha's arms held me tight. At our next meeting, God willing, he would be a free man. A tremulous kiss, Sascha was gone and I sank on to a chair, drained of all emotions. I was to have contact with no one from that day until I heard from Kolja or Lee after 15 August.

The following day I packed a small case, telling Sylvia we were going to visit friends, where she would see lots of animals.

Feeling relief at leaving Riga, I listened to Sylvia's chatter and we soon arrived at our destination. The farmer's wife greeted us warmly. The farm smelled of freshly cut grass, the sun was shining and we walked through a field covered with white daisies and yellow buttercups.

I liked the farmer's wife and the clean little cottage of two rooms with an old cooking stove in one corner and white frilly curtains blowing in the breeze at the small windows. "If you have difficulties with the wood fire I will help. My husband will bring you water. You can have all the fresh vegetables, eggs and chicken that you want."

"Mutti, can I go and look at the big cow there? And what are these?" Sylvia was pointing at a group of goats grazing close by. My daughter had spent the two years of her life in the big city, and knew most animals only from picture books. The farmer's wife laughed, and taking Sylvia's hand led her towards the goats. A small black dog appeared and jumped around their feet. I stood in the doorway watching them go, and for the first time in months (or was it years?) I felt relaxed and at peace.

Four days passed like a pleasant dream. Sylvia was ecstatic at all the new things she discovered. There were colourful butterflies, buzzing bees, birds, ducklings, lambs, even a little snake to be admired from a safe distance. The woman turned the snake over with a stick, showing us the black crosses covering her back.

Sylvia picked bunches and bunches of field flowers. We put them in glasses and I made countless rings from them which she put on her head and mine. We raided the raspberry and currant bushes, finishing up in the strawberry patch. There were hardly any regular meals. Sylvia's cheeks were rosy, her arms and legs brown, and she demanded to walk in bare feet "like Aunty farmer". I slept soundly and believed in a bright future again.

The day arrived! It was overcast, and looking at the dark clouds bunching up in the grey sky I shivered. Was it a bad omen? Sascha would arrive at Kolja's at about nine in the evening. What were his thoughts now? Was he as determined and courageous as when I last saw him? Where would he be sent to work on this day? Could anything go wrong? What *could* go wrong?

The hours dragged on. Sylvia refused to have her afternoon nap. I raised my voice and, forcing her to lie down, gave her a light smack on her thigh. Unused to punishment from me, Sylvia burst out crying. I picked her up in my arms, and walked outside into the fields. Cuddling and kissing my little daughter I carried her aimlessly from the cottage to the barns, to the fenced-in chicken yard. Soon her head sank onto my neck and she fell asleep. I searched the unfriendly sky for a patch of blue, a ray of sunshine. *Dear God, protect Sascha. For her, for his daughter.*

There was no question of sleep for me that night. Nine o'clock, ten, eleven, midnight! The clouds had not brought any rain, and now the sky was clear again, stars were twinkling and a narrow sickle of the moon was peeping just above the treetops. Everything was so quiet and peaceful. Two of the farmer's horses were grazing near the cottage door. I patted the neck of the white one. Her intelligent eyes turned to me and then she bent her head to the grass again. I needed to talk to someone, I could not pray any more. Walking inside again, I sat by Sylvia's cot, as I often had done, and let the hours go by, watching my child asleep.

I dozed off towards morning, and was awakened with, "Mutti, I am hungry. Why are you asleep in this chair?"

The new day had begun. I was pacing the floor, wondering how long I would be able to take the strain of not knowing what was happening with Sascha. Sylvia was somewhere with the farmers.

I was not sure if I had heard a knock but before I reached the door, it was opened and Lee came inside. My body was instantly bathed in a cold sweat, panic gripped me at the sight of Lee's unsmiling face. "What . . . what?" I could only stammer.

"Everything went well, Sascha is at Kolja's. Relax." Lee took a few steps into the room and I noticed a suitcase in his hand. "It's very pleasant here. I thought I might stay a few days with you."

I stared at him. "Are you mad? After what you did? How dare you! Get out!"

He put down his suitcase and calmly took out his cigarette

case. "My dear Inge, do not play the outraged innocent. Sascha is safe. I told Erna I had to go away on business. Be sensible. We're not hurting anybody."

He took hold of my arm. I shook him off, trembling with fury. "You cursed beast! Do you imagine I would let you touch me again? I hate you! You are despicable!"

Lee coolly blew rings of cigarette smoke into my face. "Let me tell you something, my silly girl. I have a perfect hiding place for Sascha, and he will be safe until the Russians arrive. I am willing to look after all his needs. Haven't I always helped you?"

By now I had found my suitcase and was throwing my things into it. "Go to hell! We always thought you were a friend. You are a snake, a dirty, vicious blackmailer. For the last time, get out! Or I'm leaving!"

"Don't be stupid. Who is going to help your Saschinka? If you walk out on me, you can forget about any help from me. There'll be no hiding place for him."

I looked at the face of this traitor, the face I thought I knew so well: his greying hair was smoothly brushed back, his cheeks flushed bluish red, his cold eyes bulging. "You call raping the wife of your friend help? You tricked me then, you knew we needed the gun desperately. Don't think you can do it again, you traitor!"

Closing the suitcase, I stormed out of the cottage, never to see Lee again. I hoped he would burn in hell.

I reached the farmhouse, where Sylvia was eating some nice-smelling pastry, and convinced the surprised farmer's wife of my need to return to Riga urgently. She did not ask any questions and took us back at a leisurely pace in a buggy with her white horse, chatting non-stop to Sylvia. She was a nice, simple person, whose heart told her to do and say the right thing at the right time. I am sure she guessed at some upheaval in my life.

I was grateful that I could remain silent. I did not stop and think of the possible danger for me in returning to Riga at this time; my anger and humiliation overrode any thought of caution. Lee wanted to have me as his mistress, in spite of knowing how I felt. He thought he could continue to blackmail me because of the help he could still give Sascha. I could not do it, I would never submit to him again. Sascha was free. Lee would not dare to betray him, as he was deeply implicated himself. I knew I was not in the same defenceless situation as I had been over the gun.

We drove through sun-flooded fields and then forest flanked the gravel road. It all seemed so peaceful and the enchanted garden in Kirbishof flashed through my mind. What had happened to that naive, happy child, that dreaming teenager? Only a few years before, I had been a loved, loving young woman, perhaps a little spoiled, stubborn at times, but I knew nothing of hatred. Now, my heart was full of it, for the Nazis and for Lee.

As we approached the outskirts of Riga, my heart hammered in my throat. A feeling of foreboding settled over me like a thick fog, through which I could not see.

As it turned out, Lee was responsible for a lot of heartache and suffering in store for me. Had he left me in peace, my month-long stay in the country would probably have changed the course of the events, and my future.

It was midday by the time I entered my apartment in Riga. After feeding Sylvia, who was not happy to have left the farm, I collected my wits while she slept.

I knew I had to restrain myself from going to Kolja's place. The tailors were on leave, Sascha would be staying quietly in the cellar, and Kolja and his mother would have the situation under control. But I had to let them know I was back in Riga.

I wrote a long and confused letter to Kolja. I begged him to find another hiding place for Sascha without delay. I asked him not to alarm Sascha by telling him that I was back in Riga. I promised to explain to Kolja my reasons for these changes later. I also urged him not to tell anybody of Sascha's new hiding place, not even myself, in case some situation would force me to divulge Sascha's whereabouts.

In the afternoon, putting Sylvia in her stroller, I went to see Nina. She was not involved in Sascha's escape and had no knowledge of my part in it. I knew I could trust her, so I gave her my sealed letter for Kolja, inventing some story why I could not go to see him myself. She told me all the news in her life, showing me the new autumn suit she had made for herself, insisting I stay for a cup of coffee and chatted with Sylvia. At last she left with my letter while I remained at her place to await a reply from Kolja.

When Nina returned, she said he had not given her anything in writing, but asked her to tell me he had understood my message and would do as I asked. He and his 'family' were well and in good spirits.

I thanked Nina, and pushing the stroller walked slowly towards home. The street lights had come on, crowds pushed past, shop windows were lit brightly. There was no darkening or fear of bombing in Riga at that time.

I stopped at a cake shop and lifting Sylvia in my arms went inside. The next day my daughter would turn two years of age. I bought the largest and most expensive cake and asked for 'Bubuly' and 'two' to be written on it in pink icing.

Arriving home I played with Sylvia, bathed, fed and put her to bed, like any normal day. But it was a special day! The first day of her father's freedom after eighteen months. She was turning two tomorrow. Would her father still be a free man when she turned three?

I tossed in our bed, sleep eluding me. Would Sascha lie next to me in this bed again? Where was he tonight? Hiding in some dark corner? Wondering why he could not stay on at Kolja's? Was he lonely, afraid, desperate? Was he thinking about his Bubuly's birthday, unhappy he could not see her on that day? Wondering when and if he would see her or me?

My head ached, I closed my eyes. Sylvia sneezed. Surely she had not wet her bed? She had not done it for a year. I got up and checked. She was dry and went on sleeping. The dawn was painting its first pink glow on my window. It was already 17 August . . .

12

The Butcher of Riga

THE BIRTHDAY CAKE was on the table, two little white candles flanking the large pink *Lebenskerze* (life candle) in the centre of the cake. Around it were several toys wrapped in a lot of paper and ribbons, to prolong the anticipation for Sylvia while she was unwrapping her presents.

I was brushing her hair, she was fidgeting.

"Bubuly's birthday? Auch! No wibbon. Mutti give Bubuli pitty dolly fo bithday?"

I managed to tie the red ribbon Sascha had given Sylvia at Christmas when a loud knock at my door made me jump. When I opened it, two men in SS uniforms confronted me. I took a step back. "What can I do for you?" I desperately hoped my face expressed only surprise, and not the naked terror I had felt the moment I saw them.

Without a greeting, ignoring my question, both men walked past me into my hallway. In silence they walked slowly through my two rooms, kitchen and bathroom. I felt my knees buckling. Sitting down I grabbed Sylvia, who was trailing after the men, telling them it was her birthday. It was clear to me these men had come here as a result of Sascha's escape. What would they ask me? I had repeatedly rehearsed my replies for just such an occasion. Kolja and Lee had gone over all possible situations I could be in after the discovery that Sascha was missing from the ghetto. But now my mind was a complete blank.

Following the movements of my intruders, I could think only of the two enlarged wedding photos of Sascha and me lying

179

on top of my wardrobe. As a necessary precaution, I had
distributed all Sascha's personal possessions, all his clothes and
photos of him alone or with me between father, Kolja and Eddy.
Since February 1942 I had had nothing on my premises
connecting me with Sascha. But I had clung to these two
reminders of our happiness, looking at them when the need
for my husband threatened to overwhelm me, especially when
I could not see or meet him for long periods of time.

I was sitting on the low stool in front of the dressing table,
Sylvia now quiet on my lap. The two SS men stood in the
middle of the room, still silent, letting their eyes casually wander
over the furniture, the walls, the ceiling, out the two windows.
Neither of them looked at me.

Strangely, while my heart was pounding with the knowledge
that I was certainly in danger from these two men, I was noticing
everything about them, as if their appearance were important.
One of them was tall and about thirty-six years old, with blond
hair visible where his cap did not cover it. His eyes were pale
blue, his nose narrow and straight, his mouth thin-lipped. He
stood very straight, his uniform immaculate, black shining boots
reaching to his knees. His rank was of an SS *Unterscharführer*,
not a high one. He wore black gloves and his hands seemed
large. He held a short stick that looked like the top end of
a leather whip. The other man was smaller, younger, and had
dark hair and eyes. He had the same rank, but looked subordinate
to the taller one.

Minutes ticked by. The tall one took off his peaked cap,
wiping the inside rim with one gloved hand. His appearance
changed. His blond hair, short all over, was receding, making
his forehead disproportionately high and his skull too big. Any
claim he might have had to being handsome when in full uniform
was now lost.

He replaced his cap, and stopping in front of me rested his
gaze on me for the first time since he had come through my
door. His mouth stretched into a frosty smile. "The Jew you
were married to has run away from *my* ghetto. What do you
know about it?"

He had said 'my ghetto' with emphasis on 'my'. That could

Eduard Roschmann, the Butcher of Riga: artist's impression.

mean only one thing—here was Eduard Roschmann, the butcher
of Riga, the current commandant of the Riga ghetto.

I pressed Sylvia to me, bracing myself for what was now to
come. The rehearsed lies tumbled from my lips while I looked
straight at Roschmann. "The Jew you are talking about was
taken away some time last year. Our marriage was annulled
at my request. I have not seen him since. I don't know anything
about him and I don't care! I realised my mistake. I am a German
after all." I was hoping against hope that I sounded halfway
convincing.

Roschmann listened to me, his head slightly inclined to one
side, his expression bored. Then he bent down to me and, taking

my arm, firmly lifted me off the stool. Sylvia jumped off my
lap and took my hand. "Mutti, Bubuly's birthday?"

"Where can you leave the child? You will accompany us to
headquarters for questioning."

"My parents live far away in Pardaugava. Can I keep my
daughter with me?"

"No! What is your parents' address?" I told him; it was the
obvious place to leave Sylvia.

His cold, pale eyes bored into mine. He turned to his
companion who had not uttered a word since their arrival.

"I will drive. You sit in the back with them." Turning to
me: "Give me your flat keys."

The nightmare had started.

"We are going to grandpa's, darling, they want to give you
your birthday present." I had my arm around Sylvia, who happily
sat between me and the SS man, ignorant, thank God, of anything
being wrong. I talked to her all during the drive of about twenty
minutes. Both men remained silent.

When we arrived at my parents' little cottage, Roschmann
remained in the car, while the other man escorted me and
Sylvia.

A patch of grass and some shrubs, two steps with a pot plant
on each one. The door. I knocked softly. The curtain on the
window next to the door was pushed aside, my mother looked
out. The calm curiosity on her face changed to fear. The door
was opened wide, and my father smiled at us.

"Inge, Bubuly, what a surprise. We did not expect you till
much later!"

He lifted Sylvia into his arms. "Come in."

Gesturing towards the SS man: "Come in, sir."

"I wait here, you can go inside for a few minutes." Roschmann's
colleague addressed me, ignoring my father.

Closing the door, I put my finger to my lips before father
could say anything. Mother was behind him, pointing to the
car, questions ready to spill out.

"It is a misunderstanding, I have to sign something about
my marriage annulment. Look after Bubuly, please. I will be
back soon."

I spoke intentionally loudly and as unconcernedly as I could manage. Somehow I conveyed a message to my disturbed parents, alarming but calming them at the same time. I cuddled and kissed Sylvia, leaving her in father's arms and shook my head when he wanted to step with me outside. Sylvia started crying, stretching her arms towards me.

"Don't worry. Go with God!" Father smiled with visible effort.

I was in the car again, next to Roschmann, the other man in the back. Tears blurred my vision as I looked at the disappearing cottage. *Sylvia, my child, will I see you again?*

When we arrived again at my apartment, the two men went thoroughly through all the drawers in my dresser, the cupboards in the kitchen, and inspected my wardrobe, taking some of my dresses and coats out, looking in pockets. They then flipped through my books and albums. To my immense relief they did not look on the top of the wardrobe. This search lasted about half an hour and was conducted in sinister silence.

I was perched miserably on the edge of a chair, and it was again Roschmann who addressed me after their search ended.

"You had better pack a case with some clothes and other necessities. You have to answer some questions, and the investigation could take some time."

I stared at him. "Where will I be questioned? I already told you. I know nothing about the Jew."

He shrugged his shoulders, a sarcastic smile stretching his lips. "You can take some of this lovely birthday cake with you. Just in case you do not like the food that will be offered to you."

He turned to the other man and they talked softly, standing by a window and ignoring me. Unable to think clearly, I put a few clothes in a small case with some toiletries. Mechanically I stopped at the table, and cutting a piece of Sylvia's cake wrapped it up and put it in the case too.

The nightmare continued.

Another drive to the Gestapo headquarters. A big office with many desks and people, some in uniforms, some in civilian clothes. Roschmann led me to an empty desk, gestured to a chair, indicating for me to sit down, and left.

My brain felt numb. Inside I was shaking. What now? Was my interrogation to begin here? I shut my eyes and prayed for strength. When I opened them, a young man was sitting opposite me. He was in an SS uniform but without a cap. He was holding a packet of cigarettes in front of me and his smile was friendly. This must be my interrogator. My hand shook when I accepted a cigarette.

"I saw you come in with Roschmann."

The man spoke Baltic German. He politely held a match to my cigarette, still smiling. "I am an interpreter here."

He seemed to sense my nervousness, and tried to put me at ease. I murmured something and looking into his face, relaxed a bit. His features were handsome and in no way threatening, and he had a pair of friendly, grey eyes.

We exchanged a few words and then Roschmann returned. He nodded to the interpreter and turned to me. "Put out the cigarette, and follow me."

Displaying his good manners, the interpreter pulled the chair for me when I rose. Roschmann strode ahead with me a couple of metres behind him. In silence we went down some stairs, along endless corridors. Not once did Roschmann look back to see whether I was following.

My mind was now racing, dozens of thoughts flashed through it. I had a little notebook in my bag with the names and addresses of all our friends. The realisation of the danger to them if this information got into the hands of the Gestapo made my heart jump. Without stopping, I opened my bag and took out a handkerchief, at the same time pressing the little notebook into the palm of my hand. Roschmann was approaching the door of the corridor; there was nobody behind me. Radiator pipes ran under the windows. I stuck my notebook behind the last radiator and went through the door Roschmann had left open.

We crossed a large empty room. Behind the next door were more stairs. There was now only artificial light and the air was stale. I realised with a shock that we were descending to the cellar of the notorious Gestapo jail.

In the grip of naked terror now, I trembled all over and wanted to vomit, my stomach in cramps. Was this the end? Was I to die? Would my baby survive? Would I betray Sascha? I saw myself screaming under torture and all my courage dissolved. We stopped at a little window and I heard Roschmann saying my full name in a loud voice. Behind the window I saw a shadowy face. A man's hand reached through. "Your handbag, watch, rings."

I handed them over. A fat woman in uniform appeared through the door. She took my case and motioned with her head for me to follow her.

I strongly believe there are times in one's life when the brain stops functioning, rendered useless by terror, helpless to find a way out in a desperate situation. At such times, I believe, the pure animal instinct present in all of us takes over. It then dictates actions the brain would reject as ludicrous if it were still capable of thinking.

There was no logical reason for what I did next, and I could never explain it to myself. To me it proved, that a sixth sense exists in us, a self-preserving instinct that acts independently of our logical brain. I am sure I owe my life to that instinct.

Roschmann was stepping back to let me and the woman pass in the narrow space. At that very moment I literally threw myself at him. I clung to him with my whole body, my arms were around his neck, my face pressing against his chest. Tears streaming down my face, I was repeating over and over the desperate plea: "Please, please, do not leave me here!"

Much later I learned from Roschmann that this appeal to him at this crucial moment decided my fate. Till then, he had no intention of handling my case personally. As Sascha was Roschmann's Jew, his escape prompted Roschmann to make the first investigation leading to my arrest. After his report to the Gestapo, they would take over. The result of their interrogation of me could have been jail, concentration camp or death, according to their pleasure.

As it was, my fate changed direction the moment Roschmann found me in his arms. He was startled and embarrassed, but my action had suddenly aroused his interest in me. The indifferent prisoner he was delivering to jail had become a quivering, crying young woman, whose soft body was pressed against him and who was appealing for his help.

He freed himself from me, but his voice was soft and his hands gentle.

"Pull yourself together. You stay here tonight. Tomorrow I will come back for you."

He stood there while the woman, who was gaping at us with an open mouth, took my arm and pushed me roughly in front of her.

Next I found myself in a small cell with two double bunks, a stool and a small table. There was a small barred window at the level of the top bunk. In the dim light of a bare bulb in the ceiling I could make out two figures.

Collapsing on to the stool, I must have cried for a long time. Eventually I became aware of two women next to me. One was wiping my face with a wet cloth while the other pressed my head against her chest and rocked me like a child. My whole body was shaking convulsively. My head was splitting with pain, my throat was dry. The women whispered soothingly to me in Russian and I felt their compassion.

The flood of tears subsided and I took a sip of water from a jar pressed to my lips. I looked into the faces bending over me. "Thank you." Two smiles answered and a hand gently stroked my head.

I spent that night, the next day and another night in that dreadful cell. It was impossible for me to lie down in the bunk; the straw mattress and the grey blanket were crawling with bedbugs. Most of the time I crouched on the stool. During the endless hours I died mentally many times over.

The two women were very kind to me. They were in their forties, peasant women, Baltic Russians with broad open faces. They told me they had been arrested a few weeks earlier, accused of being Communist sympathisers. They had dark bruises on their arms and faces but they did not speak of any interrogation.

I noticed with amazement that these unfortunate women were able to sleep, eat, joke and pray, while I just couldn't be part of it all. Several times we were taken outside the cell to a toilet and allowed to wash our faces. Food, which I did not touch, was brought on tin plates. At some stage I shared the piece of Sylvia's birthday cake with the women.

Perching on the top bunk, I tried to look through the tiny window. But it was level with the ground of some yard, and the only thing I could make out were some black boots passing occasionally.

The second day passed and my despair grew. Roschmann would not come for me as he had promised! Even knowing who and what he was I clung to the hope that he would get me out of this horrible place and I would somehow convince him that I knew nothing of Sascha. I had detected the change in Roschmann's attitude after my outburst and it seemed to me the only hope I had to cling to was that he, not the Gestapo, would interrogate me.

The window square was a pale grey on the dawn of the third day. One woman was snoring, the other sat on the top bunk and was very softly humming a Russian folksong, rocking gently. I crouched on the stool, shivering with cold and sleeplessness.

Sascha's serious face swam in front of me. Was he safe? Where was he? Had he heard about my arrest? Sylvia's dark eyes laughed at me. "Mutti, Bubuly's birthday!" I had not had time to give her her presents. The thought brought new tears. Would I ever hold my daughter in my arms again?

Time dragged on. The key was turned in the door. I did not look up. A hand grabbed my arm, pulling me off the stool. A uniformed woman I had not seen before bared her teeth at me: "Come quick." Looking back while she pushed me through the door, I saw a hand raised in the sign of the cross behind me.

The woman led me, holding my arm along a short corridor. We were at the little window again. Roschmann stood in front of it, bending over some paper he was signing. Hot blood rushed to my face then receded, leaving me faint.

Roschmann straightened up and turned towards us. He looked at the woman, and she let go of my arm. "Come with me."

We walked in silence the way we had come before, but we did not enter the big office. Roschmann opened some door and we were on the street. A car was parked at the kerb, a very young SS man at the wheel. On seeing us, he jumped out and opened the back door. Roschmann helped me in and then dropped onto the seat next to me.

So Roschmann had come for me.

Where was he taking me? What could I expect?

Later Roschmann told me laughing that he deliberately had not taken me out of jail sooner, because he wanted to soften me up. He had succeeded in that! All my courage was gone. I was distressed, dirty, tired and hungry but most of all terrified of going back to that cell.

Roschmann lit a cigarette and leaned back, relaxed. I stared out the window, trying to guess where we were going. It was an ordinary morning. Shops were opening their doors, people walking briskly. Trams were clanking, cars impatiently blowing their horns. We passed a group of Jews marching in the middle of the road with guards.

The car turned several times, and suddenly I realised with surprise we were at the gates of the ghetto. The gates opened, Jews, shabbily dressed, bowed deeply. We got out and Roschmann steered me towards a two-storey building. We climbed some stairs, and entered a large, luxurious office.

The door closed, and I was alone with the Butcher of Riga.

Roschmann motioned to me to sit down in an armchair. Taking his place in another, he shuffled through some papers in front of him, scribbling something and picking up the phone barked, "Bring it in now." Leaning back in his chair, he drummed on the desk with a pencil, looking lost in his thoughts. I hardly dared to breathe. There was a timid knock at the door and after Roschmann's "come in", a young Jew, his head bowed, entered carrying a tray with a cup and plate of sandwiches. After a gesture by Roschmann he placed the tray in front of me on the desk and, bowing deeply, backed out of the room.

Again without speaking, Roschmann indicated for me to eat. I drank some tea, but choking on the first bite of the sandwich, I pushed the plate away. My heart was racing madly in fear. I knew he was playing with me like a cat with a mouse. The tension was unbearable.

What was in store for me? He still did not speak to me. I did not dare to address him. I desperately wanted to show confidence, and lifting my head I forced myself to look at him. He met my eyes and slowly stood up.

With deliberate slowness he took out a packet of cigarettes from his pocket and lit one. Standing in front of me, he surveyed me with an amused smile. The atmosphere was eerie. Roschmann seemed to appraise me from head to toe. Exhaling smoke, he offered the cigarette packet to me. I took a cigarette, willing my hand not to shake, and he bent towards me and lit it. We smoked in silence, he standing tall and erect, me lost in the big armchair. I was very aware of my dishevelled appearance. My summer dress was crumpled, my bare legs dirty, my hair in a mess.

At last Roschmann moved. He took some sheets of paper from the desk and placed them in front of me.

"Read them both, then tell me which one is right."

He remained standing in front of me, while I read the first document.

It stated that Roschmann had interrogated me and had found evidence that I knew of and had assisted the Jew Gruschko in his escape, having been married to him. Having found me unco-operative, Roschmann was now turning me over to the Gestapo for further questioning. He was sure I knew where the filthy Jew was hiding, and who were the other helpers.

I felt cold all over. My hand was shaking badly when I picked up the other sheet of paper, holding it up to hide my face.

Stunned and bewildered, I read what it said: After questioning me himself at length, Roschmann was satisfied that I knew nothing of the whereabouts of the escaped Jew Gruschko. He got the favourable impression that I regretted my previous ignorance about Jews. After all, I was a German woman and he saw no reason to detain me any longer.

I looked up at Roschmann, questioning him with my eyes. He smiled, and bending forward stroked my bare leg from the knee down. Reaching my ankle, he gripped it hard, and said softly: "You choose the one you want me to sign."

There was of course no choice for me if I wanted to go on living. Roschmann's blackmail was blatant. My life was in his hands, like my ankle, and he knew I understood.

Wordlessly I handed him the second statement. He signed it and left it on the desk. The other one he tore up and dropped into the wastepaper basket. Opening the door he called loudly for his car.

Sitting again next to Roschmann in the back seat as we drove away from the ghetto, I realised that I had not uttered a single word since he had picked me up from the jail. It seemed hours ago. Roschmann was now in a very jovial mood, joking with the driver.

We stopped at the jail, and he sent the driver in with a note. "He will pick up your belongings and then take you home. I am sure you want a bath." He patted my hand.

He walked with me up the stairs to the door of my apartment. Unlocking the door he handed me my keys and, touching his cap, clicked his heels. "Meet me at eight in the little park on the next corner." I nodded, my mouth so dry I could not utter a word if I tried. *"Auf wiedersehen!"* With a thin smile, Roschmann turned and started down the stairs.

I entered my apartment and, flinging myself on my bed gave way to pent-up emotions. The joy of being free, alive and out of danger for the moment fought with a feeling of deep humiliation. I knew there was more to come.

I stripped and soaked in the bath, feeling that the filth of the prison was hard to remove with soap alone. At least the bath and a change of clothes helped me to stop shaking. By the time I reached my parents' home by tram, I had myself firmly in hand.

For their protection I had not told my parents about Sascha's escape or my involvement with it. Now I persisted with the story that I had had to sign some papers about my marriage annulment and that everything was now settled. They accepted my explanation, knowing my life was not normal and glad to see me again without a Gestapo escort.

I held my baby in my arms again, and life was worth living.

Father came home with me, as I said I had to go out later. We gave Sylvia her birthday presents and it was wonderful to watch her delight at every parcel she opened. We had dinner together and I put Sylvia to bed. I was aching to tell father about the last days and their horror, but I could not burden him with it. I watched him sitting by Sylvia's bed, reading to her from a storybook. He was seventy-four, a bit stooped, his hair and beard snow white. He was wise in so many ways, but politically very naive. He kept telling me of his conviction that Hitler would win the war soon and then the Jews would all be restored to their former lives and properties. He dismissed all the horrors and murders that had happened since the Nazis took over as malicious rumours, circulated only by the enemies of Hitler and friends of Communists.

I watched the time. Roschmann had said eight o'clock. I did not dare to disobey, or be a minute late. I knew only too well that his arrogance and self-assurance were justified, as he held absolute power over the fate of me and my child. At ten to eight I kissed Sylvia who was asleep, and father, who was nodding in his chair, and left.

The little park Roschmann had mentioned was only five minutes' walk from my place. It was mostly for children with a sandpit and swings, and I had often taken Sylvia there.

Reaching the bottom of my stairs, I came face to face with the interpreter from the Gestapo headquarters. Smiling, he thrust a big bunch of red roses into my hands.

I was stunned, not sure what to make of him. He seemed unsteady on his feet.

I felt like a trapped animal, afraid of being late for my meeting with Roschmann and afraid of this man, who wore the same uniform, and who obviously had something in mind for me too. Unthinking; I blurted out: "Why did you come?"

He seemed embarrassed: "I could not get you out of my mind. I heard you were released today, so I came to see you. Do you like roses?"

"Yes, thank you. But I am in a hurry, I can't ask you to stay."

He was blocking my way with an intoxicated grin, then he took my arm and mumbled that he would come with me. I freed myself and pushed past him into the street.

"I'll come back tomorrow," he said. Thank God he made no attempt to follow me.

Twilight was settling around me as I hurriedly approached the little park, not knowing what to expect, preparing myself for anything. Realising that I still had the roses in my hands, I threw them under a bush at the entrance to the park.

On one of the wooden seats Roschmann was reclining, his legs crossed, the short plaited leather stick in one of his gloved hands, beating a rhythm on his boot.

When I was right in front of him, he stood up, removed his glove, took my hand and kissed it lightly. "You look better now. Had a nice day?" His smile was friendly, his tone had no mockery. I sat down on the seat expecting him to do the same, but he remained standing.

"I will call at your place tomorrow evening. I hope you will be home."

"Of course." I winced at the sarcasm contained in his question. Our meeting tonight was obviously only to satisfy him that I would follow his orders.

"I am sorry that I can't see you home." I looked up at him to see if he was mocking me again. But his face was serious and, taking both my arms below the elbows, he made me get up. I was much smaller than he. He let go of my arms and, tilting up my face with one finger under my chin, he seemed to search it. I did not move, did not blink, hoping my face was blank. One of his hands was on my back, pressing me towards him, then his lips touched mine in a very light kiss.

"Remember, Ingelein, from now on you are mine!" He turned abruptly and walked away. I stood in the darkness, collecting my wits.

That day my involvement with the Nazi Gestapo irrevocably began: I took the first steps on a dark road and only God knew where it would lead me . . .

The morning after my meeting with Roschmann in the park, I threw caution to the wind and went to see Kolja. To my relief I learned that Sascha was safe in a new hiding place. I had telephoned Kolja on my way to my parents the day before, telling him of my release and mentioning in passing about having spent a night in jail. Kolja had many questions but I could not tell even him the truth about Roschmann and his conditions. It was too dangerous for all of us. I just told him about the fact that Roschmann had arrested, questioned and released me.

Sascha would call in on Kolja later and I begged Kolja not to worry him, assuring him that Sylvia and I were perfectly safe.

How could I possibly let Sascha even guess my true situation with the Butcher of Riga? How could he live with the knowledge that his dash for freedom had delivered me and our child into the hands of the man he had escaped from?

Kolja's mother arrived and embraced me warmly. Being the incredibly decent people they were, they both insisted that Sascha and I should meet at their place again. I pointed out how much more dangerous for them it was now, if they were found to be harbouring an escaped Jew.

"You are our friends, we want to help. It is settled," they said.

A plate of goodies was put in front of me, a glass of tea from the samovar. I will never forget these friends, and the hours of happiness they made possible for Sascha and me.

That night Roschmann arrived at my place about 8.30. He kissed my hand and handed me a bottle of wine and a parcel containing chocolate, butter and cigarettes. "Let's celebrate, Ingelein." I decided to be friendly and smiled at him, thanking him for the presents.

"It suits you when you smile, you should do it more often." I brought some glasses, and he poured the wine. We sat at the dining table that Vitja had rescued for me from the ballet dancer. We made small talk, and it was not as difficult as I had expected. I was just trying to make up my mind whether to tell him about the interpreter's visit with the roses when there was a knock at my door.

There he stood, the interpreter! He grinned widely, again thrusting a huge bunch of gladioli at me. I hesitated, Roschmann rose.

"What brings you here?" His tone was icy.

"I came to visit. I see you beat me to it. Please introduce me."

We all stood in my little vestibule. Roschmann scowled: "This is our brilliant interpreter, George." I gave George my left hand as I clutched the flowers in my right. Instead of bowing over my hand he lifted it to his lips and lingered over the kiss.

I escaped to the kitchen and took my time with a vase and the flowers. What was I to do? How was I to handle two SS men? George came into the kitchen.

"Have you got champagne glasses? Let's have a decent drink." The atmosphere in the living room was pregnant with hostility. Two bottles of champagne stood on the table. George opened one with a bang, filling three glasses, making them overflow. Roschmann pushed his glass away, his face red and angry. He lifted his wineglass and emptied it. Then he handed me my wine, pushing George's hand with the champagne for me out of the way, spilling most of it. The men glared at each other. Instinctively I knew that it was less dangerous for me to refuse George than Roschmann, and I took the wineglass.

The next hours were filled with tension, setting the pattern for a situation that was to last for the next eleven months.

From then on, Roschmann came nearly every evening. He was usually accompanied by Max Gimmlich, who appeared as devoted to him as a dog. Gimmlich had been with Roschmann at my arrest. Now he came only to the door and, after greeting me, departed. But he seemed to hang around nearby, as I often observed them walk or leave in the car together after Roschmann left me, sometimes late at night.

Roschmann always brought me gifts: perfume, cigarettes, wine, brandy and delicacies unobtainable in shops. He also gave Sylvia toys; she was usually in bed when he arrived. The innocent two-year-old did not object to him cuddling her, which to my amazement he did often. He really won her heart, though, when one day he put a grey velvet elephant into her arms. She shrieked with delight and it became her favoured toy. My heart ached looking at this little elephant, imagining a frightened Jewish child clutching it before it was torn from her by her murderers.

But to Sylvia, Roschmann and George were, as Eddy and Lee had been, just 'nice uncles'.

About a week after his first visit, Roschmann appeared with a young German Shepherd on a chain. "This is Zenta, she is three months old." Sylvia came running, and we both patted the lovely animal. Roschmann handed me the dog's chain. "It is a present for both of you." I adore dogs, but my apartment

Sylvia with Zenta, the dog Roschmann gave us, and the grey toy elephant. This gift of Roschmann's became her favourite toy.

was small, and it would be difficult to obtain food for such a big animal. I pointed this out to Roschmann, who said, "Don't worry, I will send you the food for her, and if there is any trouble with the janitor about having the dog, just tell me. Remember, Ingelein, you are under my protection."

Sylvia and I grew to love Zenta very much. I could not hold it against the faithful dog that she was a gift from Roschmann. But it was extremely embarrassing for me that on his orders a young Jew arrived every evening with a large container of food for Zenta. It upset me very much, when I saw this Jewish boy in shabby clothes, his head bowed, his eyes downcast, and all I dared to say to him was "Thank you" and press a few biscuits or a piece of chocolate into his hand. He came to my door alone but I watched him walk away down the road with a uniformed man on the footpath.

My dismay was even greater when one day several Jews appeared at my door with large cartons. "Commandant Roschmann ordered us to deliver this," one of them mumbled, eyes downcast, hat in hand. I felt humbled and degraded, as these men silently brought the cartons into my kitchen. Roschmann had not given me any warning about this delivery of food: there was butter, coffee, flour, powdered egg, powdered milk and other things, all obviously taken from the German officers' mess. These deliveries occurred every few months. All I could do was thank Roschmann and share it with my parents and friends.

George also called nearly every evening, continuing to display openly his interest in me. A handsome young man of my age, he was tall and slim with dark blond hair, grey eyes and a sensual mouth. His hands and nails were always well groomed. He was well educated and well read and good company, though he drank too much. He told me he was married to a German girl whose parents had manoeuvred him into working as in interpreter for the Gestapo. He did not belong to the Nazi party and was not a member of the SS.

The Gestapo used him to translate documents and as an interpreter for Latvians or Russians. He told me, however, he was barred from the cellars where the serious interrogations took place. Though he was not a member of the Gestapo, he wore the SS uniform most of the time, occasionally choosing civilian clothes, which were less flattering.

Roschmann and George appeared to resent each other openly, constantly making biting remarks, making clear that each wished the other to hell and not in my company. But neither actually did anything about it.

They were very competitive, particularly in their gifts and attentions to me. They were mostly civil in my presence, spending hours talking, smoking and drinking into the night.

During these endless evening hours, the conversation depended on the mood of the men and the amount of alcohol they consumed during their visits to me.

Both were, and remained, well-mannered towards me, not indulging in bad language or dirty jokes. Mostly we made small talk. We all spoke about events in our childhoods—a safe subject—as well as music, art and literature, as all three of us knew something about them. Sex was discussed, mostly flippantly. We gossiped about people, too. The progress of the German army always came up as a topic: always victorious, of course, whether the victories were real or imagined. For instance, Roschmann described the 'regroupings' of the army in the east as a brilliant tactical manoeuvre by the Führer. I had, naturally, to be full of admiration.

Sascha's name never came up during these sessions, nor was the Jewish question ever raised.

I tried to fit into the prevailing mood on any given night. I drank little, but when I deemed it advantageous I pretended to be tipsy, causing some commotion. I put on these performances when there was hostility in the air, harsh words, biting remarks and jealous outbursts between Roschmann and George. Playing the tipsy bystander, laughing and pretending to be on the verge of passing out, I frequently averted a serious quarrel between them.

Mostly they left together. On many occasions ten minutes later, Zenta would come to the door and sniff. A soft knock would follow and one of the men would be back. More often than not, the other appeared shortly after. They made a joke of it and left again. It was a show of some kind of endurance. As George drank more than Roschmann, he often left for good at the first departure. Bewildered, I eventually realised there was safety for me in numbers.

As the triangle continued, neither of the men giving ground, my nerves were stretched to the limit. They often provoked a quarrel, and then turned to me, wanting me to take sides. I usually refused, but if necessary sided with Roschmann, who was by far the more dangerous of the two.

I soon discovered that George had a good, soft character. It was also very clear that he was genuinely in love with me, and that in contrast to Roschmann, he would not hurt me, even if I rejected him.

This nervewracking, precarious situation continued, neither able to make a move without the other knowing, where I was concerned. It was extremely trying for me, requiring all my moral strength, as well as self-control and the ability to stay constantly on the alert.

The picture emerged clearly. Roschmann was very vulnerable by his association with me. Having been married to a Jew, I was 'off limits' to him. Apart from being my constant visitor and bestowing gifts on me, he also had given presents to my child, who was half Jewish. Awareness of his situation made Roschmann tolerate George, and I believe was the reason Gimmlich hung around for an alibi, if necessary. George, of course knew if he opened his mouth to Roschmann's superiors, it would mean the end of Roschmann's career and maybe his life. But it would also drag George in, although it would not have cost him as dearly.

Roschmann lived in officers' quarters not far from my flat, and always came after the evening meal. When George was not present he became very talkative. He told me he came from Graz, where he was born. He had been married, but his wife died of a brain haemorrhage. There were no children. He spoke of the beauty of Austria and sounded quite human as he described his childhood in the mountains. Sometimes I forgot who he was and listened with interest. He never mentioned the ghetto or the Jews to me.

I did not know what he had in mind for me, but I was grateful as weeks went by without any demands on me. To my amazement and relief he behaved like a perfect gentleman, displaying good manners, never telling dirty jokes or using rude words.

On arrival and when leaving he, like George, just kissed my hand. On the rare occasions when we were alone, he would lightly kiss my lips.

He only took me out on one occasion. It was to a party at the home of a Latvian Nazi collaborator and his wife. Roschmann and I arrived in his car, driven by Max Gimmlich.

Roschmann introduced me by my Christian name to the twenty or so other people who were also present. Apart from the host all the men were from the SS, but none from the Gestapo. All the men had women with them, who were also introduced by their first names. It was obvious that these women were their mistresses, and Roschmann treated me in exactly the same offhand way as the other men treated their women.

There was a lot of drinking, eating, singing and dancing that night, and I hated every minute of it.

I still don't know why Roschmann took me to that party, but I never asked him—as I never questioned him about anything.

We never went anywhere together again, but I certainly didn't mind. Much as I resented Roschmann's presence in my home, I preferred it to any more SS orgies.

So I coped as well as I could with Roschmann and George and everything their association entailed. I learned to consider it a temporary nightmare. The reality was Sascha, and the hours we could be together.

During the next two and a half months Sascha and I lived a dangerous and charmed life. Whenever possible we met at Kolja's. During the day his little kitchen provided a temporary sanctuary for us. We decided it was too big a risk to bring Sylvia. Not only would it increase the risk of our meetings, but she was now talking and in her innocence could say something to give away our secret.

I was very tense when I met Sascha for the first time after his escape from the ghetto and my arrest.

He asked so many questions: why had I not remained in the country as planned? Why did he have to leave Kolja's so suddenly? Why couldn't he go to the attic that Lee had promised? Where *was* Lee?

Most of all he worried that my arrest had been as the result of his escape. Why, he kept asking, were Roschmann and George coming to visit me? Had Roschmann threatened me? He immediately concluded that both men were interested in me as a woman. This disturbed him greatly, and he also begged me to be careful and for God's sake never to trust Roschmann.

I wove a desperate tissue of lies—the first time in six years with Sascha that I had not told him the truth about anything. I was determined to spare him the truth about Lee, about Roschmann and my situation. My desire to protect him was stronger than ever, now that he walked the tightrope of being an escaped Jew.

I was not sure that he knew I was lying to him. Outwardly he seemed to accept what I said, but sometimes I saw deep pain in his eyes, even when his lips smiled.

We would sit in the warm kitchen and chat with Kolja's mother, while Kolja attended to their customers. There was the samovar, the cakes, optimistic talk, and above all friendship and love.

When I could make it Sascha and I would spend wonderful hours alone in the cellar. It all depended when I would be left alone by my SS 'guests' in the evenings, and whether father or Tante Paschy could stay with Sylvia. I invented friends' birthdays, illnesses and other excuses. I was always afraid of being followed and took elaborate precautions before arriving at Kolja's place.

Sascha changed his hiding place several times, but we had an agreement that I would not know where he stayed, nor would Kolja and his mother.

The biggest danger for Sascha were the 'catchers'—Jews who for some extra rations or little privileges roamed the streets looking for fugitive Jews, and after spotting them pointed them out to the Gestapo. These traitors recognised their own people easily, and many knew the fugitives as former co-inmates of the ghetto.

As the weeks went by, we all became more confident. Sascha was not discovered or stopped for failing to wear the star. It also seemed that I was not being followed. But we balanced on the edge of the abyss. Each time Sascha walked the street he risked his life; each time I met him I did the same. But it never crossed my mind to abandon him, no matter what the risks. I loved him as deeply as ever, he was part of me, life without him was incomprehensible.

Since his escape Sascha, encouraged by Kolja and his mother, called on them nearly daily. Kolja had always kept several of Sascha's outfits, what better place than a tailor's shop for suits and sports jackets? Now Sascha, who had kept only the minimum while in the ghetto, took pleasure in changing from jacket to suit, to coat, with his favourite white silk scarf. He mostly used the entrance to Kolja's from the laneway, but sometimes he

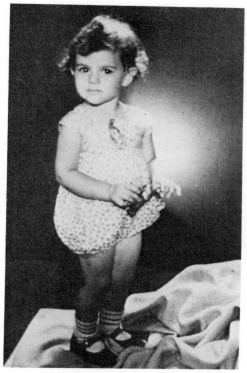

Sylvia aged two, a photograph I arranged to have taken especially for her father.

would boldly walk through the front door. If Kolja had some customers, Sascha, pretending to be one too, proceeded to look at the various materials on display as if he were waiting to be served. When he told me about these pranks he had a sparkle in his eye and the impish smile I loved so much and had not seen on him for a long time.

Sascha looked well, did not display any nervousness or fear, and at our meetings he seemed relaxed. If he had any fear, doubts and misgivings, which would be natural in his position, he hid them well. The same applied to Kolja, his mother and me. When we were together we all acted as if it were a normal gathering with our friends.

My chances of seeing Sascha were restricted by Roschmann and George, and my being able to arrange for somebody to look after Sylvia during my absence. During the day I often left Sylvia with Katja, whose son was a good playmate for her. On the few occasions that I managed to get away in the evenings, Tante Paschy mostly babysat. She visited me often and frequently stayed overnight, sharing my bed with me. Only rarely I asked my father to come. As I left everybody in complete ignorance that I saw Sascha, I always made up a plausible reason for wanting to go out without Sylvia.

There was the problem of providing Sascha with food. In his situation he could not shop, as he had no ration card. Since Lee was not there any more with his black market connections, and I had none, we relied on the provisions Roschmann kept supplying me, the cigarettes I got from him and George, and most of all on Kolja and his mother. They had relatives with a farm in the country who made sure they did not want for any food, especially meat and butter, which were scarce in the city.

Sascha had mostly to live on bread and cold cuts, but of course Kolja's mother made sure he had a hot meal when possible. As Kolja and his mother would never hear of payment for anything in any form, I insisted that they gave to their farmer relatives a lot of cigarettes from me, not divulging their source. They agreed to that.

In Kolja's kitchen we talked of the future, "when this is all over". We held hands like young lovers. I brought new photos of Sylvia, told Sascha every little thing about her. The parting was always difficult but Sascha never displayed fear or nervousness. In the inside pocket of his coat he always carried the revolver.

Lee had vanished, and Sascha and Kolja were both worried that he was in trouble. I told them that I had heard he had temporarily left Riga.

I was glad he had stayed away from us, and right in assuming he would not dare harm Sascha; he was too involved. I am sure he had friends among the SS who protected him, possibly in exchange for some Jewish loot. Many Jews must have trusted

Lee, as we did; some might have told him where they hid their valuables.

Perhaps Lee had extracted the same 'payment' for his help from other women whose position was similar to mine. I had not told anybody. Would they?

Whatever his motives and actions, Lee was evil.

Somehow I managed to live the double life I was forced into: outwardly the mistress of the Butcher of Riga, in reality the loving wife of a hunted Jew.

Since meeting Roschmann, I had unwaveringly insisted that I had known nothing about my former Jewish husband since February 1942. I stuck to it, although Roschmann tried to get something out of me, when he thought me off guard or after I had had some wine. He tried very hard to present a picture of himself as an ordinary soldier. He hinted that he really did not want his job, and personally had nothing against the 'poor Jews'. It was all a matter of following orders and doing one's duty. He took great pains to sound frank and honest, sometimes pretending (I was sure he was only pretending) to be under the influence of alcohol, when he said these things. He said his reluctance to do more than strictly necessary was the reason he was still an *Untersturbanführer*, and not promoted higher. Naturally I did not believe a word of it.

Then he came up with a new approach. One evening, when George was not present, he took my hands and, looking into my eyes, said he loved me and wanted to marry me after the war. He 'honestly' wanted to help me, and he felt my former husband's survival was what I wanted. He 'understood' me and had only my welfare and happiness at heart. I could trust him. Had he not looked after me at risk to himself? He had released me, knowing I had been involved in the escape. But he understood and only wanted to help, because he loved me. I was not safe while Sascha was at large, and he, Roschmann, could only protect me to a point.

Then came the bombshell! Roschmann offered to take my husband personally to the eastern front. He said the Russians were not far from the borders of Latvia and once he would release my husband in some forest, he could go over to the Russians and freedom.

I was speechless. It was incredible to what length Roschmann would go so I would trust him and help him to catch Sascha. But his assurances of love, his concern for me, his 'disclosure' of not really being a Nazi did not catch me off guard. I laughed and said that even if I wanted 'the Jew' to run to the Russians, I had no idea where he was, and cared less.

It was a stalemate. Roschmann obviously did not believe me; I did not trust him. My mask was so impenetrable that after this incident Roschmann stopped sounding me out about Sascha. I think I really convinced him that I did not know where he was.

George had accepted my assurance that I was not involved with my former husband in any way, and he never tried to pry into my past. I told him about Roschmann's proposal of marriage, making a joke of it. Then I casually mentioned his offer to save my ex-husband. George became very angry: "Be careful. Roschmann is two-faced."

I knew George was jealous of the man he regarded as his rival. Not knowing the real hold Roschmann had over me, George must have thought I was in some way attracted to him.

Next day George came in the morning and, grim-faced, handed me a paper. It was a page-by-page photocopy of the notebook I had hidden on the day of my arrest, with the names and addresses of my friends. A few days after my release Roschmann had brought the book back to me, saying it had been found by a cleaner. He had realised it was mine and had taken possession of it. He scolded me playfully, saying I was lucky it had fallen into his hands, and therefore I was not to worry.

Now I looked at the copies in my hands, not understanding. Bristling with indignation, George told me Roschmann kept a file on me in headquarters and George had found this paper there. He had guessed these names represented people I would like to keep out of the hands of the Gestapo. He wanted me to see for myself that I could not trust Roschmann.

It was clear to me that Roschmann had kept these copies in case he needed more power over me if I became rebellious. From then on, I was even more cautious than before.

For two months Roschmann did not make any advances towards me. I did not know what to make of this, but was grateful. He enjoyed the power he knew he had over me. It was quite obvious on many occasions. He often said to me, even in George's presence, "Ingelein, you are mine. Don't forget it."

Then one evening he made his move. It was a Sunday, and I knew George would be absent. So did Roschmann. He came early, was in good humour and played with Sylvia and the dog until it was bedtime for the child.

We had coffee and brandy, then Roschmann unwrapped a large parcel he had left by the door when he arrived. He took out a black satin dressing gown lined with purple. He threw it on a chair, and taking me by the arms, made me stand up. Then he started to undress me.

He was changed, his breath was coming in gasps as he tore off my underwear. He did not speak, reminding me of the time with him on our first encounter. He was fully dressed, I was naked. Wrapping his arms around me, he kissed and mauled me, and for the first time I felt real passion in him. Suddenly he let go of me, put the dressing gown on my nude body and pushed me into an armchair, the gown open all the way down the front.

He lit two cigarettes and handed me one. His hand was shaking, his face deeply flushed. Bending down he kissed my breast, leaving a bruise, then dropped into the armchair opposite me.

Fumbling, he undid his fly and began to masturbate. Not saying a word he stared at me, his eyes bloodshot. Our knees touched slightly. I was shaking with shock, not daring to move, like a rabbit stared at by a snake, and just as helpless.

After reaching his climax, Roschmann went into the bathroom. I stood up, wrapping the gown around me tightly. I was sickened, bewildered, shaken to the core by this new and unexpected development.

When Roschmann emerged from the bathroom he acted perfectly normally, as if nothing unusual had taken place. He asked me for coffee and poured us some brandy.

Now he was talkative, joking and stayed several hours, drinking more than usual. Leaving at last, he kissed me on the lips. "Goodnight, Ingelein, sleep well!" His tone of voice held just a hint of mockery.

From then on these strange, weird sessions took place whenever we were alone, which thanks to George was not often. Roschmann was an enigma. He never took off his own clothes, never attempted normal intercourse with me. His behaviour was humiliating to me in its perversity, but at the same time I thanked God that this man did not force his way into my body.

I spent many sleepless hours trying to fathom Roschmann's feelings for me during the terrible months of my involvement with him. I felt that the more I could understand the man, the stronger my defence would be.

He repeatedly told me he loved me, but I refused—and still refuse—to call his feeling for me 'love'. I hate to associate whatever that man felt for me with my definition of love. He was clearly obsessed with me; it was obvious that he could not stay away from me. But I never knew what to expect from him. At different times he displayed passion, possessiveness, cruelty and sometimes tenderness towards me.

There were the rare occasions when he would insist that I sit on his lap, both of us fully clothed. He would stroke my hair and cradle my head against his chest, rocking me like a child.

But there were also times when I felt brutal passion when he kissed me. He bit me, too, showing pleasure in my pain. He usually bit me on the shoulders or thighs, sometimes quite severely.

At other times I knew that he felt deeply resentful towards me. One moment he would be caressing and kissing me, the next he would grab me viciously by the hair, pulling me painfully away from him. At these times his face would distort with anger and hatred: "You witch! Stay away from me!"

After he pushed me away, he would go on raving for quite a while, his eyes bulging, occasionally shaking his fist at me. He would make terrible threats about what would happen if I cheated on him or deceived him. Much of what he said made little sense, but the meaning was always the same: if I deceived him in any way, he would turn me over to the Gestapo.

He said he would claim he had released me only to investigate me further, so that I would lead him to Jews in hiding and their accomplices.

If I thought I could wrap him around my little finger, I was mistaken; he could destroy me any time he chose.

His voice rising to screaming pitch, he would say that if he had to pay for his love for me, I would certainly die with him.

I knew of course that if any of these threats were carried out, it meant absolute disaster for me.

What caused these outbursts of fury I could never tell, and I could never foresee them.

Usually I would cry, honest tears of terror, and assure him submissively that I would do whatever he wanted me to and never, never deceive him. Mostly my tearful pleas had the desired effect; Roschmann would gradually calm down and his anger would vanish. On the very few occasions when I was unable to pacify him, he would leave, slamming the door, leaving me terrified that he would carry out his threats.

I did not know why he never did.

I am now convinced that feeling I was at his mercy gave Roschmann enormous pleasure. These outbursts towards me must have served to confirm that feeling. He also made me obey him in many trivial things. His sexual satisfaction could have derived mostly from seeing me naked, humiliated and submissive in front of him.

Roschmann's unceasing efforts to wring from me information—however inadvertently gained—about where Sascha was must also have derived from a complex mixture of motives.

For one thing, it would be a professional victory; catching an escaped Jew would be satisfying. When Roschmann offered to take Sascha to the east to save him, he was probably trying to make me trust him: another victory over me.

Those outbursts of anger could have been caused by Roschmann's deep resentment that I, the woman he wanted, had loved a Jew. Maybe the reason he never demanded sexual intercourse with me lay in this resentment—that a Jew had been there before him. One thing is certain—no matter how many Jews Roschmann killed or ordered killed, he could never

destroy the Jew who lived in my heart. Maybe Roschmann knew
it somehow. He must have been frustrated that he could not
leave me alone.

These of course are all speculations—what makes a man like
Roschmann tick is very complex. My feelings were clear, however.
I despised Roschmann for what he was, what he did, what he
stood for. I hated him fiercely because I was at his mercy.

Roschmann always carried a small revolver, which he usually
put on the table next to the food and drink. Sometimes he
played with it, picking it up, putting it down again. I had a
recurring dream—I dreamed that I was slowly picking up that
revolver and shooting him with it.

Often after he left me I cried bitterly in hopeless anger, wishing
he was dead.

The situation was nervewracking in the extreme—and I had
to cope with it alone. There was no way I could confide to
anybody this dark relationship Roschmann had thrust upon me.

13

Till Death Do Us Part

ONE MORNING AT the end of October, I called at Kolja's with food and cigarettes for Sascha. I was not sure whether Sascha would be there. Tante Paschy was with Sylvia and I had several hours at my disposal. I breezed into the kitchen and said a cheery 'hello' to Kolja. To my surprise he was gloomy and agitated: "Sascha will not come today. He is changing his hiding place again. I don't like it."

He helped me take off my coat. "Why, Kolja? What is wrong?" I could feel the cold fingers of fear reaching for me. After pouring a glass of tea for me, Kolja told me.

Sascha had called in the previous day and said he had to move again. This time he was going into a place with two other Jews who had recently escaped from the ghetto. Sascha had been ill at ease and had left his wedding ring with Kolja. He had not worn it in the ghetto but had since his escape, and I knew he felt it to be the symbol of being a free human being.

I became as alarmed as Kolja. Until then Sascha had been in about five different places; he had always been on his own, and all went well.

We knew that Jews sometimes betrayed each other when cornered, and we were ready to mistrust the Jews with whom Sascha would share his new hiding place. There was nothing Kolja or I could do. We talked and worried, then his mother arrived and as always brought warmth, wellbeing and optimism with her.

I knew that Roschmann would be prevented from visiting

me on 31 October. It was only a few days away and I asked
Kolja to tell Sascha, when he saw him again, to meet me on
that night. We hugged each other and I left with a heavy heart.
For the first time in months I had a bad premonition.

I spent the next days worrying more than usual, and the
nights brought me little sleep. The days were endless, and the
evenings with Roschmann and George more trying then ever.

At last the evening of the 31st arrived. I set the table for
the evening meal for Sylvia and my father, whom I told I was
going to a birthday party. He was talking to me, Sylvia was
chattering, but I was watching it getting dark outside, my
thoughts flying ahead of me to Kolja's place. Keeping up the
pretence, I put on a party dress. It was cold and raining. I put
on a warm coat and rubber overshoes.

"Take the umbrella. Have a good time!"

"Mutti bring Bubuly a piece of birthday cake?" Kisses and
hugs. I was outside, my eyes immediately searching the street.
I hurried to the tram.

The sky looked ominous, with dark clouds piling on each
other. Again a bad premonition squeezed my heart. But I forced
myself to show a calm face and stay alert till the third tram
brought me close to Kolja's place.

*All is in darkness. The signal knock. The door opens and shuts.
I am in Sascha's arms! Three wonderful hours pass . . . It is time
to part . . . We kiss again and again. I cling to Sascha, reluctant
to let him go. But we have stayed to the very limit of time.*

"We will meet again very soon."

"Please take care!"

"I love you so!"

"You are my life!"

*Sascha's arms press me against his chest and I feel the hard
revolver. Again I am seized by foreboding.*

*Sascha kisses my eyes. "Don't be afraid, Dusik. Remember, they
will never take me alive."*

*A few more precious minutes. His parting words, as always: "God
bless you and Bubuly. I love you both dearly."*

I am alone. My beloved husband is gone . . .

On the afternoon of 2 November, I was absentmindedly stroking Zenta, reliving in my mind my last meeting with Sascha. Sylvia was taking her nap.

There was a knock on the door. I noticed that Zenta did not bark, so the visitor must have been someone known to her. I opened the door, and automatically put a smile on my face when I found Roschmann and George standing there.

A warning bell rings. Both together? During the day? Their faces are serious, and neither makes an attempt to enter, although I have stepped back into the foyer.

"We have some news." *Roschmann bares his teeth briefly in what passes for a smile.* "I hope it will not upset you.

"The Jew Gruschko you were married to. He is dead."

I feel my body turning to stone. I am so cold, suddenly, surely all my blood is frozen. Then indescribable, agonising pain begins to tear me apart.

But I do not scream. I do not utter a word.

I hear disjointed phrases: "In a warehouse . . . a wardrobe . . . two other Jews . . . warning . . . shot the officer who opened the door of the wardrobe . . . shooting blindly . . . last bullet in his mouth . . ."

(Don't be afraid, Dusik. Remember they will never take me alive.)

George's voice sounds from miles away, reaching me through a thick fog. I try to reach for the doorframe for support, but I cannot move.

Roschmann speaks again: "Ingelein, you had better take Mausi and go to your parents. There could be trouble because of the tragic death of our comrade. Stay away for a week. If there is still a problem, I will handle it."

He sounds confident, arrogant. There follows a pregnant silence, and I know I must say something: Roschmann is giving me a penetrating look, and I know the mask of calm, learned and practised for so long, is beginning to slip off my face.

The faces of George and Roschmann are swimming, distorted, in front of my eyes . . . Roschmann's pale eyes are narrow, his lips pressed into a thin line.

I make a supreme effort.
"I understand. I will wake Mausi and go."
George gives me a sympathetic look and puts his hand on Roschmann's arm. "We had better let her get on with it."
Roschmann touches his cap in a salute, and they both turn to go. I am still standing, rooted to the floor, in the open doorway, while the men are descending the stairs.
Roschmann's cool, dismissive voice reaches me: "Das ist das Beste für die Kleine." (That is the best outcome for the little one). 'Kleine'. An expression German men often use when referring to their women.
Left alone, I am immobile, as if paralysed. Zenta licks my hand.
Das Beste für die Kleine . . . Das Beste . . . Das Beste . . .
I push the door shut with my foot. My body of stone has suddenly become a rag. The walls of the vestibule are closing in around me, the ceiling is descending. I sink to the floor shivering uncontrollably, my teeth chattering.
Das Beste für die Kleine . . .
My lips move soundlessly.
Oh, Saschinka.
Saschinka.

Eventually I woke Sylvia, dressed her and, taking nothing with me, left the apartment in a trance. I pushed the stroller aimlessly through many streets, mechanically listening to and replying to Sylvia's chatter. After a while I noticed that Zenta was with us, walking slowly beside the stroller as I had trained her to do.

I was hardly aware of my surroundings and I stopped when I found we were on the bridge leading across the Daugava. I did not want to go to my parents' as I had been advised. But I crossed the bridge and kept going, on and on.

It grew dark. Suddenly I realised I had reached Tante Paschy's cottage.

When she opened the door and saw us, she *knew*. It was such a relief to have found this true refuge.

In her comforting arms, the dam broke, the tears came at last. I shouted out my profound pain and suffering, and she understood. She said very little. There were no useless words, no promises of consolation, no urging for resignation and acceptance. There could be none, ever . . .

Later I managed to tell her what had happened (she knew about Roschmann and George, up to a point). Eventually I stood, looking out the window of Tante Paschy's living room. She was making a bed for Sylvia by pushing together two armchairs. My eyes were dry, I had no tears left. The clouds hung low, and the bits of visible sky looked grey and unfriendly. The trees and bushes in the little garden looked desolate, wintry, as if they would never again be covered in leaves.

And my beloved Sascha was gone. One little piece of metal had forever wiped out all our plans and dreams for the future. How could I face life without him?

I sit next to Tante Paschy, her arm around me, her hand holding mine.

"My life is finished! I wish I were dead too! I will go on for Bubuly, but how? She is all I have now in the world. We will be so alone. She will never again be held in her father's arms . . ."

The tears are choking me again.

"Inge, my darling, our Sascha is in heaven now. He won't find any peace while you are so unhappy."

"Heaven! Where is the Heavenly Father? Why did He take him? I prayed so much. What is there in life for me without my Saschinka? I will never, never love another man."

"My darling girl, you are so young. It will hurt for a long time. But you have to go on living. Don't bury yourself with Sascha. He would not want it. No matter how you arrange your future, you will never betray his memory. That is what counts."

Tante Pachy's voice is dear to me. It soothes but does not heal.

"I loved him so! I will always love him, as long as I live!"

"Of course you will. Don't torment yourself. You have Bubuly, Sascha's Bubuly. Life has been cruel to you. But yours is still ahead of you. Do not make it a desert."

"O, please do not talk to me of a future. How can there be one? I have lost the only man I ever loved."

We sit together long into the night.

Days followed nights. Tante Paschy and I played with Sylvia, went for walks, and I listened to Tante Paschy playing the piano (she was a brilliant pianist). At night we talked by the open fire, with all lights out and Sylvia asleep. Zenta stretched out, contented, her head on her front paws.

Very gradually Tante Paschy made me face the fact of a future without Sascha. Gently, lovingly, she helped me bury my pain deep inside me. The tears stopped flowing and I was able to present a face without emotions again.

After a week, I was ready to go on. We went home. I now had only one purpose in life: to care for, protect and love Sascha's and my child.

I never found out where Sascha was buried; I asked George, but he did not know. He gave me more details about Sascha's death, however.

Sascha's last hiding place had been a furniture storehouse. Two other Jews were with him at the time of the raid. When the Gestapo men burst into the storehouse both Jews raised their arms in surrender. They begged for mercy and one of them screamed a warning that another Jew (Sascha) was hiding in the wardrobe and that he had a gun. Dismissing the thought of any danger coming from a 'lousy Jew' one of the Nazis opened the door of the wardrobe pointed out by the traitor. Sascha shot him point blank in the forehead. After shooting blindly at the others and missing, he put the revolver into his mouth. Sascha's last bullet ended his young life.

He had not been allowed to go on living like a man, so he died as he had planned, like a man, by his own hand, not the hand of his enemies, taking one of them with him.

The tip-off about the hiding place had apparently come from a Jew.

I didn't dare ask Roschmann any questions about it, of course. All he said, casually, was that the Gestapo were going to investigate the death of their man. But he assured me that I would not be called for questioning, as his report at the time of my arrest cleared me of any suspicion. Roschmann repeatedly boasted to George and me how lucky it was that I was under his protection.

The SS man Sascha killed was given a hero's funeral. The case caused a stir: it was truly exceptional for a Jew to kill an SS man.

Outwardly, everything was the same as it had been before 2 November: the evenings at my flat with Roschmann and George continued, the flowers, the gifts, the brandy, the smoke from the cigarettes. My outward shell took part in these evenings. Obediently I smiled, I laughed, I smoked and drank and thanked them for their presents.

I only gave way to my despair and grief when I was alone.

I told my parents only the fact that Sascha had died; they knew that Roschmann and George visited me 'sometimes', and I said they had told me that Sascha had succumbed to some illness. Father was very sympathetic, and he shed tears for the Jew he had learned to love. Mother was barely affected one way or the other. I only asked father to babysit rarely; he tried to console me through religion. But I had stopped praying. God seemed unreachable.

I visited Kolja and his mother once. We talked and cried together, and Sascha seemed among us. We decided that I should stay away from them for a while.

One day George told me that several people were to be questioned as part of the investigation into the death of the SS man. They included Eddy, Kolja, his mother, the minister who had christened Sascha and Sylvia, and a number of the ghetto guards. I noticed that George did not mention Lee, whom I had not seen since our bitter quarrel. Eddy of course was on the eastern front and not able to be contacted. The minister knew nothing, and I did not expect trouble from any of the guards in the ghetto. But Kolja and his mother were deeply involved and I was very worried about them.

George told me he would be the interpreter during the questioning: that meant Russian for Kolja and his mother and Latvian for most of the guards. He seemed relaxed, not suspecting any problems for me. He asked me about my relationship with Eddy and with Kolja, but his curiosity was most likely prompted by jealousy rather than any suspicions.

After several days, there were still no arrests. The people

questioned had really known nothing about Sascha's escape, and they must have convinced the Gestapo. George made a few jokes about the questioning in Roschmann's presence, and we all laughed. But my heart was heavy, and my premonition of further trouble proved right.

Roschmann never visited me during the day, so when George wanted to see me alone, he came in the morning. One morning he arrived with a most uncharacteristically sombre expression, and I knew something was wrong.

George did not keep me in suspense. The previous day, Kolja had been summoned to Gestapo headquarters, and questioned. He appeared very nervous, constantly wiping sweat from his face and contradicting himself.

First he said he had known Sascha only at school, then he admitted he had been Sascha's tailor prior to the German occupation. He denied having seen Sascha since. All these questions were put to Kolja in German; George translated them into Russian and Kolja's replies into German again.

I knew there was more to come.

The Nazi conducting the investigation had noticed how nervous Kolja was and ordered him to come back the next day with his mother.

With the next suspect George, the interpreter, took a big chance.

It was Janis, the Latvian ghetto guard, the old drunkard who had taken Sascha to our meetings many times. He was the only guard who knew what I looked like (all the other guards took their bribes for letting Sascha in and out of the ghetto, and knew no more than that).

Janis knew nothing about Sascha's escape—he was no longer working as a guard and by this time the Riga ghetto was empty, all Jews having been transferred to Meza Parks and other camps— but when he was asked what he knew about Sascha, the old man became frightened. He blurted out in Latvian that he had taken Sascha to meet his wife many times, but before Sascha escaped; he was obviously under the impression that if he didn't know anything about the escape, he would be forgiven for other transgressions if he confessed them.

His German was very poor; he was speaking only in Latvian. George immediately realised what danger there was for me in this man's statement and did some quick thinking. He told the unsuspecting Gestapo questioner that the old man was under the influence of alcohol, knew nothing about Sascha and did not understand why he was being questioned. The guard was allowed to leave.

Now, searching my face earnestly, George implored me to trust him. "I want to help, you must believe me. But I have to know the truth. Then I promise I will do all I can to help you and your friends. But *please trust me!*"

I looked into George's honest grey eyes, at the soft line of his chin, and I was touched by his gallant and courageous action. By failing to interpret correctly the evidence of a witness, he was endangering himself.

At that point, I decided to trust George with my life.

I told him about the eighteen months I had stayed in touch with Sascha and the help we had received from Kolja and his mother. I also told the truth about Sascha's escape, letting George know how deeply they and I were involved.

It was a very serious confession, and George listened without interrupting. When I had finished, he looked pale and shaken.

At this point, Sylvia decided she wanted some of our attention. We talked and played with her, which gave us both time to compose ourselves. But we had to come to some decision very quickly; Kolja and his mother were due to be questioned that afternoon. If they caved in, it would be a certain catastrophe that would destroy us all, including George.

It was in some ways a relief for me to be frank with George, though I thought it wiser not to tell him about my true situation with Roschmann.

After considering everything, we decided that George should see Kolja and his mother before they went to headquarters. I wrote them a letter, introducing George as a friend they should trust, and do as he advised.

Kolja was shaken and his mother broke down and cried, but they listened to George, and together they worked out what to say and how to act while being questioned.

They were calm and courageous, and everything went according to plan. There were no new developments, no more suspects were called. To our relief, the investigation of Sascha's escape led to nothing, and was shelved.

But from that point on, my relationship with George changed. I grew to know, trust and like him. He was a decent man, who never used my confidences for anything but the protection of me and my child.

After Sascha's death, and because of the constant visits from George and Roschmann, I found myself quite isolated. I had to take elaborate precautions if I wanted to see Kolja and his

Sylvia at the end of 1943, shortly after her father's death. She is wearing the hair ribbon he gave her as a Christmas present the year before.

mother. It was known that I was seeing two SS men, and three of the Aryan partners of Jews, with whom I had previously kept in touch, now shunned me. I had told my friend Nina a mixture of truth and lies about why two SS men were visiting me. She remained a loyal friend, but refused to come to my apartment in case she met them; she fiercely hated the Nazis. So I could see her only when I was able to come to her. A similar situation developed with my parents: I visited them with Sylvia, but they did not come to me any more, and so they did not meet George or Roschmann.

Tante Paschy continued to visit me, always cheerful and friendly, a great comfort to me and a favourite with Sylvia. Occasionally she stayed overnight. She met Roschmann and George, and was relaxed and friendly with them. Roschmann apparently liked her, and she even read tea leaves for him on one occasion, which intrigued him. Though Tante Paschy knew more than anybody else about George and Roschmann, I never told her the whole truth about Roschmann. I knew I could trust her, even with this dark secret, but I did not want to burden her any further, as she had already shared so much trauma with Sascha and me.

Katja and I still remained friends; she was the only Aryan married to a Jew who I still saw. We did not ask each other any questions, and I had told her nothing abut Roschmann and George. She knew I had been arrested and I told her that I had been informed of Sascha's death. She was consoling and understanding.

I managed to prevent her visiting me, calling on her frequently. Usually we talked about the good old days, drank her coffee and watched Sylvia and her young son play together.

At one stage she mentioned casually that she had heard that Felix was in a work group that cleaned the Roman Cellar, a first-class restaurant. Jews were used for the dirtiest work, cleaning toilets, scrubbing floors and pots and pans. Katja expressed the hope that if he worked in the kitchen Felix at least got some food.

During one of my visits to her, early in 1944, Katja suddenly burst into tears. I knew instantly that her distress concerned

Felix. Without a word, I put my arms around her, and she told me she had not heard from him in over a month. She had been unable to find out where he was, or what had happened to him, although she had spared neither effort nor money to get information.

She lifted her head from my shoulder, her large grey eyes full of tears. "Inge, you know some SS men. Please, please will you try to find out where Felix is? I am not judging you, you must have your reasons for what you are doing. I know one of your friends is Roschmann, he must know where all the Riga Jews are. Please ask him. Please! We are friends, help me! I know how much you loved Sascha. You must know what I am going through." Tears were coursing down her cheeks, her eyes were pleading, and she was trembling.

I held her in my arms and promised to do all I could to find Felix for her. I did not ask how and what she knew of Roschmann and me, nor did I give her any explanation or justification. I comforted her as best I could, and left very disturbed.

That night and for many others I lay awake, racking my brains, trying to work out what to do. I felt deeply sorry for Katja, knowing only too well what she was suffering. But in her naivete she had set me an impossible task. She thought I had only to 'ask my SS friends' who would immediately tell me where Felix was. Nobody who was not involved with a man as dangerous and unpredictable as Roschmann could appreciate the fact that if I displayed any interest in the fate or whereabouts of a Jew, I would be not only very stupid but taking a phenomenal risk. But I desperately wanted to help Katja, so I schemed and schemed, making and discarding plans.

I finally came up with something. One night, when Roschmann and I were alone, and after he had taken his sexual pleasure, I decided to act.

By now, I knew all Roschmann's habits with me. I knew that after he had finished with me, he liked to push up the sleeves of the dressing gown he had given me, stroke my arms and kiss the inside of my wrists and elbows. Anticipating this, I was wearing a gold bracelet that Roschmann had not seen on me before. As I had expected, he noticed the thin chain and immediately asked where it had come from (thinking, no doubt, it was a present from George).

I gazed at him in carefully rehearsed, wide-eyed innocence: "I got it from my friend Katja," I said. "She smokes heavily" (which was not true) "and cannot obtain German cigarettes. Because you are so generous, I always have more than I need. I gave her six packets for this bracelet. I like it, don't you?" I rounded out the performance with a silly giggle. "I hope you don't mind?"

Then I added, "You know, Katja, like me, made the mistake of marrying a Jew. Like me, she is now looking for a new life." Another giggle, and my arms went around Roschmann's neck. "She is very pretty. Would you like to meet her? Perhaps you could introduce her to one of your colleagues?"

He laughed. "I'll do no such thing, and I don't care what you do with the cigarettes I give you. And if you want another bracelet, you have only to ask me."

Roschmann remained very amiable and poured us another brandy. He occasionally drank quite a lot; I had seen him intoxicated, but never really drunk. I consumed as little as I could, but even when the circumstances required me to appear relaxed and to drink a fair bit, as they did now, my head always remained clear. I believe my strong constitution and the ever-present tension reduced the impact of the alcohol on me.

Sipping my brandy, I gushed on about Katja's ex-husband having been a jeweller, so Katja had a lot of nice trinkets. As I had hoped, the mention of jewellery made Roschmann prick up his ears. Casually he asked me the name of the Jew, and I gave him Felix's name and surname, adding that some time ago Katja had been told that her ex-husband worked in the Roman Cellar—not that Katja was interested, because she hadn't seen him since the annulment.

Roschmann did not pursue the matter, and I changed the subject quickly. For the rest of his stay I was very nice to Roschmann and when he left I hoped fervently that the tiger had swallowed the bait.

Weeks passed; I did not dare mention Katja or Felix to Roschmann again.

Then one night, completely out of the blue as always, Roschmann turned on me in one of his fury attacks; that evening he and George had left together and Roschmann had returned alone. He hurled abuse at me, with his usual threats of turning me over to the Gestapo, and I cried helplessly, crouching in an armchair, waiting for the storm to pass.

Suddenly Roschmann leaned right over me, his face inches from mine, his voice very soft. "My little *Judenfreundin* [friend of Jews] don't think you deceived me. You are interested in this Jew, and so is his so-called ex-wife. So I went to the trouble to find out about him.

"You can tell your friend this. He did work in the Roman Cellar. He was scrubbing the kitchen floor on his knees, as a Jew should, when some officers walked in. One of them wanted to have some fun, so he spat on the floor and ordered the Jew to lick up his spittle.

"The Jew did as he was told. But the spittle of an SS officer was not to his liking, not good enough for the filthy Jew, apparently. He vomited onto the officer's boots.

"So the officer shot him, like the dog he was.

"Tell that to your friend! A lot of good his trinkets did the jeweller, eh?"

Roschmann's pale blue eyes were staring into mine. I kept my face completely expressionless, and eventually he blinked, straightened up and relaxed.

I knew the worst was over. He must have been aching to tell me about Felix all evening, and George's presence had prevented him from doing so.

I assured him I had forgotten all about the Jew. I don't think he believed me, but fortunately his anger was spent. He dropped into the other armchair and lit two cigarettes, offering one to me. Zenta, who had stood whining softly at the door during Roschmann's outburst, walked over and lay down between us. Roschmann stroked her. I knew the danger had passed and kept quiet.

Long after Roschmann left I sat at the table, my head on my folded arms, sick to my stomach.

In my mind I could see Felix, relaxing in our apartment, slim and immaculately dressed, his little son on his lap. I could hear him speaking confidently of their plans to go to Sweden. He and Katja had money in a Swiss bank, and he intended to start a business. His voice was full of hope.

I tried to hang onto this mental picture. I knew that if I let go of it the other one, the horrible one, would take over:

Felix, haggard and frightened, kneeling on the floor, scrubbing, his head bowed, hoping not to be noticed . . . some SS men, probably drunk, entering the kitchen for some reason. The 'fun' of one of them spitting next to Felix, then barking out the order to the Jew, Felix's terror and humiliation, as he did not dare to disobey. But no terror could prevent his stomach rebelling against the horror. The tormented Felix vomiting on the shiny black boot, the swift outraged reaction from the specimen of the 'master race', the gun, the shot. Felix's slight body lying in a heap next to the shiny black boots, the scrubbing brush dropping from his lifeless hand . . .

I could not shake off the terrible vision in my mind. It haunted me, for years to come.

After I had regained some of my composure, I called on Katja. I told her that I had discovered that Felix had contracted pneumonia about a month previously and had died in his bed.

I held her in my arms while she sobbed bitterly, and I hoped to God she would never learn the truth about her husband's death.

I kept in touch with Eddy via the army mail service; because we feared censorship, we never mentioned Sascha in our letters. After Sascha's death, I sent Eddy a poem which would tell him I was a widow.

He tried to get leave, but was denied it until the beginning of 1944. When he wrote to me, telling me the day and time of his arrival in Riga, I was overjoyed and went to meet him. It was wonderful to see him again, and I cried in his comforting arms. All the resentment I had felt when he joined the army disappeared at the sight of his dear, familiar face.

Eddy came home with me. His eyes were moist as he cuddled

Sylvia. He was hurt that she did not recognise him; she was now two and a half years old, very pretty, with big dark eyes and curly hair, and very talkative. But their old familiarity was re-established, and Eddy was introduced to Zenta and a large number of new toys. Sylvia also informed him that there was another Uncle Eddy (Roschmann) and an Uncle George, who had given her all the toys.

I put her down for her afternoon nap, and at last Eddy and I had time to talk. He took my hands in his and said simply: "Tell me."

I poured out everything that had happened since his departure a year before. I held nothing back, even what had happened between me and Roschmann. To share this dark secret with another human being lifted a huge weight from my shoulders. Eddy was shocked beyond words.

We sat in the same two armchairs, the only ones I had, where Roschmann and I sat while he submitted me to his sexual fantasies. After I had finished speaking we sat in silence for a moment, both emotionally drained. I sat slumped back, Eddy was leaning forward, gripping my hands so tightly they hurt.

"My poor, poor Inochka! My God, while all this was happening I wasn't here to help you and Sascha . . ."

Carried away by remorse, Eddy confessed the reason for his apparent desertion of us to join the army. The tragic fact was that Eddy had been in love with me ever since we met in 1937. Knowing from the start Sascha's and my relationship, he never, in all the years I had known him, had shown more than loyal friendship to either of us.

After Sascha was taken away from me, I had often turned to Eddy for comfort, often exposing him to physical contact with me, because I saw in him only a friend.

Eddy gradually found it impossible to cope with his feelings for me. At the same time, he could not, would not, betray his best friend. He felt he would lose control sooner or later. He also knew how young, lonely and vulnerable I was.

His only solution was to join the army, and thus put a barrier between us. As fate dictated, Sascha never knew about the conflict in his best friend's heart.

Now he said he bitterly regretted having joined the army, blaming himself for being away when I needed him most. He was outraged at Roschmann's blackmail: "I only wish I could kill that swine!" But of course we both knew there was no way he could break Roschmann's hold over me, without endangering me and my child. What could an insignificant private in a small Latvian army group do against the Butcher of Riga?

Knowing of his love for me did not shock me, though I had not suspected how he felt. I knew he respected and understood what was most important to me and he shared my grief for my husband. Besides my child, Eddy was the closest person left to me in the world. He was much closer to me than my own family.

That evening and for the next two weeks I had two SS men and a soldier around my table. Roschmann and George immediately sensed a rival, and the atmosphere remained very tense. Eddy was coldly polite, making no effort to disguise his dislike for the two men.

Eddy also spent every day with Sylvia and me. His presence gave me new strength, helping me to pick up the pieces of my shattered life. Since Sascha's death three months previously I had been an empty shell, convinced I would never know happiness again. I was thirty years old.

The time for Eddy to return to the eastern front arrived much too soon. The Russians were now very close to the Latvian border; they were advancing on a broad front and Eddy said it was a foregone conclusion that the Germans would retreat, calling it 'strategic regrouping'. Eddy and I snatched every hour we could be alone. I came to dread the thought of parting with him again. I could not really define my feelings for him at the time, except that he was part of me, part of my happy past, part of Sascha.

On the day before Eddy's departure, it happened. We made love for the first and only time. Neither of us felt regret, remorse or guilt. It had to happen. His passion and tenderness expressed really deep feeling, and I found myself responding to it.

I went with Eddy to his train. It was a clear sunny winter day. Thick snow covered everything. There were hundreds of people milling around, embracing, kissing. Many children were held by their fathers, who pressed them to their uniformed chests.

Eddy's kind blue eyes were brimming with tears when he folded me into his arms for the last time. I put my head on his chest, hiding my own tears. It was time to part again.

The couples holding hands, embracing, kissing—all sounded cheerful and loud. Colourful scarves and thick knitted gloves were evident on every soldier. Eddy wore a white woollen scarf I had given him.

The shrill train whistle was followed by a barked-out command. A hush fell on the crowd, then the soldiers scrambled on board the train and there was a struggle to get to the windows. Arms were reaching down or stretching up for a last touch. Eddy kissed me long and hard. "Take care of yourself and Bubuly. I will come back!"

But he never did . . .

14

Decisions

AFTER EDDY'S DEPARTURE, my life settled down to the usual pattern.

In April Roschmann went to Germany for four weeks. He wrote me sentimental letters, but not seeing him for a month was a wonderful break for me.

George was delighted with his absence, visiting me more often than before. He declared his love for me more and more persistently. He was very affectionate to Sylvia, whom he called 'Mausi', a popular endearment in German. He drank less than when Roschmann was present, and we often had interesting conversations. I liked him very much when he was sober. He said he understood that I was not ready for a new relationship yet, and he was willing to wait. But when he had too much to drink he insisted that I promise to marry him.

One day when he pressed me yet again, I got impatient: "You are married. Or have you forgotten?" He brushed away my remark. "You wait and see. I know what I am saying". He lifted his glass of brandy. "You will see!" After he left I forgot the conversation.

Very soon afterwards, however, George turned up with a huge bunch of gladioli and some champagne, and informed me jubilantly, "I got my divorce today. I am free. Free to marry you! All you have to do is say yes."

According to Latvian law at the time, a divorce could be obtained quickly and easily on the application of either partner, provided he or she admitted adultery. George had done that

On a street in Riga with Sylvia in April 1944. This photograph was taken by the private detective hired by George's wife. It was kept in my Gestapo file, the one started when they reopened the investigation into the death of the SS man Sascha killed.

but had not named his partner in adultery, as this information was not required by the court. His action proved disastrous for both of us. Faced with the divorce as a fait accompli George's wife and her parents were furious and bent on revenge. Later we learned that they hired a detective to follow George. The detective soon discovered where George spent his time, and who obviously was the reason for the divorce.

Occasionally George, Sylvia and I went for a walk on Sundays. On those occasions George wore civilian clothes. The detective took a photo of all three of us. My face from that photo was enlarged, my name added and a disaster set in motion. George's

An enlargement of my face from the photograph taken by the detective. George and I were unaware that the photographs existed until George's friend gave it to him with my new Gestapo file.

in-laws used their Gestapo connections to follow up what the detective had discovered. My past surfaced; my marriage to a Jew, my arrest after his escape, my release and the unheard-of crime of that Jew shooting a Gestapo officer. The file about the investigation of the shooting was dug up; it had been conducted with George as interpreter. That investigation had led to nothing.

The Gestapo became very interested. A new file was started on me. The investigation of Sascha's escape was to be reopened. And this time George would not be interpreter for the statements of the suspects. The witch hunt was on . . .

All this happened in Roschmann's absence. The detective lurking around my place saw only George coming and going. Roschmann was only mentioned as the officer who had questioned and cleared me after my arrest. George and I were ignorant of the dark clouds gathering over our heads when Roschmann returned from Germany. His rank was now that of an SS captain, and there was a new arrogance in his manner. But his obsession with me had not changed; if anything he had become more demanding and more sure of himself.

It was Roschmann who told us about the new turn of events. He made sarcastic remarks about George and his divorce and about the fury of a woman scorned. He laughed provocatively at the idea of my marrying George. One night there was an ugly scene between the two men that nearly ended in a physical fight. Roschmann told me that there was nothing for me to fear, as I had been cleared by him personally. His report on me would keep protecting me. He again urged me to send George packing.

For George and me, the next few weeks were a nightmare. Our lives were actually hanging by a thread. There was little hope that Kolja, and particularly his old mother, could withstand a thorough interrogation. If the truth came out we were all lost.

My parents were summoned for questioning, and it became apparent that my Aryan status was to be examined in an effort to find some Jewish blood in me. Mother and father were alarmed at first, but their documents were in order, and the fact that I had kept them in ignorance about so much prevented them from panicking. George went to see Kolja, warning him what to expect. Kolja thought of going to hide in the country, but decided to stay and face the ordeal.

George and I lived now from day to day. I was trying to resign myself to what was in store for me, but I was frantic about Sylvia's future. I wrote letters to Eddy, Nina, my parents and Tante Paschy, imploring each of them to care for and protect my baby. I entrusted my letters, together with the few pieces of jewellery I still possessed, to Liz, who had in no way been implicated in any of my dangerous activities over the last three years.

And so we waited, preparing ourselves for the Damocles sword to fall at last on my head, taking my true friends with me. Roschmann was still in the dark about the true situation, but even if he had known, there was no way he could help me this time. Once his association with me became common knowledge, he would find himself in serious trouble. He must have had some doubts about this new investigation, as he became conspicuous by his absence from my place, claiming pressure of work.

Salvation came at the eleventh hour.

This was spring 1944. The Russians were advancing relentlessly and there was chaos among the Nazis in Riga. More and more young men in office positions were replaced by new arrivals from Germany, disabled or old men.

The young Gestapo officer in charge of my case was transferred to the eastern front at a moment's notice. The man to succeed him and take over the unfinished investigation was on very friendly terms with George, often drinking with him. He did not take the matter seriously, thinking it was instigated by a jealous wife, and he teased George about it. Over a vodka, he handed the file over to George, with some good-natured advice to be more careful with women in future.

George rushed over to me, and our relief was enormous. Looking through the file we found to our horror that old Janis had been questioned again and had again incriminated me. Kolja or his mother had not been called yet. I cried and laughed while we tore and burned all the papers in my sink. Another link was formed between George and me.

Nobody had the time or interest to pursue the matter, and we were saved. Roschmann had heard that the investigation was shelved and, appearing again at my place, he said casually he had not expected any other outcome. Referring again to his report on me, he was taking credit not due to him. But George and I did not contradict him.

I think it was at the beginning of July when Roschmann announced that he had commandeered an apartment in the same building as mine, in fact one flight above. He said he was going to move into it, having given its occupants three days to find other accommodation. They were Latvians, not Jews, but of course they had no redress, as Roschmann was an SS captain. Until then, Roschmann had lived in the SS officers' quarters not far from my place.

His announcement dumbfounded me, but of course I was in no position to protest, having just escaped the hangman's noose.

A few days later, Roschmann took me upstairs to the apartment, which was now vacant. It was a three-room place in need of painting. Roschmann asked me what colours I liked, and which room I thought most suitable for the bedroom. It was very clear that he was building a 'love nest' for the two of us—his place, where he could order me to come and deny George admission.

During the next week, a group of Jews came and went in our building with ladders, tins of paint and tools. Roschmann made me come with him while he inspected their progress. When the painting and small repairs had been done, Roschmann brought a bottle of champagne, and I supplied two glasses. We drank to the new apartment, and Roschmann waltzed me around the rooms.

A few days later, another group of Jews appeared, this time staggering up the stairs with various items of furniture.

I dreaded the day when it would all be finished.

The apartment was looking very attractive, with a great deal of valuable furniture (no doubt Jewish), lush carpets and curtains. There was no linen, blankets, crockery or ornaments or paintings, but Roschmann told me he had already chosen them.

Fortunately he came less frequently than usual during July, saying he had to catch up with paperwork after his absence. It was George who told me that he was busily transporting large numbers of Jews out of Riga. (I had told George about Roschmann's apartment, and he was extremely annoyed.)

July brought all the summer splendour one could desire. The days were long and sunny, the parks teeming with picnickers sitting under majestic old trees on spread-out blankets. Children played in the sandpits, ran after butterflies, fed pigeons. Sylvia and I joined the crowd. We went for long walks along the banks of the City Canal, built sandcastles, threw sticks for Zenta to fetch and generally had a wonderful time. Listening to the laughter of children and the chirping of birds, it was hard to believe that not far from us savage battles were being fought.

But now the Nazis were panicking in earnest. The Allies had successfully invaded Normandy on 6 June and were advancing through France. The Russians were at the heels of the retreating, demoralised Nazi army in the east. All through that month, German and other civilians, including many collaborators, got out of Latvia and went to Germany. My parents went, too, and we all shed tears. They could not understand why I would not come with them. All I could do was to promise to follow soon, and to contact them in Germany.

But it was not so simple for me. The liberation of Latvia from the Nazis was imminent. It would come ten months too late to help Sascha, and paradoxically it constituted new peril for me.

I was in a hopeless mess. For nearly a year, my whole neighbourhood had seen two SS officers visiting me. Twice I found notes with 'Nazi whore' pinned to my door; there could be no doubt that as soon as the Russians entered Riga I would be immediately denounced as a collaborator. Who would listen to my explanations? Who would believe the tragic path I had been forced to take? Who would bother to find out the true story? Who would speak up for me?

I knew the answers to all those questions. Eddy could not stand by me even if he were still alive; Kolja and his family had gone into hiding in the country after the shock of the looming second investigation had passed. I had not seen Lee, but I knew he had left for Germany, leaving his Jewish wife and their daughter behind. Not that Lee would help me anyhow, of course.

Most of my friends shunned me, condemning me for associating with the Butcher of Riga; only Nina and Katja stayed loyal. I had nowhere to turn, being in the tragic dilemma of having Nazis as well as Communists against me.

One bright spot was that Roschmann had been caught up in the general panic and to my delight visited me less frequently.

He had his Jews to attend to. Since the liquidation of the Riga
ghetto, which took place on 25 November 1943, he was still
in charge of Jewish affairs. As far as I knew he was involved
in the administration of Meza Parks and Salaspils camps. His
special charges were a large group of Jews working for the Gestapo
and housed in a building adjoining headquarters.

He volunteered no information about his activities, and I
never asked. All he said was that he had to supervise shipments
of Jews to new locations, though he never said where.

One evening I told George about my fears of remaining in
Riga when the Russians took over. We discussed the matter
for a long time. It was clear I had to make a decision of some
kind soon, as not many ships were available for the transport
of civilians. The army had already begun to move men and
equipment to the west. There were rumours that the Germans
had gathered a large force to make a stand at Liepaja, on the
west coast of Latvia, which had a good harbour.

In case I decided to go to Germany, George made some
enquiries about a passage. His information was disturbing: my
name was on a list of people they did not want in Germany,
as I was the widow of a notorious Jew and Sylvia was his child.
That was that.

New orders were issued constantly. One was that, apart from
the military, only women, children and old people would be
shipped to Germany. All civilian males between eighteen and
sixty-five years of age were ordered to register. It was not hard
to work out why; these unfortunate men would be sacrificed,
cannon fodder for the Russians in the hope they would slow
down their advance and buy the Nazi army more time to run
to the west. Before this last order was made public, George
was ordered by his Gestapo bosses not to make any plans for
departure.

If Roschmann was aware of my predicament, he gave no sign.
He laughed at the numbers of people leaving Riga, saying they
were panicking. Riga and Latvia generally were safe and would
not be surrendered to the Russians. I agreed with him, pretending
to be unconcerned.

Roschmann knew better, of course, but insisted there was

nothing to worry about. However, once when we were alone he told me that if things grew serious he would personally see that Sylvia and I were shipped to Germany then sent on to Austria. We could stay in Graz with his parents until he was free to come to me.

One afternoon, when I was returning with Sylvia and Zenta from a day in the park, my janitor barred my way. During the eighteen months I had lived in my apartment, I had had little to do with this coarse Latvian woman. I gave her money for Christmas, as was the custom, and she had smiled and greeted me on meeting, appearing quite friendly.

Now she stood in front of me, an ugly smirk on her face. With venom in her voice, she said, "It won't be long now! Your high and mighty friends will be running like rabbits! How will you like being liberated, you filthy Nazi whore?"

All the blood drained from my face and I stumbled past her, speechless. The hatred in her words, in her face, hit me hard. I had tried not to think of what would happen when the Russians arrived.

When I told George about it, he grew very angry and wanted to rush down to tell her off. But I stopped him—what was the point? He could frighten her, Roschmann could have her shot if I told him—but why should I? In a few months, perhaps even a few weeks, the last Germans would have left Latvia, not able to frighten anybody any more. And I would be at the mercy of people like my janitor. Roschmann was absent that night. George tried to cheer me up, but I was deeply troubled.

After a prolonged silence, George said simply, "Marry me." I opened my mouth to reply, but he stopped me with a determined gesture. With a sternness unusual in him, he asked me to be quiet and to listen to what he had to say.

He felt that under the circumstances the Russians represented the greater and more immediate danger to me. Germany seemed safer temporarily. I could not enter Germany under my own name, but I could under his. So many people were coming in that I wouldn't be traced. George understood that I was still grieving for Sascha and that another marriage was not what I wanted. He respected my feelings and had been prepared to wait. But now it was a question of survival, mine and Sylvia's. George felt he had found the answer. "Don't forget, I love you both," he said.

George was offering us the protection of his name, a hiding place, possible survival. I knew he loved me, but a marriage now would give him nothing, as he well knew I would leave and he would have to stay behind. We might well be parting for good at the ship.

I had treated all his previous proposals of marriage as a joke, never considering marrying him or anybody else. But now I was grateful for his love and unselfishness.

As I listened to George, many emotions assailed me. Tears welled up and ran down my cheeks. He kissed me gently and left, without saying any more.

It was a long night.

Next day I told George I accepted his offer, and we made the necessary plans. Naturally we left Roschmann in complete ignorance of our decision.

When I saw the Butcher of Riga for the last time, he seemed nervous and preoccupied. No doubt he was considering the problem of the 'Final Solution' for the Jews in his care.

On 29 July, I packed four suitcases, which were picked up by two men George had sent. Then I locked my apartment and left the building with Sylvia in her stroller and Zenta, as if we were going for our normal walk.

Tante Paschy was the only person who knew about my impending marriage to George, and the reason for it. She approved of my decision. Leaving Sylvia and Zenta with her, I returned to the city.

George and I, being cautious, went to the registry office separately. When I arrived wearing a simple summer dress, he was waiting for me, with a bunch of gladioli. The ceremony was brief, our witnesses strangers.

A few hours later, George had secured a passage to Germany for his wife and child. He had no difficulty. The ship was leaving on 4 August.

George was taking Sylvia and me to the small seaside resort of Saulkrasti to spend the remaining days before the ship sailed.

When we said goodbye, Tante Paschy and I cried in each other's arms. She had decided to remain in Latvia, no matter what, and we knew we would never meet again.

Saulkrasti was chosen as a hideaway from Roschmann. We had been careful; as far as Roschmann knew, I was spending a week with friends in the country. George still travelled to Riga every day to the Gestapo. Apart from my clothes, nothing was missing from the apartment. The janitor had seen me leaving with Sylvia and Zenta. We hoped Roschmann would be too busy to check on me. We were afraid of his reaction to our wedding; he could stop Sylvia and me from entering Germany.

Sylvia on the beach at Saulkrasti in August 1944, a few days before our departure for Germany.

There was no telling how far he would go in his fury at being deceived.

Our few days in Saulkrasti were charged with emotion. Only Sylvia was carefree, loving every moment on the beach. It was her first experience of the sea, and she loved it. I had grown very fond of Zenta and it was hard to leave her behind; George said he would look after her.

We encountered no problems in boarding the ship; obviously nobody had time to check documents thoroughly. Because George was wearing his SS uniform, he was given priority. We were rushed through the formalities and assigned a place on the deck; no cabins were available for civilians.

The die was cast. There was no turning back. I was going with my child into the heart of the enemy, into an uncertain future. Escaping from one danger, perhaps finding a greater one . . .

The engines were started, the small ship vibrated and shook. The crowd grew restless. A woman next to me was sobbing hysterically in a man's arms. I heard somebody say loudly: "The Baltic Sea is full of mines!"

George cuddled Sylvia, then his arms were around me. "I love you very much. God willing I will get out of here too. We will have a future and be happy. Please believe it!"

As the ship steamed away from Riga harbour, George's sad and lonely figure grew smaller and smaller until I could no longer see his waving arm. Through my tears I saw the shores of my homeland recede.

Part of me remained there, in an unmarked grave. A part of me I would long for, for the rest of my life.

Over the years my thoughts and my undying love for Sascha would cross the seas and lands, searching for his soul.

Epilogue

After we left Latvia, Sylvia and I went to Dresden to visit my friend Melitta, who had lived there since 1939. We had to change trains in Stettin. The town must have been bombed shortly before our train arrived. There were burning buildings, smouldering rubble and crashing pieces of wall around the station. People were moving about with soot on their clothes and terror on their faces. It was a side of war I had not yet seen. A young Wehrmacht soldier offered to help me with my four suitcases, and stole them. Nobody I approached for help showed the slightest interest in or sympathy for my plight.

After a long delay, Sylvia and I boarded the train for Dresden. I was naturally very distressed at having lost all our possessions; I now had only my handbag and a carrybag. Apart from some necessities, the carrybag contained my most prized possessions connected with Sascha, which I had not entrusted to the suitcases. Sylvia was carrying her beloved toy elephant.

The train took us into the heart of Germany, and I could only wonder what lay ahead for me and my child.

After a few days with Melitta, I got in touch with the local refugee centre. Since their arrival in Germany several months previously, my parents had lived in a refugee camp in Panschwitz about forty kilometres from Dresden. Sylvia and I were sent to the same place, driven there by an old man in a very old car. The refugee camp consisted of a dilapidated building with many rooms and a huge kitchen. A crippled elderly SA man and an unfriendly nurse were in charge of the place.

The reunion with my parents was emotional. They were unaware of my marriage to George, as I had been too preoccupied to write to them about it. My father had aged enormously in the few months since I had seen him last. There were about forty people in the camp, mostly women and children, and a few old men. They were either refugees from the east, like our family, or bombed-out people from Berlin. We shared rooms. All ration cards were pooled; the food was atrocious.

Three months passed in these dismal surroundings.

In October 1944 George managed to leave Latvia and joined Sylvia and me. He obtained a clerical job and a house for us in Kamenz, a small town near Panschwitz. There the three of us started a new family life together. Sylvia, having experienced so many changes in location and always meeting new people, had forgotten about 'Uncle George'. When she saw him again and was told he was her 'Pappy' she accepted it without question. (Sylvia was sixteen when she learned the truth about her real father, and about the circumstances of his death.)

George had mentioned Roschmann only briefly, and as I did not want to hear about him, we never mentioned him again. I had worked hard at blotting Roschmann out of my memory, and had partially succeeded.

I was determined to make my marriage to George work. It was only a year since Sascha's death; the memories of him were still fresh, the pain at his loss still deep and strong. But I had accepted George into mine and Sylvia's lives, and I wanted to give him what feeling I was capable of. I knew I would never love any man the way I had loved Sascha. But there are so many degrees and shades of love. George deserved to be loved. He loved me and I responded the best I could with my wounded heart.

Sometimes I wanted to talk to George about Sascha, share some little episodes, just be able to mention Sascha's name. I also wanted to find some understanding in George for what I had been through. But to my sorrow and disappointment, he made it quite clear that he did not want to take any part in the memories of my life with Sascha. He reacted so strongly to any mention of Sascha that I stopped talking about him at all. His attitude made me sad; a little understanding on his part would have brought us much closer to each other.

Shared joy is double joy, but shared sorrow is half the sorrow. If I could have eased my pain by sharing it, my memories probably would have lost their intensity. But it was not to be.

As a result of George's unspoken rebuffs, I built a shrine in my heart for my beloved Sascha and buried it deep inside me, to remain there for ever. For many years I did not share with anybody my thoughts, memories and feelings about Sascha.

On 13 February 1945 I went to Dresden to see Melitta. She worked night shift in a factory and tried to persuade me to stay overnight so we could spend another day together. I agreed at first, but then decided to return home in the evening. That night Dresden was bombed for the first time in the five and a half years of war. In Kamenz we could see the sky red above Dresden from the fires. After weeks I received a letter from Melitta, telling me about the colossal casualties. She had survived in the factory bomb shelter, but the house she had lived in was completely levelled. Someone was watching over me! By coming home I had survived once more.

When I visited my parents at the end of February, my father

My parents in Panschwitz in August 1944, a few months before my father's death.

looked very tired and frail. A few days later he suffered a heart attack and passed away. Liz, who lived with her husband on the outskirts of Dresden, had not been affected by the bombing of the city. She and I rushed to Panschwitz to comfort our mother, who was very distraught and completely lost.

My father's funeral was very sad. The three of us staggered through deep snow behind the coffin on a small cart, pulled by a bedraggled old horse. We could not get any flowers. After much persuasion a pastor said a few meaningless words, while we stood shivering with cold. The ground was frozen hard as iron, the grave was shallow, and we were told the little white wooden cross Liz had managed to buy could not be erected. We put it on top of the mound of earth, after the grave was filled. I cried bitterly. In the past my father had often expressed to me his wish to be put to rest in Wolmar-Latvia, the town where he was born. Poor father. None of us were ever to visit his lonely grave again.

With George's consent I brought my mother to live with us in Kamenz. She had always been like a helpless child, turning to father for everything. Now I took his place, and she clung to me, seeking comfort and guidance. She remained with me until she died at the age of eighty-nine.

The winter of 1944–45 was exceptionally severe. From January 1945 refugees kept arriving from the east, passing through Kamenz on their flight westward. It was an endless procession. They came in horsedrawn carts, or on foot. The people of Kamenz, including me, brought out large jars of hot tea for the poor, half-frozen people, mostly women and children, as well as a few old men and crippled soldiers. It was a sorry sight. Many were crying, telling us that they had left their homes and possessions behind. They believed the Red Army to be only a few kilometres away. Day after day and all through the night, these thousands of frightened people kept streaming west. The urge to go west was unstoppable, the fear of the Russians overwhelming.

Soon after my father's death George and I also decided to go west. In the quiet of the night we could hear the distant rumblings from the east.

In response to the news that my luggage had been stolen in Stettin, George had dispatched to me two large boxes with my remaining clothes and other useful items. These boxes were misdirected and when we caught up with them, we found they had been broken open and the contents stolen. On leaving Latvia, George had managed to take quite a lot of luggage with him. Now, leaving Kamenz, we could take very little with us, just the bare essentials for the four of us. The railway station was bedlam, reminding me of June 1941 in Riga during the retreat of the Russians. Now Germans were in the same predicament. Thousands of frantic people milled around the train. Soldiers kicking anyone in the way pushed into the overcrowded wagons. Pleas for help from women with small children were unheeded. Somehow George managed to get us all into the last carriage of one of the trains.

Our train ride from Kamenz to Halle remains in my memory as a true nightmare. Countless times the train halted because of attacks by planes. Everybody rushed to some bunker or cellar nearby, where there was standing room only. Nobody worried about luggage. All we wanted was to survive this time, and the next, and the next. The bombings of the train were terrifying. The alarm over, the masses streamed back to the train, again fighting for space. Carriages that were hit were uncoupled and left behind; so were many people.

Somehow, somewhere, we got some food and water. Somehow we dozed. And somehow we arrived at our destination.

We lived in a hotel in Halle and spent most of the nights in the cellar, as the town was bombed regularly every night, and sometimes also during the day.

After a month of this nerve-wracking existence, we decided to leave. Refugees like us from the east were given passes to go to Bavaria. We left for Weiden, a sleepy little town that had been spared the ravages of war. The residents of Weiden took in the refugee families who kept arriving.

We were taken in by Sophie, a warm and kind German lady. We became one family, sharing her home and our rations with her and her two children for the next months.

After Halle, Weiden was a peaceful heaven. But every day

we could observe masses of bombers passing overhead on their way to do damage to some large city. They looked like small silver birds, high in the sky, the sun playfully reflecting on their metal bodies, carrying death.

Listening only to the German radio news we had no idea how the war was going, or how close the front was. The propaganda, the lies, continued.

One day I was walking with Sylvia when I heard what I thought was the noise of an aeroplane. I looked up in surprise and there it was, a Tiefflieger, a plane that used to fly very low and machinegunned its targets.

Stunned, following my instinct, I threw Sylvia into the ditch next to us and covered her with my body. I was not a minute too soon. The plane flew right over us and the machine gun rattled loudly . . . The pilot made only that one pass, but I remained in the ditch, covering Sylvia for quite a while. When we got out I saw with dismay that the ground around us was completely churned up by bullets. I was so shaken that I turned back home. Sylvia, not realising what had happened, cried and complained that she had been hurt when I had thrown her into the ditch.

Later we learned that the Tiefflieger had flown over the Weiden railway station and strafed it, but nobody had been hurt.

German propaganda assured the population that the battlefront had been intentionally reduced. Very soon the new secret weapon would be unleashed on the enemy and bring total victory to the Fatherland. The 'cripple' Roosevelt and the 'drunkard' Churchill would then beg for peace.

Spring arrived at last! The last patches of snow melted and snowdrops peered into the world. The trees displayed their green, young leaves ready to burst forth. Sophie's house was the last in the street, about three hundred metres from a forest. Now that the weather was mild and sunny we walked in the forest with the children. One April day we heard ominous rumblings from the direction of the forest. We were sure these were guns, and we listened with alarm as they rumbled day and night for several days. We spent those nights in Sophie's cellar that was partly filled with coal and potatoes. Naturally we had little sleep.

When we emerged from the cellar on the third morning, tired and depressed, silence engulfed us. We did not know what it meant and walked nervously in front of the house ordering the children to stay indoors. A new sound, unheard before, startled us; a deep continuous growling. Suddenly the forest seemed to part and a huge tank appeared, the long turret of its gun reaching out like the arm of some monster.

Like frightened hares we rushed inside and sat close together on the large sofa. The noise grew steadily louder, the floor under our feet trembled and the windows rattled.

Suddenly the door flew open and a very tall uniformed man stood there with his helmet pushed back, goggles hanging round his neck. His face was jet black. I had never seen a black in the flesh and gaped, fascinated. He stood in the doorway staring at us then, giving us a wide grin, said: "Wine?" We shook our heads in unison. He shrugged his broad shoulders, then made a dismissive gesture with his hand. He turned to go, then stopped and, looking back at us, threw a packet of Camel cigarettes at George. Another toothy grin and he was gone, leaving the door wide open. We looked at each other and broke into a relieved laughter. How strange and wonderful were these conquerors of the thousand-year Reich!

For Weiden and for us, the war was over. In a few weeks the unconditional surrender of Germany at last ended the monstrous slaughter of mankind in Europe.

We found ourselves in the American zone of Germany. UNRRA, later called IRO (the International Refugee Organisation), was established. All refugees became 'displaced persons' and were provided with generous rations. It was an enormous task to sort out the tens of thousands of refugees from every part of Europe: to care for the survivors of the murderous concentration camps, to restore some order to the ruins of every large town in Germany.

We rented an apartment in Weiden and moved out of Sophie's home. Sophie and I had become friends for life. We still correspond and exchange gifts.

The post-war period was difficult for all of us. The German population fared badly, on starvation rations long after the war had ended. The black market thrived and many Germans were forced to part with valuable paintings and family heirlooms for food.

The IRO staff consisted of people of many nationalities, some of whom had few scruples. Corruption flourished; food and cigarettes poured in from America and some of those who handled these enormous supplies could use part of them for their own purposes. At that time you could obtain practically anything for American cigarettes. We learned to use the black market too, and gradually obtained necessary clothes, shoes and other things.

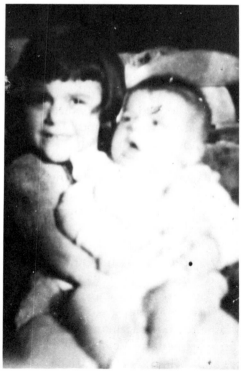

Sylvia and her three-month-old brother Alex at the end of 1945.

Working for the International Refugee Organisation in Amberg in 1947.

Our son Alex was born in Weiden. The healthy, dark-eyed baby was the pride of his father, the delight of his sister, and his grandmother's darling. Naturally I loved him dearly.

Afer Alex turned one, I applied for and was granted a position in one of the IRO offices. As a result our family was given a large apartment in one of the brick buildings belonging to IRO in Amberg, a charming little town not far from Weiden. I worked in various positions in various departments of IRO and got to know a lot of very nice people, and a few not so nice.

After I started work we employed a German woman to do the housework and cooking. She had lost her husband in the war and was struggling to bring up four children. I paid her, not with money, but with cigarettes and coffee.

When Sylvia turned six she started to attend a German school. During the years we spent in Germany the children spoke not only German and Russian, but picked up Polish and Estonian from their playmates. In the history of the world there probably has never been a greater number of different nationalities thrown together than in Germany after the Second World War.

Many men from the IRO formed relationships with German or refugee women. They were far from home, their wives and sweethearts, and no doubt homesick and lonely. Some of these relationships were shortlived, some lasted, some worked out, some had ugly endings. To mention one: a young American who held a leading position in IRO had an affair with a young, very pretty Ukrainian refugee girl. We IRO employees knew about her, as she often came to headquarters to meet him. We saw her pregnant, then she appeared with a baby in a pram. He openly made a fuss of her and the baby, and we presumed that they would get married. Then in 1948 we found out that the young American had gone home to his wife. We were all sad when his beautiful Ukrainian haunted the IRO headquarters for months, crying and imploring everybody to tell her where she could reach her beloved.

Sometime in 1948, I received a letter from a lawyer in the British zone, informing that he was writing to me at the request of his client Vitja Vanags, my former fiance. Vitja had been arrested and charged with having been commandant of a concentration camp in Germany during the war. I was asked to give a statement to the effect that I knew Vitja had been in Latvia till summer 1944, so proving that the charges were wrong. I was amazed and saddened, and replied immediately. It was true that Vitja had never left Latvia till my departure. I had kept in touch with him by phone, sometimes in person. I knew Vitja had never been anti-Semitic, and I could never imagine that kind and gentle man as being capable of any mean actions.

Two weeks later Vitja arrived at our apartment in Amberg. He looked haggard and had lost a lot of weight. He had come to thank me. As a result of my statutory declaration he had been released immediately; my testimony had weight then because I had said I was the widow of a Jew. He said the month he spent in jail had been a terrible, frightening experience. He had been kept alone in a small cell, given little food and not allowed visitors. He was lucky to be assigned a German lawyer who located me at Vitja's request.

We talked for hours. Later we corresponded, but somehow lost touch. In one of his letters he told me he intended to migrate to Australia.

From 1947 refugees started to emigrate from Germany. Canada, USA and Australia opened their doors. George and I could not see a future for us in the ravaged Germany that was recovering so very slowly. There was no question of our returning to Latvia, as our country was now occupied by the Russians, as was most of eastern Europe.

We knew refugees who wanted to migrate were screened for their past and their political views. George and I were worried that the fact he had been employed as an interpreter by the Gestapo in Riga might prove a problem; Jews who had miraculously survived the death camps were naturally bitter and

Sylvia and Alex in the summer of 1947.

anxious to find their tormentors. As the case with Vitja had shown, they did not always get hold of the guilty.

We know now that many, many real Nazi criminals with blood on their hands, including Roschmann, managed to slip through whatever screening was attempted. Apart from a few, such as Eichmann and Barbi (after many years), most of these monsters lived and died free men, enjoying the hospitality of South America and the money of ODESSA.

We had heard of a large camp established in Munich for some of the Jewish survivors of the concentration camps. I decided to pay them a visit. When I was asked my business at the gates, I said I wanted to see someone about emigration, preferably someone from Latvia. I was made to wait for a long time, ignored by people coming and going. Most were men in their twenties.

At last a jeep pulled up next to me. The driver motioned to me to get in next to him. As soon as I complied he drove off at breakneck speed. Hanging on to the sides of my seat with both hands, I looked at the driver. He was about twenty-five, his face was stern and very pale, his hair black and curly, his frame slight and his shoulders hunched. He kept silent, so I did too, presuming he was taking me to some destination where I could talk to the person I had requested.

After about fifteen minutes of frightening speed, the man pulled off the road and, stopping the car, abruptly turned to me. His eyes, set in dark circles seemed vacant, looking through me. "What is it you want?"

Suddenly I was frightened and unsure of what to say to this man. I had prepared a speech, but when I started to talk I found myself stammering. I related the death of my Jewish husband, my predicament in trying to get out of Latvia and the fact that George had helped me and my child by marrying me. I said I was happy with him, we had a son, and George was good to my daughter and mother. We wanted to emigrate to America or Australia, where we could start a new life. I had come here to get an assurance from some representative of the Jewish people that they would not hold it against George that he had worked as an interpreter for the Gestapo in Riga.

I put my hand on his arm and he shook it off immediately.

"I know you hate the Nazi criminals, so do I. But I beg you to understand my situation. Please believe me. My husband was only an interpreter, he has hurt nobody and has married me, a widow of a Jew and adopted my child, a half-Jew."

All the time I was talking, I had the strong feeling my words were bouncing off a stone wall. The man had not interrupted me. There had not been the slightest gesture or word to indicate his reaction to what I was saying. He had been sitting erect, staring straight ahead. Now he slowly turned his head and looked at me, as if seeing me for the first time. His face was without expression; it held no hostility or hatred, no interest or sympathy. It was a blank mask. His voice, when he at last spoke was very soft, and like his face completely lacking in any emotion.

"Why do you come to us with your petty problems? Do you expect sympathy for the death of your Jewish husband? He is only one of six million! You have replaced him, replaced the dead Jew! How dare you ask of us to guarantee your new man a safe passage into a new country? You are stupid! Stupid! Leave your husband, the Gestapo serf. If he is innocent of any crimes, nothing will happen to him. But do not expect us to help him. If you leave him I guarantee that we will arrange sponsorship for you, your children and mother to go to the States. Decide now. I promise, you and your children will want for nothing."

We sat in silence for a long time. His words had sunk in slowly. Not for a moment did I consider his offer; the thought of deserting George was inconceivable. But what had I really expected to achieve by coming here? It was truly stupid of me, as he had said, to appeal for sympathy from people who had survived the most terrible cruelty imaginable. Most likely the man I was appealing to had lost his family in some death camp. How could he possibly have compassion left in him for my situation?

I broke the heavy silence: "I will not abandon my husband. Please let us go back."

There was no reply. I had not given my name, he had not asked. When we stopped at the gates of the camp again, after the same insane speed, I got out a bit shakily. The young man did not give me another glance and there was no goodbye. I slowly made my way back to the Munich railway station.

I told George of my fiasco in Munich, and we decided in spite of it to go ahead with our plans to emigrate. We filled in the emigration papers for Australia; at that time it was the only country that would accept families with dependants, otherwise we would have had to leave my mother behind. We knew very little about this country. In our schools we had been told about its isolation, its unique flora and fauna, and that it had black people who were the original inhabitants. We also learned that the country had originally been settled by convicts and was part of the British Commonwealth.

After being subjected to a health and political screening, our application was accepted.

I gave up my job in IRO and we started packing again. We were excited and hopeful for the future. My mother, as always, accepted our decision as right. The children never stopped asking questions. Sylvia was doing well at school, and was sad to part with her many friends. Alex was a bright and mischievous child, spoiled by all of us. But he was too young to understand the mangitude of our decision. Sylvia had some idea. She was quite mature for her years and already displayed a strong character. Deciding that she was now grown up, she had given her grey toy elephant, for so many years her constant companion, to her brother. For some reason it became his favourite toy too.

And so we waited.

Liz and her husband, who found themselves at the end of the war in the British zone, found a sponsor in New York and were leaving for the States. She came to Amberg and we said goodbye. We were not to see each other for fourteen years.

In June 1949 we at last boarded a train in Amberg and were on our way. On arriving in Italy we spent some time in several camps consisting of tents, Sinegalia, a village by the Adriatic Sea and some time in Capua and Bagnolli. The weather in Italy was sunny and warm, the people were friendly and we did not mind the stopovers. We travelled by train and eventually arrived in Naples. There was another delay, less pleasant. In mid July, we finally boarded the *Fairsea* destined for Australia.

Alex at our last Christmas celebration in Germany (1948).

The month-long voyage was very difficult. The ship was overcrowded, the food was poor, we were all seasick, except George. The heat in the Red Sea was unbearable. As many of us who could were crowded on deck, gasping for air. The Indian Ocean was stormy.

After a short stopover in Fremantle, where we stayed on board, we landed in the port of Newcastle.

On 19 August 1949, we stepped ashore. Australia—our new homeland!

BALTIC
SEA

ESTONIA

RUSSIA

Kirbishof (Kirbeli)
Rujen (Ruijena)

Wolmar (Valmiera)

Saulkrasti
Meluzi

Riga

LATVIA

Leipãja

LITHUANIA

A Note on Latvia

WITH ESTONIA ON its northern border, Russia on the east and Lithuania and Poland to the south, Latvia borders on the Baltic Sea to the west.

With Estonia and Lithuania, it forms what are known as the Baltic States, which have always been vulnerable to invasion. The great powers wrangled over Latvia and its capital, Riga, for centuries. At different times, the country has looked for protection to Poland, Germany and Russia, as well as Sweden.

In the mid seventeenth century, after a period of Polish dominance of the Baltic lands, the Swedes wrested the Riga settlements from the Poles and converted the city into one of the most powerful Baltic fortresses.

Because the Russian Tsar Peter the Great wanted 'a window to the Baltic', he was soon at war with Sweden over Latvia. In 1710 Riga was under siege, and after the city fell the entire territory of Latvia was incorporated into the Russian Empire.

During the nineteenth century Riga expanded, becoming a large industrial city. Latvia became one of Russia's most prosperous occupied territories, and Riga a vital foreign trade port. Towards the end of the century, the walls encircling the old city of Riga were demolished, and the old and new city became one. Railways were spanning Latvia, connecting it with Russia, and with Europe. Soon the feudal Riga was transformed into a modern city.

Latvia dreamed of liberation from the Russian Empire, but this did not materialise for a long time. During World War I, Latvian troops joined the Russians against the Germans, and Latvia suffered damage. In 1917 the Germans briefly occupied Riga and other Latvian territory, but were forced out.

On 18 November 1918, Latvia was proclaimed an independent

state and a provisional government was established, under the chairman Janis Cakste. But the following year, the Latvian army was fighting the Bolsheviks and the Red Army occupied the country, proclaiming it a Soviet republic and applying ruthless measures of control. Latvia sought help from the Allies, and on 1 February 1920 an armistice was declared between Latvia and Russia, though unrest continued for about another year.

On 18 March 1921, the world recognised Latvia as an independent sovereign country, and Janis Cakste became the first president of the country under a democratic constitution. For the first time, Latvia had its own national anthem and its own national flag.

For almost twenty years, Latvia was a stable, sovereign country. It advanced in leaps and bounds.

Land reform legislation returned the soil to those who worked it, and the new farmers prospered. With independence, too, came a tremendous upsurge of national pride, and education became very important. There were remarkable achievements in culture, as well as education. Research into the Latvian language, which derives from Sanskrit, as well as literature, art, history and law, was greatly encouraged. The official government language was proclaimed to be Latvian, not Russian. Ethnic minorities had their own elementary and secondary schools, as well as theatres, hospitals and clubs.

There was complete freedom of religion. The state religion was Lutheran, but there were Catholic churches, a beautiful Russian Orthodox cathedral and a large synagogue in Riga, as well as churches for other denominations.

In the 1930s, Latvia's population consisted of 63 per cent Latvians, 10 per cent Germans, 9 per cent Russians and 4 per cent Jews, as well as other minorities.